Praise for *Moses: Called by God*

"*Moses: Called by God* is a beautiful and inspiring look at the primary character of the Old Testament. It's encouraging to be reminded that with many flaws and mistakes, Moses was still called a friend of God. In a culture that reveres youth, it's hopeful to see that Moses spent the first two-thirds of his life preparing for the primary work of his life. With the speed of our daily lives, Moses's story offers a gentle reminder to be listening for those burning bush moments when God can clarify our purpose and calling. This book will clear the smoke to allow your own face-to-face encounters with God."

—**Dan Miller**, *New York Times* bestselling author of *48 Days to the Work You Love*, and host of the 48 Days Podcast

"Marilynn Hood's *Moses: Called by God* is an inspiring journey into the heart of the very purpose of our lives: knowing God and making Him known. The insights and questions Marilynn offers help us understand that, like Moses, we can experience a deep and extraordinary relationship with God, which is exactly what He created us for!"

—**Meredith Perryman**, speaker, Bible teacher, and author of *The Whole Story*

"When you have an encounter with God and get in His presence, the experience will shake the foundation of your view of God *and* your view of yourself in relationship to a holy God. In *Moses: Called by God*, Marilynn Hood takes you on a faith-filled adventure that will fire up your soul. She unpacks Moses's life story—his doubts, fears, and the deep faith he developed as a result of his encounter with God. From the relevant insights she offers, you'll learn how you, like Moses, can have a personal connection with God. If you're wondering if God has called you or what His purpose is for you, this reflective study will help you find the answers."

—**Bill Rieser**, pastor, author, evangelist, and founder of Encounter Ministries

"If you enjoy digging into the Scriptures and connecting the historical dots linking biblical stories to each other and to us today, you'll love Marilynn Hood's new book on Moses. Marilynn's research and personal insights will enrich your appreciation of Moses and how his life relates to our walk with God. Bible students and teachers alike will find lots of helpful information and inspiration in *Moses: Called by God*."

—**Debbie W. Wilson**, author of *Little Strength, Big God*

MOSES
CALLED BY GOD

Living by Faith through the Journeys of Life

by Marilynn E. Hood

These books are available at special discounts when purchased in bulk for use as premiums, promotions, fundraising, or group studies. For inquiries and details, contact us: info@courageousheartpress.com.

Published by Courageous Heart Press

Paperback ISBN: 978-1-950714-27-8
eBook: 978-1-950714-28-5
LCCN: 2023937647

To my mother, Marie LaThelle Hasty Edmiston (July 17, 1920–June 14, 2022), someone who truly lived her life by faith through the journeys of life.

Contents

Author's Note

God has no grandchildren. These words spoken by our class discussion leader resonated deeply with me. Your faith in God, like your soul, is uniquely yours. It's not something you can inherit. While other people and circumstances may influence you, your faith remains yours alone. It's something you must develop for yourself—or not.

As a young adult striking out on my own, one of my objectives in life had been to find God for myself. From my parents and grandparents, I learned a deep reverence for the Scriptures. From my own studies, I believed the Bible to be the inspired Word of God. That would be my source for learning more about God.

While studying the Bible, I noticed there were people with whom God developed personal relationships. Both Abraham and Moses were called the "friend of God." King David was known as "a man after God's own heart." The prophet Daniel was "esteemed" by God.

How did these people develop such personal relationships with God? They lived in different eras, and each had unique life stories, yet they shared a commonality: a great faith in God. They believed He would do what He said He would do. They trusted in Him fully as they set about fulfilling what He had called them to do in life.

The purpose of this book is to study the life of Moses and the personal relationship he developed with God. In so doing, may you be encouraged to deepen your faith and further develop your own personal relationship with Him. May you aspire to become, like Moses, someone whom God Himself would name as a friend as you trust in Him through all of your life's journeys!

God's Word contains a fascinating collection of literary works. The depth of the Scriptures continues, as it has for centuries, to challenge scholars, historians, clergy, and ordinary people alike. Its message, however, remains elegantly simple: *God loved us so much that He gave His Son, Jesus, as the perfect sacrifice for our sins so that whoever believes in Him should not perish but have eternal life* (John 3:16, paraphrased).

The Law, which Moses received from God at Mount Sinai and delivered to the Israelites, helped prepare the way for Jesus to enter the world centuries later. When Moses read the Law to the people, they understood its meaning and agreed to its terms. Then, when Jesus came to earth, He presented His teachings to the great multitudes.

In keeping with the tenor of God's Word, this book is for you. Whether you have studied the Bible much or not at all, it is my prayer that these lessons will enrich your life, deepen your faith, and draw you closer to your Creator as you, too, travel the journey He has set before you.

How to Use This Book

Moses is a big topic! His life spans four books of the Old Testament: Exodus, Leviticus, Numbers, and Deuteronomy. He is credited with writing these books as well as the book of Genesis, making him the single greatest contributor to our Bible.

Understandably, the life of Moses is intertwined with the story of the Israelite people, whom God called him to lead, and with the precepts of the Law, which he faithfully delivered to them. In order to better study the character of Moses, this book seeks to filter through this great amount of material and separate out the narrative of his life.

- For individual study, the forty-three lessons plus the intro and epilogue could easily serve as six to seven weeks of daily devotionals.

- For group study, depending on the duration of your class, the lessons could be broken down into perhaps five per week for nine weeks or three per week for fifteen weeks. The outline below groups the chapters into blocks of five lessons each. It also lists the Scripture passages covered in each chapter, along with a suggested song to help the instructor create a syllabus for the class. (A sample syllabus is available at marilynnhood.com/moses.)

God Prepares Moses for His Calling

Chapter Title	Scripture Reading	Suggested Song	Song Links
Setting the Scene	Exodus 1 (NIV)	In the Desert of Sorrow and Sin	tinyurl.com/km6xt36h
1: The Baby Drawn Out of the Water	Exodus 2:1–10 (ESV)	I Know the Lord Will Find a Way	tinyurl.com/2s89cz9w
2: Moses Escapes From Egypt	Exodus 2:11–15 (HCSB)	Where He Leads Me	tinyurl.com/2b277sr4
3: Moses Finds a Family among the Midianites	Exodus 2:16–22 (HCSB)	This World Is Not My Home	tinyurl.com/r4tcna64
4: Moses's Call to Leadership	Exodus 2:23–3:10 (ESV)	Take My Life and Let It Be	tinyurl.com/2tebvs5e

God Redirects Moses's Life

Chapter Title	Scripture Reading	Suggested Song	Song Links
5: God Reveals His Plan to Moses	Exodus 3:11–22 (HCSB)	Great I Am	tinyurl.com/45mfyf3k
6: God Equips Moses for His Role	Exodus 4:1–17 (NIV)	Anywhere with Jesus	tinyurl.com/27ecvwch
7: Moses Leaves for Egypt	Exodus 4:18–26 (ESV)	Savior, Teach Me Day by Day	tinyurl.com/mr2r3v95
8: Moses Becomes a Leader	Exodus 4:27–31; 5:1–21 (HCSB)	After the Midnight	tinyurl.com/2vdyxh2s
9: Moses Questions God	Exodus 5:22–6:13; 7:1–7 (NLT)	A Shelter in the Time of Storm	tinyurl.com/2p8e2wfk

God Displays His Power

Chapter Title	Scripture Reading	Suggested Song	Song Links
10: The Plagues Begin	Exodus 7:8–8:15 (HCSB)	Living by Faith	tinyurl.com/2zenjy4k
11: Gnats and Flies	Exodus 8:16–32 (NIV)	Into My Heart	tinyurl.com/5t43fnrr
12: Livestock, Boils, and Hail	Exodus 9 (NLT)	Standing on the Promises of Christ Our King	tinyurl.com/573dpndp
13: Locusts	Exodus 10:1–20 (NIV)	I Love to Tell the Story	tinyurl.com/24x7n2ma
14: Darkness and a Final Warning	Exodus 10:21–11:10 (NIV)	Heavenly Sunlight	tinyurl.com/yeyjydjx

God Rescues His Chosen People

Chapter Title	Scripture Reading	Suggested Song	Song Links
15: God Establishes the Passover	Exodus 12:1–28 (NLT)	Redeemed by the Blood of the Lamb	tinyurl.com/5n8bc9p3
16: The Final Plague	Exodus 12:29–51 (HCSB)	The Gospel Is for All	tinyurl.com/5b3scne5
17: Out of Egypt	Exodus 13:17–14:12 (NKJV)	Turn Your Eyes Upon Jesus	tinyurl.com/3r97df5e
18: Crossing the Red Sea	Exodus 14:13–31 (NKJV)	Be Still and Know That I Am God	tinyurl.com/32ku2twd
19: A Song of Praise to the Lord	Exodus 14:30–15:21 (ESV)	The New Song	tinyurl.com/4kvk2deh

God Provides for His People

Chapter Title	Scripture Reading	Suggested Song	Song Links
20: The Israelites Grumble	Exodus 15:22–16:8 (NLT)	Trust and Obey	tinyurl.com/bdhs66et
21: Manna and Quail	Exodus 16:9–36 (NLT)	He Knows Just What I Need	tinyurl.com/2p9c7psa
22: Water from a Rock and the Battle at Rephidim	Exodus 17 (NIV)	God Our Banner	tinyurl.com/2hye3auy
23: The Beginnings of a Judicial System	Exodus 18 (NKJV)	Far and Near the Fields Are Teeming	tinyurl.com/56c9syen
24: God's Covenant with the Israelites	Exodus 19 (HCSB)	All to Jesus, I Surrender	tinyurl.com/mr3kdh2r

God Reveals His Character and Calls His People to Holiness

Chapter Title	Scripture Reading	Suggested Song	Song Links
25: The Ten Commandments	Exodus 20:1–17 (HCSB)	Amazing Grace	tinyurl.com/3dafehpt
26: Moses Intercedes for the Israelites	Exodus 20:18–21; Deuteronomy 5:1–5, 22–33 (HCSB)	The Love of God	tinyurl.com/bdhsp6br
27: Ratifying the Covenant	Exodus 24 (NKJV)	What Can Wash Away My Sin?	tinyurl.com/jwevmtys
28: The Golden Calf	Exodus 31:18–32:14 (HCSB)	Dear Lord and Father of Mankind	tinyurl.com/y63fprf5
29: Moses Smashes the Tablets	Exodus 32:15–35 (HCSB)	The Great Redeemer	tinyurl.com/43m954r9

God Reestablishes the Relationship

Chapter Title	Scripture Reading	Suggested Song	Song Links
30: Moses's Friendship with God	Exodus 33 (NIV)	If Jesus Goes with Me	tinyurl.com/yhz8jfry
31: The New Tablets	Exodus 34:1–11, 27–35 (NIV)	Nearer, Still Nearer	tinyurl.com/5zey3zxn
32: Becoming a Nation	Numbers 9:1–5, 15–23; 10:1–28 (NLT)	Lamb of God	tinyurl.com/2p9xn8vc
33: Leaving the Mountain of God	Numbers 10:33–36; 11:1–35 (NKJV)	Does Jesus Care?	tinyurl.com/ywvj5rbw
34: Miriam and Aaron Criticize Moses	Numbers 12 (NLT)	Humble Thyself in the Sight of the Lord	tinyurl.com/4ymrpeft

God Never Leaves His People

Chapter Title	Scripture Reading	Suggested Song	Song Links
35: Exploring the Promised Land	Numbers 13 (NIV)	Jesus, Savior, Pilot Me	tinyurl.com/4k3u442w
36: Forty Years of Wandering!	Numbers 14 (NIV)	O for a Faith That Will Not Shrink	tinyurl.com/5ef44bju
37: Korah's Rebellion	Numbers 16:1–35 (ESV)	As the Deer	tinyurl.com/y83kpkxe
38: God Reaffirms His Leaders	Numbers 16:36–17:13 (ESV)	Holy, Holy, Holy! Lord God Almighty	tinyurl.com/27x9asn3
39: Moses Strikes the Rock	Numbers 20:1–13, 22–29 (NLT)	Lord, Speak to Me	tinyurl.com/244dumzk

God's Plan Is Greater than We Can Imagine

Chapter Title	Scripture Reading	Suggested Song	Song Links
40: Moses's Death Draws Near	Numbers 21:4–9; 27:12–23; Deuteronomy 3:23–29 (HCSB)	Jesus, Keep Me Near the Cross	tinyurl.com/yf5dtub7
41: God Gives Moses a Song	Deuteronomy 31 (HCSB)	He Gave Me A Song	tinyurl.com/6bdfc7xs
42: The Death of Moses	Deuteronomy 32:44–52; 34 (HCSB)	Hold to God's Unchanging Hand	tinyurl.com/52kfamk2
43: Preparing the Way for the Messiah	Deuteronomy 18:15-22 (HCSB)	He Paid a Debt He Did Not Owe	tinyurl.com/32wn3ve5
Moses, A Faithful Servant of God		The Lord Bless You and Keep You	tinyurl.com/mrxw74f4

At the end of each lesson (except for the last two) are three Thoughts to Ponder to help foster your personal study or to use for group discussions. The author's answers or thoughts on these questions are available at the website, marilynnhood.com/moses.

May this study of Moses truly bless you as you journey through your own life and accomplish all that God has called you to do!

The God who made the world and everything in it is the Lord of heaven and earth and does not live in temples built by human hands. And he is not served by human hands, as if he needed anything. Rather, he himself gives everyone life and breath and everything else. From one man he made all the nations, that they should inhabit the whole earth; and he marked out their appointed times in history and the boundaries of their lands. God did this so that they would seek him and perhaps reach out for him and find him, though he is not far from any one of us.

—Acts 17:24–27, NIV

Moses's Family Tree

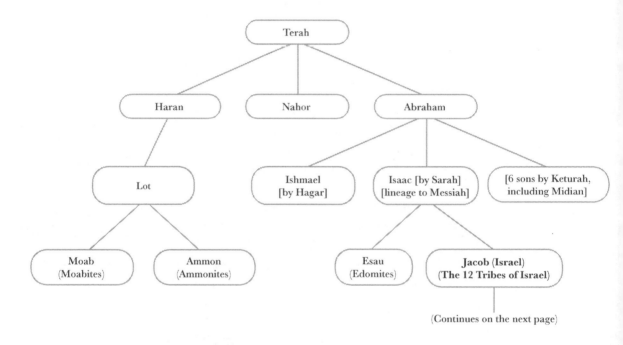

Terah
- Haran
  - Lot
    - Moab (Moabites)
    - Ammon (Ammonites)
- Nahor
- Abraham
  - Ishmael [by Hagar]
  - Isaac [by Sarah] [lineage to Messiah]
    - Esau (Edomites)
    - **Jacob (Israel)** **(The 12 Tribes of Israel)**
  - [6 sons by Keturah, including Midian]

(Continues on the next page)

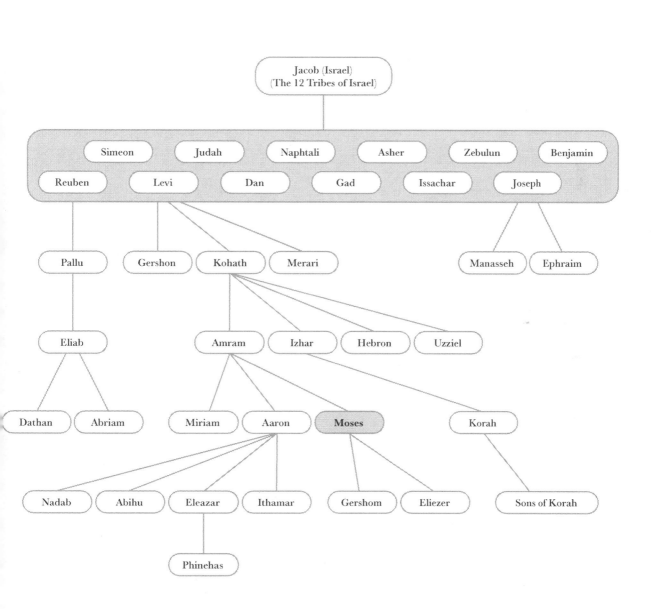

GOD PREPARES MOSES FOR HIS CALLING

Setting the Scene

Now the LORD said to Abram, "Go from your country and your kindred and your father's house to the land that I will show you. And I will make of you a great nation, and I will bless you and make your name great, so that you will be a blessing. I will bless those who bless you, and him who dishonors you I will curse, and in you all the families of the earth shall be blessed."

—Genesis 12:1–3, ESV

Suggested Song

"In the Desert of Sorrow and Sin"

(tinyurl.com/km6xt36h)

Moses's story actually begins in Mesopotamia, a region that lies, as the crow flies, about a thousand miles to the east of his birthplace in Egypt. It was there, several centuries before Moses's birth, that God revealed His plan to make Abram's family a great nation. In that revelation, God promised to make Abram's descendants as numerous as the stars in the sky, and through him and his lineage, all peoples of the earth would be blessed. When God later established His covenant of circumcision with Abram, He changed his name to Abraham, which means the father of many nations or of a multitude.

Moses was one of those descendants God had promised to Abram. Regardless of your ancestral lineage, today, you also have access to the ultimate blessing of that promise: Jesus.

God's promise to Abraham was specific. It would come about through a son born to his wife, Sarah. Despite the fact that both he and Sarah were elderly when God made the promise, Abraham believed God. That belief earned Abraham and Sarah a place in Hebrews 11 as people of faith, but believing wasn't always easy.

An Infertile Beginning

For a nation to become great, it must first have people. For several decades after God made His promise to Abraham, infertility remained a distinct problem. When God told Abraham that Sarah would become the mother of nations and that kings of peoples would come from her, Abraham laughed. Such a thing seemed impossible, given their advanced years and the fact that Sarah had never been able to have children. Later, when the Lord visited Abraham and told him that within a year, Sarah would have a son, *she* was the one who laughed.

In response to their astonishment at the improbable news, God asked, "Is anything too hard for the LORD?" (Genesis 18:14, NIV). The answer became evident the next year. When Abraham was 100 and Sarah 90 years old, Isaac was born—just as God had promised.

> "Is anything too hard for the LORD?"

It took time for Isaac to become a father as well. He was already forty years old when he married Rebekah. Like Sarah, Rebekah remained childless for many years. Isaac prayed for his wife to conceive, and finally, when Isaac was sixty, Rebekah gave birth to twins, Esau and Jacob.

Esau was the firstborn of the twins, but God determined that His promise to Abraham would continue through Jacob. Like his brother, Esau became the founder of nations, but the blessing for all humanity would come through Jacob.

Finally, after many years, Abraham's family began to increase significantly. Jacob fathered twelve sons and at least one daughter, but even that took time. Jacob worked seven years to wed Rachel, whom he loved. Laban, Rachel's father, deceived Jacob and, on his wedding night, gave him Leah, Rachel's older sister, instead. Laban then agreed to give Rachel to Jacob after Leah's bridal week, but, in return, he required Jacob to work another seven years. God enabled Leah, the one who was unloved, to bear children. Rachel, however, remained childless for many years. She eventually gave birth to Joseph, then later died while giving birth to her second son, Benjamin.

Jacob Becomes Israel

After working for Laban for twenty years, Jacob returned to Canaan with his family and flocks. During the journey to his homeland, Jacob wrestled one night with someone he thought was a man. At daybreak, however, he realized it was God with whom he had struggled. God then affirmed His blessing on Jacob's life and changed his name to Israel.

Jacob's twelve sons fathered the twelve tribes of the Israelite nation. None lived long enough to claim the land promised to Abraham; in fact, a famine forced Jacob's family to move from Canaan to Egypt. Years before the famine, the ten older boys had sold their brother Joseph into slavery. Bought by a military captain in Egypt and later thrown into prison, Joseph endured one hardship after another. That struggle, however, positioned Joseph perfectly to rise to be second in command of the whole nation of Egypt. It was there that he reunited with his brothers, who had come to buy grain. After a tearful reunion, Joseph brought his entire family, including his father Jacob, to Egypt.

Seventy Souls

When they came to Egypt, the number of Israelites (Jacob's family) totaled a mere seventy souls. While living there, Abraham's descendants began to multiply greatly. When a new ruler came into power—one who knew nothing about the great things Joseph had done for Egypt—the sheer number of the Israelite people concerned him. The new pharaoh forced the Israelites into slavery.

Moses was born during this time of great oppression.

The Israelite people continued to multiply—just as God had promised. Fearful that the Israelites would outnumber the Egyptians and revolt, Pharaoh ordered the midwives to kill every newborn Israelite boy. The midwives, however, feared God more than Pharaoh and refused to murder the infants. They claimed the Israelite women gave birth before the midwives could arrive.

Thus, baby Moses escaped death.

When Moses's mother could no longer hide him at home, she put him in a basket and hid him among the reeds along the Nile River. The Pharaoh's own daughter found him there. She had pity on the child and raised him as her son. She even employed Moses's mother to nurse and care for him. So Moses, who was born a Hebrew slave, grew up as Egyptian royalty, the adopted grandson of one of the world's most powerful rulers.

The Making of a Leader

Several significant events became turning points in Moses's life. The first came when he witnessed an Egyptian beating one of his own people. Thinking he would be able to conceal his actions, he killed the Egyptian and hid him in the sand. Pharaoh learned of Moses's deed and sought to have him killed.

Moses, at the age of forty, fled Egypt, escaping to the land of the Midianites. He lived in Midian for the next forty years of his life. While there, he married the daughter of a Midianite priest, had two sons, and tended his father-in-law's flocks. That relatively peaceful phase of his life ended when God called to him from a burning bush.

During the encounter, God told Moses to lead the Israelite people out of Egyptian bondage. Reluctantly obedient, Moses brought together the slaves who had been scattered across Egypt. As one people, they witnessed God's miracles and marched out of Egypt to freedom. Moses then spent the next forty years of his life leading the Israelites (also known as the Hebrew people) to the land God had promised to Abraham so many years earlier. Like Abraham, Moses would never witness the Israelites taking possession of the Promised Land, a land flowing with milk and honey. It would be the following generation who would finally see the fulfillment of God's promise to Abraham.

The first chapter of Exodus helps set the scene for the birth of Moses. It offers insight into the difficult conditions facing the Hebrew people at the time.

Exodus 1, NIV

(1) These are the names of the sons of Israel who went to Egypt with Jacob, each with his family: (2) Reuben, Simeon, Levi and Judah; (3) Issachar, Zebulun and Benjamin; (4) Dan and Naphtali; Gad and Asher. (5) The descendants of Jacob numbered seventy in all; Joseph was already in Egypt.

(6) Now Joseph and all his brothers and all that generation died, (7) but the Israelites were exceedingly fruitful; they multiplied greatly, increased in numbers and became so numerous that the land was filled with them.

(8) Then a new king, to whom Joseph meant nothing, came to power in Egypt.

(9) "Look," he said to his people, "the Israelites have become far too numerous for us. (10) Come, we must deal shrewdly with them or they will become even more numerous and, if war breaks out, will join our enemies, fight against us and leave the country."

(11) So they put slave masters over them to oppress them with forced labor, and they built Pithom and Rameses as store cities for Pharaoh. (12) But the more they were oppressed, the more they multiplied and spread; so the Egyptians came to dread the Israelites (13) and worked them ruthlessly. (14) They made their lives bitter with harsh labor in brick and mortar and with all kinds of work in the fields; in all their harsh labor the Egyptians worked them ruthlessly.

(15) The king of Egypt said to the Hebrew midwives, whose names were Shiphrah and Puah, (16) "When you are helping the Hebrew women during childbirth on the delivery stool, if you see that the baby is a boy, kill him; but if it is a girl, let her live." (17) The midwives, however, feared God and did not do what the king of Egypt had told them to do; they let the boys live. (18) Then the king of Egypt summoned the midwives and asked them, "Why have you done this? Why have you let the boys live?"

(19) The midwives answered Pharaoh, "Hebrew women are not like Egyptian women; they are vigorous and give birth before the midwives arrive."

(20) So God was kind to the midwives and the people increased and became even more numerous. (21) And because the midwives feared God, he gave them families of their own.

(22) Then Pharaoh gave this order to all his people: "Every Hebrew boy that is born you must throw into the Nile, but let every girl live."

The Names of God's People

Hebrew—Abram (later Abraham) is referred to as a "Hebrew" for the first time in Genesis 14:13. This term must have become widely accepted for the descendants of Abraham because Joseph and the rest of the Israelites were referred to as Hebrews while living in Egypt.

Some Bible scholars believe the name was derived from Eber, the great-grandson of Shem (Genesis 10:24) and ancestor of Abraham. (See Abraham's genealogy in Genesis 11:10–26. Eber is mentioned in verses 14–17.)

Other scholars believe the word "Hebrew" means someone from the other side. In Abraham's case, it may have meant someone who came from the other side of the Jordan River or the Euphrates River. Speaking to the people in Joshua 24:2–3 (NIV), Joshua told them: "This is what the Lord, the God of Israel, says: 'Long ago your ancestors, including Terah the father of Abraham and Nahor, lived beyond the Euphrates River and worshiped other gods. But I took your father Abraham from the land beyond the Euphrates and led him throughout Canaan and gave him many descendants.'"

Israelite—As Jacob was returning home after spending twenty years working for his father-in-law, Laban, he spent a night wrestling with God. At that time, God changed Jacob's name to Israel, and evidently, his family became known as the Israelites from that point forward. (See Genesis 32:22–32 for the account of Jacob wrestling with God and his name being changed to Israel.)

Jew—This name was derived from Judah, one of Jacob's twelve sons and whose descendants became one of the twelve tribes of Israel. When the nation later became divided, the Southern Kingdom consisted of the tribes of Judah and Benjamin and was referred to collectively as Judah. The Northern Kingdom was made up of the other ten tribes and was known as Israel.

The term "Jew" is not used in the Bible until later in their history, particularly around the time of their exile into Babylonian captivity and beyond. It eventually came to refer to all the Israelites, not just the ones from the kingdom of Judah.

For more information, see *Bible Study Tools Dictionary* (tinyurl.com/4xvkph9s). Use their "Quick Reference Dictionary" page to select the first letter of what you would like to look up. Then on the page for that letter, scroll down to the offerings for that letter and select a particular name or term.

Also, see "Bible Hub Bible Timeline" (tinyurl.com/5b65355c). This timeline provides the approximate dates for various occurrences in both the Old and New Testaments and gives Scripture references for the events.

Thoughts to Ponder

Evidently, Abram had no children until the birth of Ishmael. At that time, he was 86 years old (Genesis 16:16). When Isaac was born, Abraham was 100 years old (Genesis 21:5). How many other children did Abraham have, and what were their names? (See Genesis 25.)

_____

_____

_____

_____

_____

If Moses wrote the book of Exodus, why do you suppose so little of the first eighty years of his life is mentioned in these writings?

_____

_____

_____

_____

In Exodus 1:15, the names of the two midwives are recorded. What does this tell you about their significance in the history of the Hebrew people?

_____

_____

_____

Chapter 1

The Baby Drawn Out of the Water

Exodus 2:1–10, ESV

(1) Now a man from the house of Levi went and took as his wife a Levite woman.

(2) The woman conceived and bore a son, and when she saw that he was a fine child, she hid him for three months. (3) When she could hide him no longer, she took for him a basket made of bulrushes and daubed it with bitumen and pitch. She put the child in it and placed it among the reeds by the riverbank. (4) And his sister stood at a distance to know what would be done to him.

(5) Now the daughter of Pharaoh came down to bathe at the river, while her young women walked beside the river. She saw the basket among the reeds and sent her servant woman, and she took it. (6) When she opened it, she saw the child, and behold, the baby was crying. She took pity on him and said, "This is one of the Hebrews' children."

(7) Then his sister said to Pharaoh's daughter, "Shall I go and call you a nurse from the Hebrew women to nurse the child for you?" (8) And Pharaoh's daughter said to her, "Go." So the girl went and called the child's mother. (9) And Pharaoh's daughter said to her, "Take this child away and nurse him for me, and I will give you your wages." So the woman took the child and nursed him.

(10) When the child grew older, she brought him to Pharaoh's daughter, and he became her son. She named him Moses, "Because," she said, "I drew him out of the water."

◇◇◇

────── 1 ──────

Although she is not named here in this passage, Exodus 6:20 and Numbers 26:59 state that Moses's mother was named Jochebed.

────── 2 ──────

The Nile is known for not only fish but great numbers of other animals as well, including crocodiles, monitor lizards, hippos, and rhinos. For more information, see the article "Animals Living in and around the River Nile" at RiverNile.info (tinyurl.com/t7my4tab).

Moses was born into treacherous times. His family lived as slaves in Egypt and had no political standing, no laws to protect them, and no civil rights. The Egyptian slave masters oppressed the Hebrews, working them ruthlessly.

The Hebrews had become so numerous that Pharaoh feared they would revolt. If that happened, the loss would hurt both his reputation as a revered leader and the nation's economy. As slaves, the Hebrews were free labor, which he used to build his empire. To quell their numbers and crush their spirits, Pharaoh decreed that all Hebrew boys were to be killed at birth.

Imagine the fear and dread Moses's mother, Jochebed, felt as she gave birth and then tried to hide her newborn son.[1] She knew she could not keep him hidden for long, so when he was three months old, she came up with a plan. Determined to protect and preserve her child's life, she placed Moses in a water-proofed basket and placed him in the Nile River.

Jochebed had to have been desperate to set her infant afloat in a river teeming with untold dangers.[2] She was desperate but smart. She chose a place by the river's edge where the reeds would hide the basket and prevent it from washing downstream. She also chose a location where Pharaoh's daughter and her attendants came to bathe. Most importantly, she stationed her daughter, Miriam, nearby to watch over the basket.

God Provides a Way When There Is No Way

When Jochebed placed that basket in the water, she placed Moses in God's hands. She had gone as far as she could on her own in keeping him alive. Gently rocking on the water, his fate was up to the Lord.

God responded to Jochebed's faith in an amazing way.

Before any harm could come to Moses, Pharaoh's daughter found the child. She had compassion for him and boldly went against her father's edict to kill the Hebrews' baby boys. When

Miriam approached her with the offer to fetch a Hebrew nurse, she agreed, which meant Moses's own mother got to care for him—and Pharaoh's daughter paid her to do so. Pharaoh's daughter then raised the boy as her own son rather than as a slave.

It's doubtful Moses's mother could have ever imagined such a fate for her baby boy. Nor could she have known he would one day lead the Israelites out of slavery. Pharaoh had decreed death for Jochebed's child, yet God provided a way for him to live. Instead of dying at birth or living as a slave, Moses grew up as the grandson of the king of Egypt, one of the most powerful and richest rulers in the world at that time.

> Pharaoh had decreed death for Jochebed's child, yet God provided a way for him to live.

Have you ever felt like you've gone as far as you can go?

You may feel that way right now. Take comfort in knowing that God will meet you wherever you are. Think about Jochebed and the untenable circumstances she and her family faced. When she turned her situation over to God, He worked things out in a way she could never have dreamed of or accomplished on her own.

When you face difficult times, spend time in prayer and call upon God's strength. Like a friend, God desires to help you. Like a father, He desires to provide and care for you.

As King David wrote, "Cast your burden on the LORD, and He will sustain you; He will never allow the righteous to be shaken" (Psalm 55:22, HCSB). God is worthy of your trust. Like Jochebed, have the faith to go ahead and place your basket in the water.

Moses's Adopted Mother

The Pharaoh at the time Moses fled may have been particularly difficult. The following article provides more information about Egypt around the time Moses lived there: "Queen Hatshepsut, Moses' Egyptian Mother" (tinyurl.com/mwuf5xwb).

Now to him who is able to do immeasurably more than all we ask or imagine, according to his power that is at work within us, to him be glory in the church and in Christ Jesus throughout all generations, for ever and ever! Amen.

—Ephesians 3:20–21, NIV

Thoughts to Ponder

In Exodus 2:2, when Moses's mother gave birth, she saw that he was a "fine child." (Other versions use various terms, such as beautiful, healthy, special baby, goodly child.) Consider that the birth of a healthy child was a precious gift, especially during these desperate times. Do you think God had a hand in his birth as well?

In Hebrews 11:23 (NIV), the writer includes Moses's parents among those who showed great faith: "By faith Moses's parents hid him for three months after he was born, because they saw he was no ordinary child, and they were not afraid of the king's edict." What did these people know about God that gave them such faith in Him? Contrast the knowledge and resources available to you today to learn about God with those available to people living during the time of Moses's parents.

Do you feel like you're only supposed to bother God with the hard stuff, the problems you can't handle on your own? Why do you feel that way? What if you decided to turn your burdens over to God sooner? Read and comment on these scriptures: Matthew 11:28–30, 1 Peter 5:6–7, and Philippians 4:6–7. Perhaps you have other favorite scriptures that you can share.

Chapter 2

Moses Escapes from Egypt

Exodus 2:11–15, HCSB

(11) Years later, after Moses had grown up, he went out to his own people and observed their forced labor. He saw an Egyptian beating a Hebrew, one of his people. (12) Looking all around and seeing no one, he struck the Egyptian dead and hid him in the sand. (13) The next day he went out and saw two Hebrews fighting. He asked the one in the wrong, "Why are you attacking your neighbor?"

(14) "Who made you a leader and judge over us?" the man replied. "Are you planning to kill me as you killed the Egyptian?"

Then Moses became afraid and thought: What I did is certainly known. (15) When Pharaoh heard about this, he tried to kill Moses. But Moses fled from Pharaoh and went to live in the land of Midian, and sat down by a well.

◇◇◇

Do you ever wonder what Moses's life was like before he became the leader of the Israelites? Exodus 2 covers roughly the first 80 of his 120 years. A mere ten verses are dedicated to his first forty years. Even though Moses was a key figure in the Old Testament, almost everything recorded about him occurred during the last forty years of his life.

The early years of anyone's life greatly influence their remaining years. Thankfully, Moses's own mother nursed him through his formative years, and because of that, he was able to develop a relationship with his older siblings, Miriam and Aaron.

At some point, however, his mother turned him over to Pharaoh's daughter, who raised him as her own son. Who do you think his friends were then? The other

Hebrew children were busy being slaves. Pharaoh's daughter probably associated with Egyptian royalty. Do you think their children warmly embraced the Hebrew boy as their playmate? Human nature being what it is, it's likely Moses had difficulty fitting in anywhere during the years he lived in Egypt. At the very least, he was different from his peers. Perhaps feeling like an outsider is, at least in part, why Moses was reluctant to accept God's call to be the leader of the Israelites.

Regardless of his circumstances, Moses obviously felt a real connection with the Hebrews. He was willing to kill an Egyptian for abusing one of his people. The only known witness was the one he had defended, yet by the very next day, Moses realized his deed had already become widely known. He also realized his position of privilege and royalty did not sit well with his fellow Hebrews. You can almost hear the contempt in their voices. "Who made you a leader and judge over us? . . . Are you planning to kill me as you killed the Egyptian?" (Exodus 2:14, HCSB). In other words, *Who do you think you are? You are not the boss of us!*

Moses's deed did not sit well with the Pharaoh either. Presumably, Moses was not a royal favorite. As king, Pharaoh could easily have excused Moses's action; instead, he sought to have him killed. With no place to hide in Egypt, either among the royalty or among the Hebrews, Moses fled the country and finally stopped in the land of the Midianites.

The route Moses took when he left Egypt is not known, but somehow he had to cross the Sinai Peninsula. This region was also under Egyptian rule, and Moses needed to get beyond Pharaoh's powerful reach. Whatever his course, the distance he traveled was significant, at least several hundred miles.

Think of how physically demanding Moses's escape was. Here was a man, all alone, crossing a sparsely populated, inhospitable landscape. It's likely he fled on foot with little more than the clothes on his back. When he finally reached Midian, what better place for a tired and possibly emaciated soul to rest than by a well of cool, refreshing water?

Running into the Unknown

Very little is known about the faith of the Hebrew people prior to Moses's return to Egypt. Even less is explained about Moses's life and personal faith. When Moses fled Egypt into Midian, what did he know of God? Did he associate with his birth family or other Hebrews as he got older? If so, did they instruct him about God? What did they know about God, and how did they worship Him while living as slaves?

When Moses fled into an unknown land and an unknown future, it wasn't faith that drove him; it was fear and exhaustion that surely overwhelmed him. The ruler of one of the mightiest kingdoms on earth wanted him dead and had great resources at his disposal to go after him. Moses did not yet know God as he would in the years to come, nor was his faith in God nearly as developed as it would become later. Imagine how lonely he must have felt when he arrived in Midian, depleted in every way—spiritually, physically, and emotionally.

> When Moses fled into an unknown land and an unknown future, it wasn't faith that drove him; it was fear and exhaustion that surely overwhelmed him.

God waits for you in the lonely places.

Have you ever been forced to run or at least step out into the unknown? What compelled you to do so? What sustained you as you faced the uncertainty? Dealing with a new situation can be unnerving, particularly one that's suddenly thrust upon you.

Perhaps you've found yourself in a circumstance that seems as dire as what Moses faced so long ago. You, too, may feel depleted in every way.

Where your life differs from Moses's is that you have access to spiritual resources that were not available to him. Today, we have

Where was the land of the Midianites?

Pull up this map to get a better idea of how far Moses had to travel through Egyptian-controlled areas before reaching Midian: "Midian" (tinyurl.com/5y82mcpf).

This map identifies various locations and landmarks in the area: "Exodus Route Map" (tinyurl.com/2rtjxs8d).

the Bible, and by reading and studying it, we can know God. *Yes, those who have the desire to know God can truly know Him!* God will make sure of it. Remember Jesus's promise: "Ask, and it will be given to you; seek, and you will find; knock, and it will be opened to you. For everyone who asks receives, and the one who seeks finds, and to the one who knocks it will be opened" (Matthew 7:7–8, ESV).

If you find yourself thrust upon a path not of your choosing, remember that God's people can step out in faith. Christians never have to walk or run alone. Moreover, wherever your path may lead, you can rest assured that God is already there.

Where can I go from your Spirit?
Where can I flee from your presence?
If I go up to the heavens, you are there;
if I make my bed in the depths, you are there.
If I rise on the wings of the dawn,
if I settle on the far side of the sea,
even there your hand will guide me,
your right hand will hold me fast.
If I say, "Surely the darkness will hide me
and the light become night around me,"
even the darkness will not be dark to you;
the night will shine like the day,
for darkness is as light to you.

—Psalm 139:7–12, NIV

Thoughts to Ponder

Moses had royal standing, so why did he not use his status to command the Egyptian to stop beating the Hebrew? What might have compelled Moses to kill the slave master?

_____

_____

_____

_____

How many pharaohs reigned during Moses's life up until the Exodus? Ancient timelines vary, but it's possible that the pharaoh when Moses fled to Midian was not the same pharaoh whose daughter had adopted Moses. Compare a Bible timeline, such as the "Bible Hub Bible Timeline" (tinyurl.com/5b65355c), with a timeline of the pharaohs, such as the "Pharaoh Timeline" (tinyurl.com/bdet3mmu). Dates differ among various timelines, so you might want to research several to get a broader picture of the time period.

_____

_____

_____

_____

The Law that was later given to Moses on Mount Sinai was the first written law given to God's people. In the years prior to the Law being given, how did the Hebrews receive instruction from God? How did they learn about God, particularly while they lived as slaves in Egypt?

_____

_____

_____

_____

Chapter 3

Moses Finds a Family Among the Midianites

Exodus 2:16–22, HCSB

(16) Now the priest of Midian had seven daughters. They came to draw water and filled the troughs to water their father's flock. (17) Then some shepherds arrived and drove them away, but Moses came to their rescue and watered their flock. (18) When they returned to their father Reuel he asked, "Why have you come back so quickly today?"

(19) They answered, "An Egyptian rescued us from the shepherds. He even drew water for us and watered the flock."

(20) "So where is he?" he asked his daughters. "Why then did you leave the man behind? Invite him to eat dinner."

(21) Moses agreed to stay with the man, and he gave his daughter Zipporah to Moses in marriage. (22) She gave birth to a son whom he named Gershom, for he said, "I have been a foreigner in a foreign land."

◇◇◇

Little is known about Moses's personal life, but these few verses provide just a glimpse. His stay in Midian spanned roughly forty years of his life (from age forty to age eighty), and it was during this time that Moses found a wife and fathered two children.

— 1 —

Several other Bible versions of this passage state these animals were sheep.

— 2 —

See Genesis 17 for God's covenant with Abraham. In verses 4–8, God promises to make Abraham the father of many nations.

— 3 —

See Genesis 17:19–21.

— 4 —

See Genesis 25:12–18 for a listing of Ishmael's twelve sons who became tribal rulers.

— 5 —

See Genesis 25:1–6 for a listing of Abraham's sons by Keturah.

It's interesting to note that Moses's first recorded encounter in Midian involved another conflict. His strong sense of right and wrong compelled him to defend the young women who had come to the well to water their father's flock.[1] The same character trait that had him running from Egypt took him right into the home of Jethro (also called Reuel), the father of the young shepherdesses. Even though the women believed he was Egyptian, they invited him to their home because he had defended them. He later became part of their family when he married Zipporah, one of Jethro's daughters.

Who were these Midianite people with whom Moses found refuge? The book of Genesis provides the answer, and it's there we learn that Abraham was truly the father of many nations.[2] Although God chose Isaac to be the one through whose lineage Christ would eventually enter the world,[3] Abraham fathered other children.

Abraham's first wife was Sarai (whose name God later changed to Sarah). As Sarai got older and saw that she was unable to conceive, she gave her Egyptian servant, Hagar, to Abraham (who was still called Abram at the time). The son born of this union was Ishmael. Although he was Abraham's firstborn child, he was not the one through whom God would fulfill His covenant. God promised, however, to make Ishmael into a great nation and that he would become the father of twelve rulers.[4]

At some point in his life, Abraham took another wife, Keturah. It's uncertain when this union occurred, but she is not mentioned in the Scriptures until after the death of Sarah. By Keturah, Abraham fathered six sons, one of whom was Midian.[5] Like Moses, the Midianites with whom he found a home were descendants of Abraham.

Finding Refuge in a Foreign Land with the "Friend of God"

The Scripture reading for this lesson provides a glimpse into the interesting character of Reuel, the head of this Midianite household.[6] He is called a priest, and from all indications here and in later scriptures, he worshiped the same God as the Hebrews.[7] Even his name means "friend of God" in Hebrew. As a descendant of Abraham, the knowledge he had of God had evidently been passed on to him through the generations.

Another important thing to note about Reuel was the hospitality he readily extended to a stranger. He had cause to be hospitable, of course, because Moses had defended his daughters, but hospitality also seems to be characteristic of God's people through the ages. Recall how Abraham welcomed strangers in Genesis 18:1–15. Then later, when God set His laws before the Israelites, He included this admonition in Exodus 22:21 (NIV): "Do not mistreat or oppress a foreigner, for you were foreigners in Egypt."

Evidently, Moses made a lasting impression on Reuel and his family. They invited him to dinner, and he stayed for forty years![8] Reuel even allowed Moses to marry his daughter, Zipporah, and become a permanent member of his household. This all speaks to the mutual admiration and trust that must have developed between these two men. Later references in the Scriptures also seem to confirm that these men held one another in high regard.

> They invited him to dinner, and he stayed for forty years!

At this point in his life, Moses had no inkling of what God had in store for him later. When he named his firstborn son Gershom, he acknowledged, however, that he had become a foreigner in a foreign land.[9] Although he lived in a welcoming household, had taken a wife, and even had a child, he still considered himself a foreigner in the land of

6

Reuel is also called Jethro later on, and both names identify him as Moses's father-in-law (Exodus 3:1). Perhaps one of the names was more of a title because he was a priest, and the other his proper or given name. Depending on which reference you consult, the name Jethro means "abundance" or "his excellence," while Reuel means "friend of God." For more information on these names, see "Jethro" at *Smith's Bible Dictionary* (tinyurl.com/529jrdm7) and "Reuel" at *Behind the Name* (tinyurl.com/y4af5syb).

7

See Exodus 18, particularly verses 9–12, where Jethro gives praise and offers a sacrifice to God.

8

The number of years Moses lived in Midian can be derived from several scriptures. In reviewing Jewish history before he was stoned to death, Stephen stated in Acts 7:23–30 that Moses was forty years old when he struck down the Egyptian and that he then lived as an exile in Midian for another forty years. This would align with Exodus 7:7, which states that Moses was eighty when he went back to Egypt to speak to the reigning Pharaoh.

9

Other Bible versions use the word "sojourner" or "stranger" instead of "foreigner."

Midian. Perhaps Moses knew this place would not be his lasting home.

Considering the whole of Moses's life, his years in Midian may have been the only time he experienced a somewhat normal life. He certainly seemed to fit in better among these fellow descendants of Abraham than he had in Egypt. Back there, he hadn't really belonged in either Pharaoh's family or among the Hebrew slaves. When he later led the Israelites through the wilderness for forty years, he encountered one hardship or disaster after another. Immense responsibility, the constant grumbling from the people, a revolt against his leadership, and ridicule from his own brother and sister about his wife were only a few of the things he faced after his time in Midian. But, as a foreigner in a foreign land, he found a place of rest, if only for a while, thanks to Reuel's hospitality.

Christians are encouraged to be hospitable.

Romans 12:9–21 (NIV) provides a wonderful blueprint for living and specifically states in verse 13: "Share with the Lord's people who are in need. Practice hospitality." Jesus described the hospitable nature of those who will inherit the Kingdom of Heaven in Matthew 25:35–36 (HCSB): "For I was hungry and you gave Me something to eat; I was thirsty and you gave Me something to drink; I was a stranger and you took Me in; I was naked and you clothed Me; I was sick and you took care of Me; I was in prison and you visited Me."

You never know what may become of even a small amount of kindness or hospitality. What you are able to provide may be desperately needed by someone else. Even if it doesn't seem significant or appreciated at the time, your generosity may prove to be pivotal down the road. Reuel had no idea that the stranger he took in would later become one of God's greatest leaders. He simply invited him to dinner and let him spend the night. As opportunities arise, remember Reuel's example—offer what you have, and let God do the rest.

Above all, maintain an intense love for each other, since love covers a multitude of sins. Be hospitable to one another without complaining. Based on the gift each one has received, use it to serve others, as good managers of the varied grace of God.

—1 Peter 4:8–10, HCSB

Do not neglect to show hospitality to strangers, for by this some have entertained angels without knowing it.

—Hebrews 13:2, NASB

The Importance of Hospitality in Bible Times

Outside of the cities or villages, few of the accommodations we take for granted today existed in ancient times. Travelers often depended on the hospitality of the residents of the area. Particularly in harsher climates, food, water, and shelter may have been hard to find. The hospitality residents showed others was more than a nicety—it often became vital to the well-being and survival of travelers and strangers.

This article discusses hospitality customs during Bible times: "Travelers and Strangers: Hospitality in the Biblical World" (tinyurl.com/59nz65p6).

See also Deuteronomy 10:17–19, where God explained to the Israelites how they were to treat foreigners and the less fortunate among them.

Thoughts to Ponder

What was Sarai's heritage? See Genesis 20:12.

_____

_____

_____

_____

_____

Jethro asked why his daughters returned so soon. What does this imply about what may have been the norm in caring for their flock?

_____

_____

_____

_____

Other than being the firstborn, how was Ishmael different from the six sons of Keturah? For further information, see the BibleHub.com commentary page for Genesis 25:1 (tinyurl.com/48r8kxv3).

_____

_____

_____

_____

_____

Chapter 4

Moses's Call to Leadership

Exodus 2:23–3:10, ESV

(2:23) During those many days the king of Egypt died, and the people of Israel groaned because of their slavery and cried out for help. Their cry for rescue from slavery came up to God. (24) And God heard their groaning, and God remembered his covenant with Abraham, with Isaac, and with Jacob. (25) God saw the people of Israel—and God knew.

(3:1) Now Moses was keeping the flock of his father-in-law, Jethro, the priest of Midian, and he led his flock to the west side of the wilderness and came to Horeb, the mountain of God. (2) And the angel of the LORD appeared to him in a flame of fire out of the midst of a bush. He looked, and behold, the bush was burning, yet it was not consumed. (3) And Moses said, "I will turn aside to see this great sight, why the bush is not burned." (4) When the LORD saw that he turned aside to see, God called to him out of the bush, "Moses, Moses!" And he said, "Here I am." (5) Then he said, "Do not come near; take your sandals off your feet, for the place on which you are standing is holy ground." (6) And he said, "I am the God of your father, the God of Abraham, the God of Isaac, and the God of Jacob." And Moses hid his face, for he was afraid to look at God.

(7) Then the LORD said, "I have surely seen the affliction of my people who are in Egypt and have heard their cry because of their taskmasters. I know their sufferings, (8) and I have come down to deliver them out of the hand of the Egyptians and to bring them up out of that land to a good and broad land, a land flowing with milk and honey, to the place of the Canaanites, the Hittites, the Amorites, the Perizzites, the Hivites, and the Jebusites. (9) And now, behold, the cry of the people of Israel has come to me, and I have also seen the oppression with which the Egyptians oppress them. (10) Come, I will send you to Pharaoh that you may bring my people, the children of Israel, out of Egypt."

Suggested Song

"Take My Life, and Let It Be"

(tinyurl.com/2tebvs5e)

What began as an ordinary day for Moses turned out to be one that changed the course of his life and shifted the flow of events for what would become the nation of Israel. This was the day God called Moses to be a leader and, in so doing, set in motion one of the greatest journeys of all time.

A handful of crucial days shaped Moses's entire life. First, there was the day his mother set him afloat in a basket in the Nile River. Because of her desperate faith that God would provide, Pharaoh's daughter rescued Moses, and he went from being a slave child condemned to death to a privileged member of the royal household.

Forty years later, the day he killed an Egyptian sent him on another life-changing journey. He went from being royalty to being a fugitive. Moses fled Egypt and found sanctuary and, for another forty years, made a home living among the Midianites. He established a new life, took a wife, and fathered children.

Then, one ordinary day, while tending his father-in-law's sheep in the wilderness, he saw a burning bush. On that day, Moses encountered God. Little did he know that he would go on to develop a close friendship with the Almighty. Life would never be the same: not for Moses, not for his family, and not for the nation of Israel.

Coming to the Mountain of God

As Moses led his flock toward Mount Horeb, a fire caught his attention. He quickly realized this was no ordinary occurrence. An angel of the Lord appeared among the flames, and the bush itself remained unharmed, even though it was covered in flames. The strange sight compelled Moses to draw closer. When he did, God spoke to him from within the bush.

Not since the time of Jacob and Joseph had God spoken directly to any of His people.[1] No one presently living on the

---

1

God spoke to Joseph through dreams and also gave him the ability to interpret dreams. See Genesis 37:1–11 for Joseph's dreams as a young man. See Genesis 40 and 41 for the account of Joseph interpreting the dreams of the cupbearer, the baker, and Pharaoh while living in Egypt. See Genesis 32:22–32 for the account of Jacob wrestling with God and his name being changed to Israel. See Genesis 46:1–4 for the account of God speaking to Jacob and telling him to go to Egypt. God promised him that He would go with them and that Joseph's hand would close his eyes when he passed away.

earth had heard the voice of God. (If someone did, it's not recorded in Scripture.)

Even though God had not spoken, He had been listening. He had heard the cry of the Israelites, He saw their affliction and oppression, and He knew it was time to free them. He chose Moses to be the one to lead His people out of Egypt and on toward the Promised Land. God's ultimate goal was the fulfillment of His promise to Abraham.

Moses was uniquely qualified for the journey that lay ahead. Unlike the other Hebrews who had been living as slaves, Moses had been raised by Pharaoh's daughter. It's likely he received the highest quality education and cultural training of the time. Few, if any, of the Hebrew slaves would have traveled outside Egypt or have firsthand knowledge of the area to which they would soon be fleeing. Moses had already traversed the area and established contacts with Jethro's household and possibly others while living in exile.

Consider, in particular, Moses's relationship with Jethro.[2] It was no accident that Moses landed where he did. Being privileged to live among a priest's household for forty years provided Moses with spiritual knowledge and insight that may well have been missing or, at best, underdeveloped while living among the Egyptians. Jethro became a father figure to Moses. While Moses may have kept in contact with his biological family during the first forty years of his life, he was certainly not raised in a traditional household or with his Hebrew father. Perhaps God purposely sent Moses to Midian to be nurtured and trained by this wise man.

God had been preparing Moses his entire life for the role to which He called him on that not-so-ordinary day from the burning bush. That role was to be the leader of the Israelite people. The duration of their servitude, which God had foretold to Abraham centuries earlier, was drawing to a close.[3] As promised, God would deliver them out of Egypt. The Israelite people had

———— 2 ————
Exodus 18 tells of Jethro's visit to Moses after the Israelites had escaped Egypt. This chapter provides more insight into the character of Jethro and the relationship he had with Moses.

———— 3 ————
See Genesis 15 for God's covenant with Abraham. Note verses 13–14 (NLT): "Then the LORD said to Abram, 'You can be sure that your descendants will be strangers in a foreign land, where they will be oppressed as slaves for 400 years. But I will punish the nation that enslaves them, and in the end they will come away with great wealth.'"

What Are the Dispensations?

Bible history can be divided into distinct periods of time, often referred to as "dispensations." This word is not found in the Bible, but it does prove helpful in discussing the Scriptures. Bible scholars, at their discretion, have used it to denote various time periods, and they may differ on the number and names of the dispensations.

The Patriarchal Dispensation existed from the time of the creation of Adam until the giving of the Law of Moses. During that era, God gave instructions to and dealt with the family heads of households or patriarchs, such as Noah, Abraham, Isaac, and Jacob.

The Mosaic Dispensation began when God gave the children of Israel a written law. This consisted of the Ten Commandments as well as other recorded laws and directives (the book of Leviticus contains many of His instructions and commands).

When Jesus came, He offered Himself as the perfect sacrifice for sin, once and for all time. Thus, when He defeated death and rose from the grave, the Law of Moses was fulfilled. He ushered in the **Christian Dispensation** by establishing a spiritual, rather than an earthly, kingdom.

For more information, see the definition provided by BibleStudyTools.com: "Dispensation" (tinyurl. com/2p9szstu).

reached a turning point in their history, and through Moses's leadership, God would transform them from a group of slaves into a nation. There, on the Mountain of God, Moses stood upon the cusp of a new era for the Israelite people.

God continues to call people to do His will today.

Have you ever wondered why you are living now, at this point in time? It isn't by accident or coincidence. As the Apostle Paul explained to the people of Athens in Acts 17:26–27, it is God who determines when and where each person should live. He desires so much for you to reach out to Him that He has selected the most opportune time and place for you to live.

> He desires so much for you to reach out to Him that He has selected the most opportune time and place for you to live.

Just as it was no accident that Moses landed where he did, it's no accident that you are alive today and living exactly where you are. Your days may seem ordinary, but like Moses, you will experience moments that change everything. During those moments, you have the choice to respond to God's call or to disregard it and go on about your life.

And if you're wondering why God would call you, the answer is simple: You have characteristics and experiences that are unique to you. God has a special role for you, but it is up to you to decide whether you will respond, as Moses did so long ago, "Here I am."

The God who made the world and everything in it is the Lord of heaven and earth and does not live in temples built by human hands. And he is not served by human hands, as if he needed anything. Rather, he himself gives everyone life and breath and everything else. From one man he made all the nations, that they should inhabit the whole earth; and he marked out their appointed times in history and the boundaries of their lands. God did this so that they would seek him and perhaps reach out for him and find him, though he is not far from any one of us.

—Acts 17:24–27, NIV

Thoughts to Ponder

Why do you suppose God commanded Moses to remove his shoes? How does this fore-shadow some of the directives God will give later concerning priests?

_____

_____

_____

_____

_____

Are we to consider Mount Horeb (also called Mount Sinai) as holy ground today? Why or why not?

_____

_____

_____

_____

_____

Have you ever had a day when the whole trajectory of your life changed? Did you initiate the change, or was it thrust upon you? What life lesson did you learn? Perhaps you know of others who have had such an experience from which you can draw inspiration or gain insight.

_____

_____

_____

_____

_____

GOD REDIRECTS
MOSES'S LIFE

Chapter 5

God Reveals His Plan to Moses

Exodus 3:11–22, HCSB

(11) But Moses asked God, "Who am I that I should go to Pharaoh and that I should bring the Israelites out of Egypt?"

(12) He answered, "I will certainly be with you, and this will be the sign to you that I have sent you: when you bring the people out of Egypt, you will all worship God at this mountain."

(13) Then Moses asked God, "If I go to the Israelites and say to them: The God of your fathers has sent me to you, and they ask me, 'What is His name?' what should I tell them?"

(14) God replied to Moses, "I AM WHO I AM. This is what you are to say to the Israelites: I AM has sent me to you." (15) God also said to Moses, "Say this to the Israelites: Yahweh, the God of your fathers, the God of Abraham, the God of Isaac, and the God of Jacob, has sent me to you. This is My name forever; this is how I am to be remembered in every generation.

(16) "Go and assemble the elders of Israel and say to them: Yahweh, the God of your fathers, the God of Abraham, Isaac, and Jacob, has appeared to me and said: I have paid close attention to you and to what has been done to you in Egypt. (17) And I have promised you that I will bring you up from the misery of Egypt to the land of the Canaanites, Hittites, Amorites, Perizzites, Hivites, and Jebusites—a land flowing with milk and honey. (18) They will listen to what you say. Then you, along with the elders of Israel, must go to the king of Egypt and say to him: Yahweh, the God of the Hebrews, has met with us. Now please let us go on a three-day trip into the wilderness so that we may sacrifice to Yahweh our God.

(19) "However, I know that the king of Egypt will not allow you to go, unless he is forced by a strong hand. (20) I will stretch out My hand and strike Egypt with all My

miracles that I will perform in it. After that, he will let you go. (21) And I will give these people such favor in the sight of the Egyptians that when you go, you will not go empty-handed. (22) Each woman will ask her neighbor and any woman staying in her house for silver and gold jewelry, and clothing, and you will put them on your sons and daughters. So you will plunder the Egyptians."

◇◇◇

Suggested Song

"Great I Am"

(tinyurl.com/45mfyf3k)

Moses's knowledge of God up to this point had depended entirely upon information passed on to him from others. Now, during this, his first encounter with God, Moses had witnessed a miracle, heard the voice of God, and learned that God had a plan for his life. Thus began Moses's relationship with God, one of the closest ever recorded in Scripture.

Others might have been rendered speechless by what he'd seen or by God's life-changing proposal. Moses, instead, uttered the immortal words—*Who am I that I should . . .?* With that question, he verbalized his self-doubt. It's one of the greatest stumbling blocks of all time—one that people continue to place in their own way today. Fill in the blank with whatever seems too difficult, and you'll be using the same excuse Moses offered so long ago.

In all fairness to Moses, he had his reasons for asking this question of God. He knew full well that he would be confronting the world's most powerful ruler. Twice his life had been placed in the crosshairs by the pharaoh, and it's doubtful he wanted to be in that position again.[1] Then, there was the matter of the Israelite people. Uniting this vast multitude of slaves into a nation would be a monumental task. Moses doubted they would even accept him as their leader. Years earlier, they had taunted him after he had struck down the Egyptian taskmaster, asking him, "Who made you a leader and judge over us?" (Exodus 2:14, HCSB). Even forty years later, it's doubtful Moses had forgotten the sting of those words.

1

It is unknown whether the pharaoh who ordered all the Hebrew boy babies killed was the same one who later sought Moses's life after he killed the Egyptian. Historical accounts vary concerning the names of the pharaohs and the dates they ruled. By the time God called Moses to return to Egypt, however, He told him in Exodus 4:19 that all those who had sought to kill him were now dead.

God, of course, was prepared for Moses's objection. He immediately countered Moses's self-doubt by promising to be with Moses and offered him a sign: Moses would bring the Israelite people back with him to this very mountain, and here they would all worship God. Moses's return, alive and intact, accompanied by the Israelite people, would serve as proof that God had sent him. How else could a mission so difficult and implausible be successful, except by divine intervention?

With that concern addressed, Moses moved down his list of reasons why he believed God had chosen the wrong person. Would the Israelites even believe it was God who had sent him? Moses knew the Israelites had been living among the Egyptians for several centuries, immersed in a culture that worshiped false gods.[2] How would Moses convince them that it was the true God who had sent him? He needed to know the name by which the Israelites would recognize God.

God responded to Moses with this statement in verse 14: "I AM WHO I AM." He then instructed Moses to simply tell them, "I AM has sent me to you."

> "I AM has sent me to you."

In this statement, God expresses Himself in two words: one subject, referring to Himself, and one verb, the first person singular present tense of *be*. No matter the time period, He is the God who exists, infinite and eternal, always in the present tense.[3]

God then took the explanation of His identity from the theoretical to terminology the Israelites would easily recognize. Moses was to tell them the Lord—*Yahweh*, the God of their fathers, Abraham, Isaac, and Jacob—had sent him. God explained, "This is My name forever; this is how I am to be remembered in every generation" (Exodus 3:15b, HCSB).

With that long-standing relationship established, God assured Moses the elders of Israel would listen to him. Once he had their attention, Moses was to deliver God's message: God

<hr>

2

Joseph, the first of the children of Israel to enter Egypt, was given a wife by Pharaoh. She was the daughter of a pagan priest (Genesis 41:45). So from their early days in Egypt on to the present, the Israelites had lived among those who worshiped false gods. This article at BibleArchaeology. org provides more historical insight into Joseph's life in Egypt: "Joseph in Egypt: Part IV" (tinyurl.com/stz4t6em).

<hr>

3

Jesus also expressed His eternal nature to the Jews in a similar manner when he told them in John 8:58 (NIV)—"before Abraham was born, I am!"

———— 4 ————

Genesis 15:13–14 (NIV):
"Then the LORD said to him, 'Know for certain that for four hundred years your descendants will be strangers in a country not their own and that they will be enslaved and mistreated there. But I will punish the nation they serve as slaves, and afterward they will come out with great possessions.'"

The Mountain of God

Mount Horeb and Mount Sinai appear to be the same place. Mount Horeb is mentioned for the first time in the Bible in Exodus 3:1 and is called the mountain of God. Mount Sinai is named in Exodus chapters 19–20 as the mountain where the Ten Commandments were given to Moses by God. In Deuteronomy 5:2, these same events are described as having transpired at Mount Horeb.

The geographic location of Mount Horeb or Mount Sinai is up for debate. The site that is identified on many Bible maps as Mount Sinai, located on the Sinai Peninsula, does not seem to fit the description or

had been watching over them, He had seen their misery, and He would deliver them out of Egypt to a land flowing with milk and honey. They would witness God's mighty hand performing wonders so great that, ultimately, Pharaoh would be compelled to let the Israelites go. Not only that, but they would also leave with great wealth! It would all come about just as God had promised Abraham so long ago.[4]

"I will certainly be with you."

Those reassuring words should have been enough for Moses. But remember: Moses did not know God very well yet. They had just met! So Moses questioned God. He simply could not understand how he could accomplish the task God had set before him. It seemed too big, too dangerous, too unreasonable.

From that day forward, Moses repeatedly witnessed the power and peace of God's presence. With God's help, he fulfilled the calling he received that day in the wilderness, standing barefoot in front of a burning bush. Yes, God called Moses to do the seemingly impossible, but He never expected him to do it alone.

> God called Moses to do the seemingly impossible, but He never expected him to do it alone.

God does not expect you to walk alone.

We are blessed today to have easy access to know about God through His Holy Word, the Bible. It is filled with His promises and wisdom. By studying the Bible, we can know and understand God so much better than Moses did during the earlier years of his life. Moses, Abraham, Isaac, Jacob, the prophets, the apostles, and all of God's people who have gone before us have laid a foundation of faith. Their lives continue to inspire and bless all who come after. We can see how God worked in their lives and accompanied them through all He had called them to do.

That same God continues to work in our lives today. He is *Yahweh*, the Great I Am. He was *Yahweh* then, He remains *Yahweh* now, and He will be *Yahweh* forevermore. He has proven Himself faithful to His people throughout the ages, and His faithfulness will continue throughout eternity. You can know that *Yahweh* will always walk with His people, no matter how difficult their path. Call upon Him, and allow *Yahweh* to walk with you.

The LORD makes firm the steps
of the one who delights in him;
though he may stumble, he will not fall,
for the LORD upholds him with his hand.

—Psalm 37:23–24, NIV

Where can I go from your Spirit?
Where can I flee from your presence?
If I go up to the heavens, you are there;
if I make my bed in the depths, you are there.
If I rise on the wings of the dawn,
if I settle on the far side of the sea,
even there your hand will guide me,
your right hand will hold me fast.
If I say, "Surely the darkness will hide me
and the light become night around me,"
even the darkness will not be dark to you;
the night will shine like the day,
for darkness is as light to you.

—Psalm 139:7–12, NIV

characteristics given in Scripture. Many Bible scholars feel Mount Sinai is actually located in Arabia. Adding to the confusion, it seems Horeb may also refer to the whole range of mountains, while Sinai may refer to an individual peak. Sometimes Sinai may also refer to the region surrounding Mount Sinai.

Because of the uncertainty of the location of Mount Horeb, or Mount Sinai, for the purposes of this book, the term "mountain of God" will often be used instead.

This site, WyattMuseum.com, presents archaeological information on Mount Sinai, including this article: "The Traditional Mt. Sinai" (tinyurl.com/28vjn7hv).

JewishEncyclopedia.com provides a great deal of information in this article: "Sinai, Mount" (tinyurl. com/mrymvus4).

Thoughts to Ponder

Why do some versions of the Bible use "Yahweh" for the name of God in these passages while others use LORD in capital letters? When is "Jehovah" used? Discuss these names and how Bible translators have influenced the names by which we call God. These articles provide further insight:

- "Is Jehovah the true name of God?" (tinyurl.com/bdk37ph5).

- "Ex 3:15" (tinyurl.com/2b3akrh2).

_____

_____

_____

God instructed Moses to tell the elders that He would bring the Israelites out of Egypt to the land of Canaan. He listed all the various groups currently living there. Who were these people? Whenever God promised the land of Canaan to Abraham, why did he not immediately give the land to him? How did God use the Israelites' time in Egypt to set them up for their future life in Canaan?

_____

_____

_____

Consider the debt of gratitude Christians owe Moses and the many people of faith who lived before us. They helped lay the foundation on which Christianity has been built, with Christ Himself serving as the chief cornerstone. Read Hebrews 11 and discuss the faith exhibited by these people and how their lives still impact us today.

_____

_____

_____

Chapter 6

God Equips Moses for His Role

Exodus 4:1–17, NIV

(1) Moses answered, "What if they do not believe me or listen to me and say, 'The LORD did not appear to you'?"

(2) Then the LORD said to him, "What is that in your hand?"

"A staff," he replied.

(3) The LORD said, "Throw it on the ground."

Moses threw it on the ground and it became a snake, and he ran from it. (4) Then the LORD said to him, "Reach out your hand and take it by the tail." So Moses reached out and took hold of the snake and it turned back into a staff in his hand. (5) "This," said the LORD, "is so that they may believe that the LORD, the God of their fathers—the God of Abraham, the God of Isaac and the God of Jacob—has appeared to you."

(6) Then the LORD said, "Put your hand inside your cloak." So Moses put his hand into his cloak, and when he took it out, the skin was leprous—it had become as white as snow.

(7) "Now put it back into your cloak," he said. So Moses put his hand back into his cloak, and when he took it out, it was restored, like the rest of his flesh.

(8) Then the LORD said, "If they do not believe you or pay attention to the first sign, they may believe the second. (9) But if they do not believe these two signs or listen to you, take some water from the Nile and pour it on the dry ground. The water you take from the river will become blood on the ground."

(10) Moses said to the LORD, "Pardon your servant, Lord. I have never been eloquent, neither in the past nor since you have spoken to your servant. I am slow of speech and tongue."

(11) The LORD said to him, "Who gave human beings their mouths? Who makes

them deaf or mute? Who gives them sight or makes them blind? Is it not I, the LORD? (12) Now go; I will help you speak and will teach you what to say."

(13) But Moses said, "Pardon your servant, Lord. Please send someone else."

(14) Then the LORD's anger burned against Moses and he said, "What about your brother, Aaron the Levite? I know he can speak well. He is already on his way to meet you, and he will be glad to see you. (15) You shall speak to him and put words in his mouth; I will help both of you speak and will teach you what to do. (16) He will speak to the people for you, and it will be as if he were your mouth and as if you were God to him. (17) But take this staff in your hand so you can perform the signs with it."

Suggested Song

"Anywhere with Jesus"
(tinyurl.com/27ecvwch)

It's one thing to witness miracles, but can you imagine being able to perform them? God knew how extraordinary this mission of leading the Israelites out of Egypt was going to be. He did not expect Moses to accomplish this great feat alone, nor did He expect him to go ill-equipped. God enabled Moses to perform miraculous signs to show that the one true God had sent him.

The first sign frightened Moses. At the sight of his staff becoming a snake, his survival instincts kicked in, and he ran. Fortunately, upon God's command, he had enough faith to reach down and grasp the snake by its tail. Just as miraculously, the snake turned back into his staff.

The sign of leprosy must have been just as fearful. Leprosy brought great stigma on people, leaving them isolated from society and physically disfigured. Seeing his hand infected with this dreaded disease must have alarmed Moses. As with the snake, however, God showed Moses that He had power over the disease.

God knew the Israelites would demand further proof and equipped Moses with yet another miracle to demonstrate that he was there by God's authority. He told Moses that when the people asked for another sign, he was to take some water from the Nile River and pour it onto the dry ground, where the water would turn into blood. (Later, God would use this same miracle in one of the plagues He inflicted upon the Egyptians.)

God promised Moses that He would be with him. Then He armed Moses with these three miraculous signs that would surely convince the Israelites he had been sent by God. Still, Moses did not want to accept the mission. So he offered yet another excuse, and it was perfect: He had an inherent defect. Surely this would prove to be the fatal flaw he needed to disqualify himself!

What was it that Moses considered such a problem?[1] It could have been a lack of eloquence or even an actual speech impediment. Or perhaps, having lived among the Midianites for the past forty years, he had lost some of his command of the Hebrew and Egyptian languages. Regardless, Moses told God his speech would hinder his ability to communicate effectively. Perhaps it slipped his mind that he was speaking to his Creator. God immediately, in no uncertain terms, set him straight, assuring him that He would help him speak.

Now out of excuses, Moses resorted in verse 13 to begging: "Please send someone else!" He knew that accepting God's call meant leaving the comfort zone in which he'd been living for the past forty years. God, on the other hand, knew that Moses's entire life had been lived in preparation for this role, and no one else could fulfill it as he could.

It was at this point in his newly developing relationship with God that Moses learned two important things about the Almighty:

1) He is not easily dissuaded.
2) His patience has its limits.

God made it clear that the discussion was over. He did, however, make an important concession: Moses's brother Aaron would accompany him and perform the speaking duties. Having a partner would provide support for Moses, and who better than his brother, who had been living among the Israelites? With

---
1

This article presents numerous Bible translations of Exodus 4:10: "The Speech Problem of Moses" (tinyurl.com/mtz5rnwt).

Scroll down and read the "Conclusion" concerning Moses's speech problem.

that, Moses was equipped for what lay ahead. And then, God reminded him—*Don't forget your staff!*

God Equips His People

Moses was acutely aware of his flaws and his fears and, as a result, felt far from perfect for the mission God called him to do. He knew he was out of touch with the Israelite people if, indeed, he had ever been considered one of them. The only thing he was accustomed to leading was sheep. But, in God's eyes, Moses was the one, and He would see to it that Moses was fully equipped for the job.

God continues to call imperfect people to serve Him today.

Maybe you can relate to Moses's reluctance to do what God has called you to do. You can offer a list of reasons why you aren't the right person for the job. You are sure you don't have what it takes to succeed. But here's what Moses had to learn and what you may need to hear as well: All that's required to serve God is a willing heart and a commitment to obey Him. Your divine Creator knows your needs and has promised to supply them. He knows where the gaps in your ability lie, and He can effortlessly fill them in.[2]

> All that's required to serve God is a willing heart and a commitment to obey Him.

The Apostle Paul likened humans to earthen vessels, fragile jars of clay that are easily chipped or broken. When God's people proclaim the Word and allow His light to shine in their lives, they glorify Him rather than themselves. Their imperfections make it all the more evident that a message as powerful as the gospel of Christ could only come from God and not from them.[3]

Remember that God does not send out His people ill-equipped. You have the Bible, the written Word of God. It serves as the most invaluable resource, providing instruction and equipping God's people for every good work.[4] Not only that, but Christians also receive the Holy Spirit. Christ left this beautiful gift to provide His people with comfort and strength.[5] And, of course, Christians are part of the family of God. They have one another from whom they are able to draw encouragement and support.[6]

Serving God may well take you out of your comfort zone, just as it did Moses so long ago. But there are things that only you can do, and there are people that only you can reach. God has prepared many good works for you. He will go with you, and He will equip you, but it's up to you to step out in faith and choose to do them.[7]

Now may the God of peace, who through the blood of the eternal covenant brought back from the dead our Lord Jesus, that great Shepherd of the sheep, equip you with everything good for doing his will, and may he work in us what is pleasing to him, through Jesus Christ, to whom be glory for ever and ever. Amen.

—Hebrews 13:20–21, NIV

——— 5 ———

"And I will pray the Father, and He will give you another Helper, that He may abide with you forever—the Spirit of truth, whom the world cannot receive, because it neither sees Him nor knows Him; but you know Him, for He dwells with you and will be in you" (John 14:16–17, NKJV).

"I pray that from his glorious, unlimited resources he will empower you with inner strength through his Spirit. Then Christ will make his home in your hearts as you trust in him. Your roots will grow down into God's love and keep you strong" (Ephesians 3:16–17, NLT).

——— 6 ———

"Now, therefore, you are no longer strangers and foreigners, but fellow citizens with the saints and members of the household of God, having been built on the foundation of the apostles and prophets, Jesus Christ Himself being the chief cornerstone" (Ephesians 2:19–20, NKJV).

——— 7 ———

"For we are His workmanship, created in Christ Jesus for good works, which God prepared beforehand that we should walk in them" (Ephesians 2:10, NKJV).

Egypt

The ancient Egyptians worshiped many gods. The signs and miracles God gave Moses to perform were meant to show Pharaoh and the Egyptian people that the Israelites' God, Yahweh, was real. He could do what their lifeless gods could not.

Egypt had been the preeminent civilization in the Mediterranean region for centuries. At this point in their history, during the period known as the New Kingdom, Egypt was likely the greatest country in the known world.

These articles present more information on ancient Egypt:

"Egypt" (tinyurl.com/3yufkh5b). Read the "Encyclopedia" entry and then click on the map to see a larger map of the whole area.

"List of Ancient Great Powers" (tinyurl.com/53aerj3n).

"Ancient Egypt: History, Dynasties, Religion and Writing" (tinyurl.com/3ndpuakj).

Find approximate dates for various events: "Bible Timeline" (tinyurl.com/5b65355c).

Thoughts to Ponder

Consider Moses's response to God's calling. He used every excuse he could think of to get out of doing what God wanted him to do. At this point in his life, Moses did not have the faith to take even the first step, so God had to shove him. People who end up accomplishing great things for God are not necessarily larger-than-life characters with a burning desire to serve. Who else did God use in His service in the Scriptures who fits this description?

_____

_____

_____

_____

While he was out tending the flock, he probably didn't carry much with him other than his staff. God used this common object, something that was right there in Moses's hand, to equip him for service. What common things can we use today in God's service?

_____

_____

_____

How can God use us even when we feel like that fragile jar of clay that Paul talks about in 2 Corinthians 4:7?

_____

_____

_____

Chapter 7

Moses Leaves for Egypt

Exodus 4:18–26, ESV

(18) Moses went back to Jethro his father-in-law and said to him, "Please let me go back to my brothers in Egypt to see whether they are still alive." And Jethro said to Moses, "Go in peace." (19) And the LORD said to Moses in Midian, "Go back to Egypt, for all the men who were seeking your life are dead." (20) So Moses took his wife and his sons and had them ride on a donkey, and went back to the land of Egypt. And Moses took the staff of God in his hand.

(21) And the LORD said to Moses, "When you go back to Egypt, see that you do before Pharaoh all the miracles that I have put in your power. But I will harden his heart, so that he will not let the people go. (22) Then you shall say to Pharaoh, 'Thus says the LORD, Israel is my firstborn son, (23) and I say to you, "Let my son go that he may serve me." If you refuse to let him go, behold, I will kill your firstborn son.'"

(24) At a lodging place on the way the LORD met him and sought to put him to death. (25) Then Zipporah took a flint and cut off her son's foreskin and touched Moses's feet with it and said, "Surely you are a bridegroom of blood to me!" (26) So he let him alone. It was then that she said, "A bridegroom of blood," because of the circumcision.

◇◇◇

What thoughts must have been racing through Moses's mind as he made his way back to Jethro with the sheep? He had experienced something few mortals ever would: a direct encounter with God. Beyond that, God had charged him with leading a mission that, to achieve, would require divine intervention. And now, Moses would have to tell Jethro, the head of the family who had become Moses's own, that he intended to take Jethro's daughter and grandsons on a journey to a place where Moses hadn't been in forty years.

With each step he took, Moses must have felt another page turning in this chapter of his life. His sojourn among the Midianites had reached its end.

Following cultural protocol, Moses didn't just pack up and go. Even though he was eighty, he asked Jethro's permission to leave. Interestingly enough, the reason he gave for this trip was *not* that he had received a charge from God. Rather, he stated that he wanted to see if his relatives were still alive, something Jethro would surely understand.

With Jethro's blessing, Moses loaded up his wife and sons and embarked on a journey that would last the rest of his life. It is for this role in uniting a people into a nation and leading them out of slavery to the land God had promised them that we remember Moses. Fortunately, he remembered to take his staff because he was going to need it.

God had prepared Moses for what he would face upon his return to Egypt. He had equipped Moses with miracles and explained how Pharaoh would respond. He even gave him the words and the warnings he was to speak to the Egyptian leader.

But there was something for which Moses wasn't prepared. Something that, to us, seems shocking. God tried to kill Moses!

Why, after selecting Moses for this mission, would God do this? The answer starts back in Genesis 12 with God's covenant with Abram. Among the blessings that God promised him were land, many descendants, and that all families of the earth would be blessed through him. Later, in Genesis 17, God changed his name to Abraham and instructed him concerning male circumcision. This was to serve as a physical sign of God's covenant, and it was to be binding on Abraham and all of his offspring.

Moses, of all people, needed to be in compliance with God's directives. Not only was he a descendant of Abraham, but he would also be the one leading the Israelites to the land God had promised to Abraham. God could not allow someone who had defied His covenant to help Him fulfill one of the integral components of His promise to Abraham.

Scripture provides only a brief account of this encounter, but it's clear that Moses had failed to circumcise one of his sons. Moses had lived among the Midianites for forty years, but how long he had been married or how old his two sons were is not recorded. It would seem that one son, presumably the older one, had been circumcised. It's possible Zipporah had witnessed the first circumcision because she knew what to do. These are all suppositions, however, because the Bible simply does not provide the details of this incident.

Regardless, Zipporah understood why God was trying to kill Moses. She performed the circumcision herself, something Moses should have done already. Her actions were sufficient to cause God to relent and not kill Moses. Her words about Moses being a bridegroom of blood to her seem to reveal her disdain for the act of circumcision. Even so, she circumcised her son in order to save Moses's life.

Moses Learns the Importance of Obeying God

The importance of this incident of God trying to kill Moses cannot be overstated. We know what Moses went on to become—one of the greatest leaders in Bible history. Later, when Jesus was transfigured on the mountain and His divine glory revealed, only two people appeared and spoke with Him—Moses and Elijah. (See Matthew 17:1–13.) Moses is referenced repeatedly in both the Old and New Testaments because of the role he played and the example he set for God's people.

God's Promise to Abraham

Although God made His original covenant with Abraham, He repeated His promise to Isaac in Genesis 26:2–5 and again to Jacob in Genesis 28:10–15. This could be why God, on numerous occasions, states the names of all three patriarchs and not just Abraham. After God told Jacob to go down to Egypt in Genesis 46:1–7, there is no record in the scriptures of God speaking to anyone until His encounter with Moses on the mountain in the burning bush.

God called Abram in Genesis 12:1–3. In Genesis 13:14–17, God promised to give the land to Abram and his descendants forever. In Genesis 15, God made His covenant with Abram and defined the land which He would give him in verses 18–21. In Genesis 17, God changed Abram's name to Abraham and instituted circumcision as the sign of His covenant with Abraham and his descendants.

As Moses found out,

circumcision was not optional for Abraham and his male descendants. God told Abraham in Genesis 17:9–14 (NIV):

"As for you, you must keep my covenant, you and your descendants after you for the generations to come. This is my covenant with you and your descendants after you, the covenant you are to keep: Every male among you shall be circumcised. You are to undergo circumcision, and it will be the sign of the covenant between me and you. For the generations to come every male among you who is eight days old must be circumcised, including those born in your household or bought with money from a foreigner—those who are not your offspring. Whether born in your household or bought with your money, they must be circumcised. My covenant in your flesh is to be an everlasting covenant. Any uncircumcised male, who has not been circumcised in the flesh, will be cut off from his people; he has broken my covenant."

God knew when He called Moses what he *could* become. But at the very point of his transition from a shepherd into the leader of a nation, God stood ready to squelch him. All that Moses was set to accomplish almost didn't happen. God had done His part in preparing Moses: He had watched over him, cared for him, and directed certain events throughout his life. Moses, however, had a part to fulfill as well, and that was to obey God's commands. He had failed to keep God's covenant of circumcision regarding his son, and God could not and would not overlook that omission. Now, as Moses stood on the threshold of his new role, God refused to allow him to cross over until His covenant had been honored.

> All that Moses was set to accomplish almost didn't happen.

What can we learn from Moses's encounter with God?

Think of the mitigating factors in Moses's life: He was raised by Pharaoh's daughter rather than in an Israelite household; he had been living among the Midianites for the past forty years; there was currently no written law for him to study. You can probably think of other reasons, but the point is this: If anyone should have been given a little slack, it should have been Moses. Any excuse we may come up with today for not obeying God is simply that—an excuse.

How do you learn about what God expects of you? By studying His Word. Many things have transpired since the time of Moses, namely that God sent His Son, Jesus, to serve as the perfect sacrifice for sin, once and for all time. With Jesus's resurrection, He ushered in the New Covenant under which we live today. God has done His part, just as He promised. But like Moses, we have a part, and that is to obey His Word and keep His commands.

My dear children, I write this to you so that you will not sin. But if anybody does sin, we have an advocate with the Father—Jesus Christ, the Righteous One. He is the atoning sacrifice for our sins, and not only for ours but also for the sins of the whole world.

We know that we have come to know him if we keep his commands. Whoever says, "I know him," but does not do what he commands is a liar, and the truth is not in that person. But if anyone obeys his word, love for God is truly made complete in them.

—1 John 2:1–5a, NIV

This article, "What is the Abrahamic Covenant?" (tinyurl.com/mtn4ufzn), discusses the various aspects of the special covenant God made with Abraham.

Thoughts to Ponder

Why do you think Moses did not tell Jethro his real reason for returning to Egypt, that he had been given a charge by God?

_____

_____

_____

_____

_____

Why do you think Moses had not circumcised his son? Is circumcision required today?

_____

_____

_____

_____

When Zipporah used the term "bridegroom of blood," how does that remind you of Christ?

_____

_____

_____

_____

Chapter 8

Moses Becomes a Leader

Exodus 4:27–31; 5:1–21, HCSB

(4:27) Now the LORD had said to Aaron, "Go and meet Moses in the wilderness." So he went and met him at the mountain of God and kissed him. (28) Moses told Aaron everything the LORD had sent him to say, and about all the signs He had commanded him to do. (29) Then Moses and Aaron went and assembled all the elders of the Israelites. (30) Aaron repeated everything the LORD had said to Moses and performed the signs before the people. (31) The people believed, and when they heard that the LORD had paid attention to them and that He had seen their misery, they bowed down and worshiped.

(5:1) Later, Moses and Aaron went in and said to Pharaoh, "This is what Yahweh, the God of Israel, says: Let My people go, so that they may hold a festival for Me in the wilderness."

(2) But Pharaoh responded, "Who is Yahweh that I should obey Him by letting Israel go? I do not know anything about Yahweh, and besides, I will not let Israel go."

(3) Then they answered, "The God of the Hebrews has met with us. Please let us go on a three-day trip into the wilderness so that we may sacrifice to Yahweh our God, or else He may strike us with plague or sword."

(4) The king of Egypt said to them, "Moses and Aaron, why are you causing the people to neglect their work? Get to your work!" (5) Pharaoh also said, "Look, the people of the land are so numerous, and you would stop them from working."

(6) That day Pharaoh commanded the overseers of the people as well as their foremen: (7) "Don't continue to supply the people with straw for making bricks, as before. They must go and gather straw for themselves. (8) But require the same quota of bricks from them as they were

making before; do not reduce it. For they are slackers—that is why they are crying out, 'Let us go and sacrifice to our God.' (9) Impose heavier work on the men. Then they will be occupied with it and not pay attention to deceptive words."

(10) So the overseers and foremen of the people went out and said to them, "This is what Pharaoh says: 'I am not giving you straw. (11) Go get straw yourselves wherever you can find it, but there will be no reduction at all in your workload.'" (12) So the people scattered throughout the land of Egypt to gather stubble for straw. (13) The overseers insisted, "Finish your assigned work each day, just as you did when straw was provided." (14) Then the Israelite foremen, whom Pharaoh's slave drivers had set over the people, were beaten and asked, "Why haven't you finished making your prescribed number of bricks yesterday or today, as you did before?"

(15) So the Israelite foremen went in and cried for help to Pharaoh: "Why are you treating your servants this way? (16) No straw has been given to your servants, yet they say to us, 'Make bricks!' Look, your servants are being beaten, but it is your own people who are at fault."

(17) But he said, "You are slackers. Slackers! That is why you are saying, 'Let us go sacrifice to the LORD.' (18) Now get to work. No straw will be given to you, but you must produce the same quantity of bricks."

(19) The Israelite foremen saw that they were in trouble when they were told, "You cannot reduce your daily quota of bricks." (20) When they left Pharaoh, they confronted Moses and Aaron, who stood waiting to meet them.

(21) "May the LORD take note of you and judge," they said to them, "because you have made us reek in front of Pharaoh and his officials—putting a sword in their hand to kill us!"

Before heading to Egypt, Moses met Aaron at the mountain of God. This was the same mountain where Moses had encountered God at the burning bush. And it was where God had promised that Moses would return with the Israelite nation in tow and worship Him there. (See Exodus 3:12.) In the near future, this mountain would become the scene for even more momentous events as well.

Meeting on this mountain represented much more than a long-awaited family reunion for Moses and Aaron. It was here that the two brothers who had been apart for at least forty years united as leaders of God's people; their lives would never be the same.

Like Moses, Aaron had been called by God to come to this mountain. He needed little (if any) convincing when Moses explained God's instructions and told him about the signs with which he had been equipped. Likewise, the elders of the Israelites were quick to believe Moses and Aaron when the people witnessed the signs. Relieved and hopeful that God had heard their prayers and seen their misery, they bowed down and worshiped Him. The leaders had proven their worthiness to their new followers.

Soon, however, their leadership would be put to the test. Their meeting with Pharaoh became a confrontation. Regardless of how respectfully he and Aaron may have approached him, for slaves to come before the ruler of this great kingdom with a request of any kind would have been seen as an affront to his power. Adding to the insult, they demanded three days off work—for all of the slaves and their families—not to worship an Egyptian god but this unknown Yahweh.

Their request infuriated Pharaoh. Even worse, the Israelites' coming together under a centralized leadership threatened his authority, something he immediately sought to quell by increasing their workload.

Pharaoh's retaliation proved effective. His demand for the same output while requiring the Hebrews to gather their own materials did two things. First, it scattered them throughout the land. Fewer slaves concentrated in any one area made an insurrection against the Pharaoh less likely to occur and also easier to control, should that happen. Second, it made meeting the quota for bricks impossible—and the beatings inevitable. In response, the people immediately turned on Moses and Aaron.

Moses's Wife and Children

The scriptures do not record much concerning Moses's family. Exodus 2:21–22 tells us that Jethro gave Moses his daughter Zipporah in marriage and that she gave birth to a son whom Moses named Gershom. Then, in Exodus 4:20–26, Moses took his wife and sons (plural) and put them on a donkey and headed back to Egypt. It was during this trip that Zipporah was forced to circumcise one of her sons in order to save Moses's life.

In Acts 7, Stephen made his speech before the council, after which he was stoned to death. In his speech, he summarized the history of the Jewish people and mentioned in verse 29 that Moses had two sons during his sojourn in Midian. The name of Moses's second son, Eliezer, is mentioned in Exodus 18:2–6. Jethro took Zipporah and her two sons back to Moses after the Israelites' exodus from Egypt while they were encamped at the mountain of God. Then,

Moses's Leadership Challenged

Leaders often receive the glory when things go well, but they're the first to catch the blame when events turn sour. The Israelites faulted Moses and Aaron for their plight, even calling upon God to judge them. They likened what these new leaders had done in confronting the Pharaoh to handing him the sword with which to kill them. Strong words indeed, but they were the ones who had been placed in such an impossible situation. They, not Moses and Aaron, were the ones being squeezed in this power play.

Moses and Aaron knew their charge to lead the Israelites had come from the one true and living God. In turn, they had convinced the people of this as well. Now, during Pharaoh's challenge to their leadership, the people threw it back in their faces. At this point, Moses and Aaron had a choice. They could walk away. They had tried. Who would fault them for withering under this onslaught of resistance and criticism? Had they done so, God could have created another means by which to accomplish His will.

They, indeed, may have considered walking away from the people who were so quick to turn on them. But if they had faltered and not stood firm, think of the unbelievable opportunity Moses and Aaron would have missed in allowing God to work through them.

They made their choice to stay, perhaps not for the people's sake or even their own, but because of what they believed God could do.

> The Israelites faulted Moses and Aaron for their plight, even calling upon God to judge them.

Leading or standing up for what you know is right can lead to attacks.

It's easy to become discouraged when your words or actions are challenged. Yet, when you have committed your life to following God, be determined to stay the course. Like Moses, your journey on this earth will one day define your life. At the end, you know that your reward will be eternal life with God. But for every day you're still here, be courageous and keep the faith. You don't want to miss out on the many ways God has planned to work His will through your life.

My enemies have trampled upon me all day long,
For they are many who fight proudly against me.
When I am afraid,
I will put my trust in You.
In God, whose word I praise,
In God I have put my trust;
I shall not be afraid.
What can mere mortals do to me?

—Psalm 56:2–4, NASB

I have fought the good fight, I have finished the race, I have kept the faith. Now there is in store for me the crown of righteousness, which the Lord, the righteous Judge, will award to me on that day—and not only to me, but also to all who have longed for his appearing.

—2 Timothy 4:7–8, NIV

in the genealogy given in 1 Chronicles 23:15, Gershom and Eliezer are listed as the sons of Moses.

The only other mention of Moses's wife occurs in Numbers 12 when his sister, Miriam, and his brother, Aaron, talk against Moses because of his Cushite wife. Whether this wife was Zipporah or someone else is not known.

Thoughts to Ponder

Consider the journey Moses and his family made to the mountain of God through the eyes of Zipporah and the children. What do you think they were feeling? How much of a part would they play in the future in Moses's life?

_____

_____

_____

Consider Moses and Aaron's leadership through the eyes of the Israelites, whose lives had quickly gone from bad to very bad. What choices did they have? What power did they hold over their own lives? What do you think they were feeling?

_____

_____

_____

_____

Moses spent eighty years preparing for his signature role as the leader of the Israelite nation, but he did not realize that until the day of the burning bush. Seeing as how he lived to be 120, his life at this point was two-thirds over! Most of the things he's known for throughout the Bible he accomplished during the last third of his life.

It's the same for you: You have been preparing for your future your entire life, and everything up to this moment serves as a prelude to what will follow. Think of examples of people of various ages in the Bible who allowed God to work through their lives. How can you serve God with the rest of your life, no matter how much or how little is left?

_____

_____

_____

_____

Chapter 9

Moses Questions God

Exodus 5:22–6:13; 7:1–7, NLT

(5:22) Then Moses went back to the LORD and protested, "Why have you brought all this trouble on your own people, Lord? Why did you send me? (23) Ever since I came to Pharaoh as your spokesman, he has been even more brutal to your people. And you have done nothing to rescue them!"

(6:1) Then the LORD told Moses, "Now you will see what I will do to Pharaoh. When he feels the force of my strong hand, he will let the people go. In fact, he will force them to leave his land!"

(2) And God said to Moses, "I am Yahweh— 'the LORD.' (3) I appeared to Abraham, to Isaac, and to Jacob as El-Shaddai—'God Almighty'—but I did not reveal my name, Yahweh, to them. (4) And I reaffirmed my covenant with them. Under its terms, I promised to give them the land of Canaan, where they were living as foreigners. (5) You can be sure that I have heard the groans of the people of Israel, who are now slaves to the Egyptians. And I am well aware of my covenant with them.

(6) "Therefore, say to the people of Israel: 'I am the LORD. I will free you from your oppression and will rescue you from your slavery in Egypt. I will redeem you with a powerful arm and great acts of judgment. (7) I will claim you as my own people, and I will be your God. Then you will know that I am the LORD your God who has freed you from your oppression in Egypt. (8) I will bring you into the land I swore to give to Abraham, Isaac, and Jacob. I will give it to you as your very own possession. I am the LORD!'"

(9) So Moses told the people of Israel what the LORD had said, but they refused to listen anymore. They had become too discouraged by the brutality of their slavery.

(10) Then the LORD said to Moses, (11) "Go back to Pharaoh, the king of Egypt, and tell

him to let the people of Israel leave his country."

(12) "But LORD!" Moses objected. "My own people won't listen to me anymore. How can I expect Pharaoh to listen? I'm such a clumsy speaker!"

(13) But the LORD spoke to Moses and Aaron and gave them orders for the Israelites and for Pharaoh, the king of Egypt. The LORD commanded Moses and Aaron to lead the people of Israel out of Egypt.

(7:1) Then the LORD said to Moses, "Pay close attention to this. I will make you seem like God to Pharaoh, and your brother, Aaron, will be your prophet. (2) Tell Aaron everything I command you, and Aaron must command Pharaoh to let the people of Israel leave his country. (3) But I will make Pharaoh's heart stubborn so I can multiply my miraculous signs and wonders in the land of Egypt. (4) Even then Pharaoh will refuse to listen to you. So I will bring down my fist on Egypt. Then I will rescue my forces—my people, the Israelites—from the land of Egypt with great acts of judgment. (5) When I raise my powerful hand and bring out the Israelites, the Egyptians will know that I am the LORD."

(6) So Moses and Aaron did just as the LORD had commanded them. (7) Moses was eighty years old, and Aaron was eighty-three when they made their demands to Pharaoh.

Suggested Song

"A Shelter in the Time of Storm"

(tinyurl.com/2p8e2wfk)

Moses had obeyed God's calling. He had done *everything* God told him to do, and now the very people he was supposed to deliver had turned on him—and rightly so. Instead of making their lives better, he had made things so much worse, and they called upon God to judge him.

Distressed at these happenings, Moses cried out to God and questioned why he had even been sent. So far, God had done nothing to rescue the Israelites, and now they were hurting more than ever. Moses had not yet developed the trust and confidence in God that he would later on.

> So far, God had done nothing to rescue the Israelites, and now they were hurting more than ever.

In response, God told Moses he would soon see what all He would do! The time had come for Him to fulfill what He had promised to Abraham, Isaac, and Jacob centuries earlier. Moses and the Israelite people would be more than witnesses—they would be participants in these long-awaited events. God would deliver the Israelites from Egyptian slavery with His mighty hand. He would claim them as His people, and the land of Canaan would soon be theirs.

Unfortunately, in their state of despondency, the Israelites paid little attention to Moses when he told them what God had said. God had to prod even Moses to get him to take action and carry out His commands. But just as darkness often precedes a storm, things sometimes have to get worse before they can get better. At the moment, God's people were engulfed in the darkness. They were unable to see through their gloom and comprehend the significance of the moment.

God Reassures Moses

God reassured Moses during this difficult time by repeating to him His name, Yahweh. A name above all names, Yahweh speaks to His eternal nature. He is the Great I AM, the everlasting God—He always was, and He always will be. God's name is powerful, and like His very nature, it sets Him apart from all other gods.

The Egyptians worshiped many gods that took on various forms, such as that of an animal or the sun. Even the pharaohs were deemed to be deities. The Israelites worshiping only one God was, in itself, remarkable. Even more so was the fact that He was the Creator of all the animals and objects that personified the Egyptian gods. His name was truly above those false gods.

No other god had ever been nor ever would be like Yahweh. And it was only He who could deliver the Israelites from Egyptian captivity. What reassurance the very name of God—the LORD,

The Names of God

God addresses several of His names in Exodus 6:2–3. Here is the reading from the New Living Translation: "And God said to Moses, 'I am Yahweh— "the LORD." I appeared to Abraham, to Isaac, and to Jacob as El-Shaddai— "God Almighty"—but I did not reveal my name, Yahweh, to them.'"

Several commentaries suggest that possibly this statement was meant to be a question, something like this—but by my name Yahweh was I not known to them? This would make sense with the overall meaning of this discourse. Here are the same verses in the New International Version: "God also said to Moses, 'I am the LORD. I appeared to Abraham, to Isaac and to Jacob as God Almighty, but by my name the LORD I did not make myself fully known to them.'"

While the patriarchs had known the name of God, they had not known the full significance and power that His name implied. God had not fully revealed Himself to them.

The Israelites, however, were about to witness firsthand His great power. They would come to know God—both His nature and His power—to a much greater extent than the patriarchs ever had.

Yahweh, the Great I AM—gave to Moses during these seemingly hopeless and desperate times.

The name of God continues to reassure His people today.

By His name, we recognize His matchless power and the constancy of His being. He is the one true God, the God who always cares for His people. He is the God who kept His promises from long ago, and He is the God who sent Jesus Christ, His Son and our Redeemer, into the world.

When the dark clouds of life engulf you, remember the power and majesty of the name of God. He is the God who created the universe. He is the God who delivered the Israelites out of Egyptian bondage. He is the God you can trust, no matter what storms you may encounter. Call upon His name, and let His very name bring you peace and comfort.

As for me, I will call upon God; and the LORD shall save me.

—Psalm 55:16, KJV

For whosoever shall call upon the name of the Lord shall be saved.

—Romans 10:13, KJV

No longer will there be a curse upon anything. For the throne of God and of the Lamb will be there, and his servants will worship him. And they will see his face, and his name will be written on their foreheads.

—Revelation 22:3–4, NLT

Moses: Called by God

Thoughts to Ponder

Have you ever had a time in your life when you were caught up in the darkness before the storm and were unable to see how things could possibly work out? What did you learn from that experience? What could you see after the storm passed that you couldn't see before?

_____

_____

_____

Various religions and cultures have deified the created rather than the Creator. Why do you think the Egyptians had so many gods? What does that say about the scope of power of any one of their gods? Name other religions or philosophies that worship what has been created.

_____

_____

_____

_____

God is God, and the various names given in the Bible emphasize His different characteristics. These articles will help you research further the names of God and what they mean:

- "What Are the Names of God Found in the Bible?" (tinyurl.com/y55fkd3z)

- "What Are the Different Names of God, and What Do They Mean?" (tinyurl.com/4z7hfzwy)

Which of God's names are your favorites? How do they speak to you?

_____

_____

_____

_____

GOD DISPLAYS HIS POWER

Chapter 10

The Plagues Begin

Exodus 7:8–8:15, HCSB

(7:8) The LORD said to Moses and Aaron, (9) "When Pharaoh tells you, 'Perform a miracle,' tell Aaron, 'Take your staff and throw it down before Pharaoh. It will become a serpent.'" (10) So Moses and Aaron went in to Pharaoh and did just as the LORD had commanded. Aaron threw down his staff before Pharaoh and his officials, and it became a serpent. (11) But then Pharaoh called the wise men and sorcerers—the magicians of Egypt, and they also did the same thing by their occult practices. (12) Each one threw down his staff, and it became a serpent. But Aaron's staff swallowed their staffs. (13) However, Pharaoh's heart hardened, and he did not listen to them, as the LORD had said.

(14) Then the LORD said to Moses, "Pharaoh's heart is hard: he refuses to let the people go. (15) Go to Pharaoh in the morning. When you see him walking out to the water, stand ready to meet him by the bank of the Nile. Take in your hand the staff that turned into a snake. (16) Tell him: Yahweh, the God of the Hebrews, has sent me to tell you: Let My people go, so that they may worship Me in the wilderness, but so far you have not listened. (17) This is what Yahweh says: Here is how you will know that I am Yahweh. Watch. I will strike the water in the Nile with the staff in my hand, and it will turn to blood. (18) The fish in the Nile will die, the river will stink, and the Egyptians will be unable to drink water from it."

(19) So the LORD said to Moses, "Tell Aaron: Take your staff and stretch out your hand over the waters of Egypt—over their rivers, canals, ponds, and all their water reservoirs—and they will become blood. There will be blood throughout the land of Egypt, even in wooden and stone containers."

(20) Moses and Aaron did just as the LORD had commanded; in the sight of Pharaoh and his officials, he raised the staff and struck the water in the Nile, and all the water in the Nile was turned to blood. (21) The fish in the Nile died, and the river smelled so bad the Egyptians could not drink water from it. There was blood throughout the land of Egypt.

(22) But the magicians of Egypt did the same thing by their occult practices. So Pharaoh's heart hardened, and he would not listen to them, as the LORD had said. (23) Pharaoh turned around, went into his palace, and didn't even take this to heart. (24) All the Egyptians dug around the Nile for water to drink because they could not drink the water from the river. (25) Seven days passed after the LORD struck the Nile.

(8:1) Then the LORD said to Moses, "Go in to Pharaoh and tell him: This is what Yahweh says: Let My people go, so that they may worship Me. (2) But if you refuse to let them go, then I will plague all your territory with frogs. (3) The Nile will swarm with frogs; they will come up and go into your palace, into your bedroom and on your bed, into the houses of your officials and your people, and into your ovens and kneading bowls. (4) The frogs will come up on you, your people, and all your officials."

(5) The LORD then said to Moses, "Tell Aaron: Stretch out your hand with your staff over the rivers, canals, and ponds, and cause the frogs to come up onto the land of Egypt." (6) When Aaron stretched out his hand over the waters of Egypt, the frogs came up and covered the land of Egypt. (7) But the magicians did the same thing by their occult practices and brought frogs up onto the land of Egypt.

(8) Pharaoh summoned Moses and Aaron and said, "Ask Yahweh to remove the frogs from me and my people. Then I will let the people go and they can sacrifice to Yahweh."

(9) Moses said to Pharaoh, "You make the choice rather than me. When should I ask on behalf of you, your officials, and your people, that the frogs be taken away from you and your houses, and remain only in the Nile?"

(10) "Tomorrow," he answered.

Moses replied, "As you have said, so you may know there is no one like Yahweh our God, (11) the frogs will go away from you, your houses, your officials, and your people. The frogs will remain only in the Nile." (12) After Moses and Aaron went out from Pharaoh, Moses cried out to the LORD for help concerning the frogs that He had brought against Pharaoh. (13) The LORD did as Moses had said: the frogs in the houses, courtyards, and fields died. (14) They piled them in countless heaps, and there was a terrible odor in the land. (15) But when Pharaoh saw there was relief, he hardened his heart and would not listen to them, as the LORD had said.

Just as God had foretold, Pharaoh hardened his heart against the Israelites. Why should he care about the strange God these lowly slaves worshiped? Their labor provided fuel for the Egyptian economy and helped him maintain his magnificent kingdom. He knew any concessions made to them now would open the door for even greater demands in the future.

God Makes Himself Known

Rather than reveal His might all at once, God planned a progression of miracles. Certainly, He wanted to show His power to Pharaoh and the Egyptians, but just as importantly, He needed the Israelite people to understand who He was and what He could do. He also needed to give Moses time to grow into his role as a leader.

> Rather than reveal His might all at once, God planned a progression of miracles.

The first miracle Aaron performed to show God's great power had little impact. Pharaoh simply summoned his magicians, who likewise were able to turn their staffs into snakes. The fact that Aaron's staff-snake then swallowed theirs seemed totally inconsequential to Pharaoh, but it's likely his magicians took note and were probably alarmed.

Why wasn't this miracle enough? Why wouldn't it have struck fear and awe into anyone who witnessed it? For centuries, the Egyptian culture had been steeped in magic, witchcraft, and various beliefs in the supernatural. As king, Pharaoh had likely witnessed numerous acts of sleight-of-hand magic. It would take more than another snake act to impress him.

Aaron turning his staff into a snake was a miracle to be observed—a simple show of power. The ten plagues that followed not only revealed God's power, but they also created discomfort, misery, and loss.

The first involved the Nile River, which served as an enormous artery of life coursing through Egypt. The river supplied water for humans, livestock, and crops and provided an important means of transportation throughout the land. When the Nile and other water sources were turned into blood, the entire country suffered, and the stench must have been unbearable.

Although devastating and disgusting, this first plague failed to impress Pharaoh. After all, his magicians were able to mimic this miracle. The suffering of his people and the livestock seemed of no concern to him.

Then, after seven days, came the second plague: the invasion of the frogs. Massive amounts of them came up out of the Nile and other bodies of water, making their presence inescapable. Frogs invaded the people's homes, hopped on their beds, the tables where they prepared their food, and even on their bodies. This plague went beyond disgusting to being up close and personal. The noise alone had to have been deafening.

Again, Pharaoh's magicians were able to simulate this miracle, but this time, the frogs got Pharaoh's attention. He acknowledged God's power by asking Moses to have Yahweh remove them. In response, Moses told Pharaoh to name the time when they should leave. He wanted to make sure Pharaoh understood the extent of God's control.

The following day, the frogs died as Pharaoh had requested. The only ones that remained were those in the Nile. The country reeked from the enormous piles of dead frogs, but once again, Pharaoh hardened his heart against the Israelites.

Moses and Aaron acted in faith and obeyed God.

Approaching one of the most powerful rulers in the world, especially from the position of being slaves, took great courage on the part of Moses and Aaron. Their faith in God, however, proved stronger than their fear of Pharaoh. They understood

God's power, revered and obeyed His instructions, and believed He would do what He said He would do.

Christians today are called to act in faith as well. When you study God's Word, you come to know God. When you live your life in obedience to God, you learn to trust in Him. No matter how great the challenges you may face, you can live in confidence, knowing that God has promised to never leave His people. He will see you through.

Fear not, for I am with you;
be not dismayed, for I am your God;
I will strengthen you, I will help you,
I will uphold you with my righteous right hand.
—Isaiah 41:10, ESV

For we walk by faith, not by sight.

—2 Corinthians 5:7, ESV

Magic in Ancient Egypt

Magic was not only widely accepted in the ancient Egyptian culture, but it was infused into almost every aspect of their lives and also their afterlives. *The Egyptian Book of the Dead* provided magic spells that a soul would need after death to safely reach paradise. This article explains more about their belief in magic and the supernatural: "Magic in Ancient Egypt" (tinyurl.com/3wj7446p).

How were Pharaoh's magicians able to perform some of the same miracles that Aaron and Moses performed? They were probably highly skilled in sleight of hand, much like modern-day magicians. This article explores some of the possible ways they were able to perform miracles: "How Were Pharaoh's Magicians Able to Perform Miracles?" (tinyurl.com/4asa4jfb).

Thoughts to Ponder

What is a miracle? Does it need to happen instantly to be called a miracle, or can it happen over time?

_____

_____

_____

_____

_____

Why did God have Moses inform Pharaoh ahead of time as to what would occur?

_____

_____

_____

_____

Pharaoh seemed unimpressed by the miracles Moses and Aaron performed, but what do you think was going on in the minds of his magicians? How do you think these miracles affected the Egyptian people?

_____

_____

_____

_____

_____

Chapter 11

Gnats and Flies

Exodus 8:16–32, NIV

(16) Then the LORD said to Moses, "Tell Aaron, 'Stretch out your staff and strike the dust of the ground,' and throughout the land of Egypt the dust will become gnats." (17) They did this, and when Aaron stretched out his hand with the staff and struck the dust of the ground, gnats came on people and animals. All the dust throughout the land of Egypt became gnats. (18) But when the magicians tried to produce gnats by their secret arts, they could not.

Since the gnats were on people and animals everywhere, (19) the magicians said to Pharaoh, "This is the finger of God." But Pharaoh's heart was hard and he would not listen, just as the LORD had said.

(20) Then the LORD said to Moses, "Get up early in the morning and confront Pharaoh as he goes to the river and say to him, 'This is what the LORD says: Let my people go, so that they may worship me. (21) If you

do not let my people go, I will send swarms of flies on you and your officials, on your people and into your houses. The houses of the Egyptians will be full of flies; even the ground will be covered with them.

(22) "'But on that day I will deal differently with the land of Goshen, where my people live; no swarms of flies will be there, so that you will know that I, the LORD, am in this land. (23) I will make a distinction between my people and your people. This sign will occur tomorrow.'"

(24) And the LORD did this. Dense swarms of flies poured into Pharaoh's palace and into the houses of his officials; throughout Egypt the land was ruined by the flies.

(25) Then Pharaoh summoned Moses and Aaron and said, "Go, sacrifice to your God here in the land."

(26) But Moses said, "That would not be right. The sacrifices we offer the LORD

our God would be detestable to the Egyptians. And if we offer sacrifices that are detestable in their eyes, will they not stone us? (27) We must take a three-day journey into the wilderness to offer sacrifices to the LORD our God, as he commands us."

(28) Pharaoh said, "I will let you go to offer sacrifices to the LORD your God in the wilderness, but you must not go very far. Now pray for me."

(29) Moses answered, "As soon as I leave you, I will pray to the LORD, and tomorrow the flies will leave Pharaoh and his officials and his people. Only let Pharaoh be sure that he does not act deceitfully again by not letting the people go to offer sacrifices to the LORD."

(30) Then Moses left Pharaoh and prayed to the LORD, (31) and the LORD did what Moses asked. The flies left Pharaoh and his officials and his people; not a fly remained. (32) But this time also Pharaoh hardened his heart and would not let the people go.

◇◇◇

Suggested Song

"Into My Heart"

(tinyurl.com/5t43fnrr)

--------- 1 ---------

The King James Version, along with several others, calls them lice, while other versions call them gnats. Various Bible commentaries suggest they could have been mosquitos. Read the interesting commentaries on Exodus 8:16 at Biblehub.com (tinyurl.com/frrd46eu).

No sooner had the Egyptians piled the dead frogs into heaps when along came another plague. This time, however, God didn't give Pharaoh a warning. At God's command, Aaron stretched out his staff and struck the dust of the ground. The dust became gnats, and the gnats came upon the people and animals.

Bible translations vary as to whether these insects were gnats, mosquitos, lice, or some other type of tiny, obnoxious creatures.[1] Regardless, they invaded the people's personal space. Imagine them in your eyes and ears, up your nose, and even trying to get in your mouth. If they were lice or mosquitos, they would also be biting or stinging. Whatever the insects were, they were pervasive and inescapable.

With this third plague, Pharaoh's magicians realized they were outdone. They had probably suspected the miracles Moses and Aaron performed weren't simple tricks, but now they knew for sure. They admitted defeat and told Pharaoh in verse 19, "This is the finger of God." Nevertheless, Pharaoh refused to heed his own people's warning. As a result, the tiny creatures were soon followed by larger insects.

For the fourth plague, God sent forth flies—swarms and swarms of flies. This time, however, Pharaoh received an advance notice. Upon God's instruction, Moses approached Pharaoh in the early morning as he came out to the river. As he had before, Moses delivered God's message: Pharaoh was to let His people go so that they could worship Him. Moses then warned Pharaoh that if he refused, the land would be inundated with flies—on the people, in their houses, and covering the ground. And, just to make sure Pharaoh understood the extent of God's power, there would be no flies in Goshen, the area of Egypt where the Israelites lived.

Of course, Pharaoh refused to let his slaves go, and the next day, just as Moses had promised, dense swarms of flies invaded the land. They came into Pharaoh's palace and the homes of his officials. This massive amount of flies was more than an annoyance; they ruined the land.[2] They were everywhere *except* in Goshen.

Finally, Pharaoh relented. For the first time, he told Moses the Israelites could go sacrifice to the Lord, but they had to stay within Egypt's borders. Moses insisted they needed to travel at least a three-day journey into the desert. He argued that their sacrifices would be detestable to the Egyptians, so they needed to get far enough away where they would not be observed.

Desperate to have the flies gone and knowing that only the God of Moses could make that happen, Pharaoh agreed to allow the Israelites to go into the desert to offer sacrifices. His stipulation was that they couldn't go far. And then, in verse 28, the mighty king of Egypt made this request of Moses: "Now pray for me."

Indeed, Moses did pray, and God removed every one of the flies. Feeling relief from the pests, Pharaoh once again hardened his heart. He went back on his word and refused to let the Israelites go.

———— 2 ————
These swarms may have been a type of beetle that chewed and destroyed. See what various commentaries have to say about Exodus 8:24 at Biblehub.com (tinyurl.com/46pashd7).

A Heart Hardened by Pride

As the ruler of Egypt, Pharaoh was one of the most powerful and influential people in the world. Conceding to the demands of slaves would have made him appear weak and vulnerable in the eyes of other countries. Even worse, he would have lost face with his own people.

Added to that was the financial cost. Pharaoh could not afford to let the Israelites go. If he did, he risked losing them and the economic benefits they provided to his country. As he saw it, he had nothing to gain in letting them go but much to lose.

> Pharaoh could not afford to let the Israelites go.

Little did he know how much he and his country would ultimately lose because of his stubborn, prideful heart.

Pride continues to be a stumbling block to people today.

It is easy to become vested in certain positions or ideas. Can you think of a time when you refused to concede or back down, even when you knew you were wrong? No one likes to admit they've made a mistake, and too often, pride keeps us from changing course, even when we know we should.

God's people are called to do the right thing, even if it means they must give up an opinion they've held onto for a long time or disagree with a belief that is popular with the world. When God reveals what is right, God's people must follow Him and His ways.

How will you know what is right? Search the Scriptures with an open heart. Pray for wisdom to discern what is right and to have the courage to act upon it. Know that wise people can and do change their minds, while fools often do not.

The way of a fool is right in his own eyes,
But he who heeds counsel is wise.

—Proverbs 12:15, NKJV

Pride goes before destruction,
And a haughty spirit before a fall.
Better to be of a humble spirit with the lowly,
Than to divide the spoil with the proud.

—Proverbs 16:18–19, NKJV

Thoughts to Ponder

Before the fourth plague of the flies, God sent Moses early in the morning to speak to Pharaoh as he went down to the river. He had also done this with the earlier plague of turning the water into blood (Exodus 7:15). Going down to the river was likely part of the king's morning routine. This may have been an easier time for Moses to approach him directly. What impact do you think it made on Pharaoh to have Moses appear before him first thing in the morning before he even had a chance to wash himself off? How does it make you feel to have to confront something early in your day?

_____

_____

_____

_____

What do you think Pharaoh desired when he asked Moses to pray for him? Was he showing signs of humility, or was he only selfishly asking for relief from the plagues?

_____

_____

_____

Scripture has much to say concerning Pharaoh's hard heart. As the study of the plagues continues, watch for passages that indicate his state of mind and heart. Did God preordain him to act this way, or did God, as his Creator, already know how he would react?

_____

_____

_____

_____

Chapter 12

Livestock, Boils, and Hail

Exodus 9, NLT

(1) "Go back to Pharaoh," the LORD commanded Moses. "Tell him, 'This is what the LORD, the God of the Hebrews, says: Let my people go, so they can worship me. (2) If you continue to hold them and refuse to let them go, (3) the hand of the LORD will strike all your livestock—your horses, donkeys, camels, cattle, sheep, and goats—with a deadly plague. (4) But the LORD will again make a distinction between the livestock of the Israelites and that of the Egyptians. Not a single one of Israel's animals will die! (5) The LORD has already set the time for the plague to begin. He has declared that he will strike the land tomorrow.'"

(6) And the LORD did just as he had said. The next morning all the livestock of the Egyptians died, but the Israelites didn't lose a single animal. (7) Pharaoh sent his officials to investigate, and they discovered that the Israelites had not lost a single animal! But even so, Pharaoh's heart remained stubborn, and he still refused to let the people go.

(8) Then the LORD said to Moses and Aaron, "Take handfuls of soot from a brick kiln, and have Moses toss it into the air while Pharaoh watches. (9) The ashes will spread like fine dust over the whole land of Egypt, causing festering boils to break out on people and animals throughout the land."

(10) So they took soot from a brick kiln and went and stood before Pharaoh. As Pharaoh watched, Moses threw the soot into the air, and boils broke out on people and animals alike. (11) Even the magicians were unable to stand before Moses, because the boils had broken out on them and all the Egyptians. (12) But the LORD hardened Pharaoh's heart, and just as the LORD had predicted to Moses, Pharaoh refused to listen.

(13) Then the LORD said to Moses, "Get up early in the morning and stand before Pharaoh. Tell him, 'This is what the LORD, the God of the Hebrews, says: Let my people go, so they can worship me. (14) If you don't, I will send more plagues on you and your officials and your people. Then you will know that there is no one like me in all the earth. (15) By now I could have lifted my hand and struck you and your people with a plague to wipe you off the face of the earth. (16) But I have spared you for a purpose—to show you my power and to spread my fame throughout the earth. (17) But you still lord it over my people and refuse to let them go. (18) So tomorrow at this time I will send a hailstorm more devastating than any in all the history of Egypt. (19) Quick! Order your livestock and servants to come in from the fields to find shelter. Any person or animal left outside will die when the hail falls.'"

(20) Some of Pharaoh's officials were afraid because of what the LORD had said. They quickly brought their servants and livestock in from the fields. (21) But those who paid no attention to the word of the LORD left theirs out in the open.

(22) Then the LORD said to Moses, "Lift your hand toward the sky so hail may fall on the people, the livestock, and all the plants throughout the land of Egypt."

(23) So Moses lifted his staff toward the sky, and the LORD sent thunder and hail, and lightning flashed toward the earth. The LORD sent a tremendous hailstorm against all the land of Egypt. (24) Never in all the history of Egypt had there been a storm like that, with such devastating hail and continuous lightning. (25) It left all of Egypt in ruins. The hail struck down everything in the open field—people, animals, and plants alike. Even the trees were destroyed. (26) The only place without hail was the region of Goshen, where the people of Israel lived.

(27) Then Pharaoh quickly summoned Moses and Aaron. "This time I have sinned," he confessed. "The LORD is the righteous one, and my people and I are wrong. (28) Please beg the LORD to end this terrifying thunder and hail. We've had enough. I will let you go; you don't need to stay any longer."

(29) "All right," Moses replied. "As soon as I leave the city, I will lift my hands and pray to the LORD. Then the thunder and hail will stop, and you will know that the earth belongs to the LORD. (30) But I know that you and your officials still do not fear the LORD God."

(31) (All the flax and barley were ruined by the hail, because the barley had formed heads and the flax was budding. (32) But the wheat and the emmer wheat were spared, because they had not yet sprouted from the ground.)

(33) So Moses left Pharaoh's court and went out of the city. When he lifted his hands to the LORD, the thunder and hail stopped, and the downpour ceased. (34) But when Pharaoh saw that the rain, hail, and thunder had stopped, he and his officials sinned again, and Pharaoh again became stubborn. (35) Because his heart was hard, Pharaoh refused to let the people leave, just as the LORD had predicted through Moses.

Plague number five brought great destruction, but not without warning. Even though Moses relayed God's command and consequences, Pharaoh again refused to let the Israelites leave to worship their God.

The day after Moses's visit, just as he had promised, the livestock of the Egyptians died.[1] When Pharaoh sent his officials to check on the livestock of the Israelites, he probably knew they would find them alive, just as Moses had said, but he had to be sure. Even when presented with such strong evidence of God's power, Pharaoh still did not relent. He refused to let the Israelites go.

As with the gnats (the third plague), plague number six came unannounced. God simply instructed Moses to take handfuls of soot from the furnace and then throw the soot into the air while in Pharaoh's presence. The soot, as it spread throughout the land, caused festering boils to break out on both people and animals alike.[2] This plague caused painful sores, such that even Pharaoh's magicians could not stand in Moses's presence. Nevertheless, Pharaoh refused to listen to Moses or yield to God's request.[3]

Then came plague number seven, sheer destruction falling from the skies. With this plague, God revealed His purpose to Pharaoh as well as Pharaoh's role in God's overall plan. God told the king He could have easily destroyed him and his people with one powerful blow. Instead, God chose to use the plagues to make Himself and the extent of His power known throughout the earth. This revelation must have come as a rude shock to Pharaoh that the God of the Hebrews could use him, a powerful Egyptian king, for *His* purposes.

Never before had the Egyptians experienced anything like the continuous lightning, terrifying thunder, and unrelenting hail that came

> God revealed His purpose to Pharaoh as well as Pharaoh's role in God's overall plan.

Suggested Song

"Standing on the Promises of Christ Our King"

(tinyurl.com/573dpndp)

1

These animals provided transportation and carried loads. Some were used for food, and others were used in Egyptian worship. Losing so many animals must have dealt a huge blow to the Egyptian economy.

2

What animals were left after the fifth plague? Presumably, some survived. Also, fowl, domesticated animals, such as cats, and wild animals were not named among those listed in Exodus 9:3 that were to be affected. The Scriptures do not state how much time passed between plagues. It's possible the Egyptians were able to go purchase animals from somewhere else or maybe even from the Israelites. We are not told.

3

Plague number six was quite personal. Were Pharaoh and his family also inflicted with festering boils? We know they were not spared from the frogs (Exodus 8:3–4) or the flies (Exodus 8:24), which came up into the palace. It seems likely that Pharaoh himself was also affected by the boils, but evidently, he was able to still stand and talk with Moses, unlike his magicians.

with the seventh plague. The perils of the preceding plagues had convinced at least some of Pharaoh's officials to fear God. Those who heeded Moses's warning brought their people and animals under shelter. The Egyptian people had already endured so much, but with this storm, it seemed there was nothing left. Everything had been destroyed—everywhere, that is, except in the land of Goshen, where the Israelites lived.

A Brief Display of Humility

At long last, after much of his country lay ruined, Pharaoh confessed in verse 27, "This time I have sinned." Without expressing remorse for all the other times he had refused to let the Israelites go, Pharaoh relented due to the level of devastation this plague had caused. Not only did he agree to let the Israelites go, but he also acknowledged that God was right and he was wrong. Think of the pride he had to swallow in order to utter those words!

As Pharaoh requested, Moses then prayed to God for the hailstorm to cease, even though he doubted Pharaoh's sincerity. "But I know that you and your officials still do not fear the LORD God," he told him in verse 30, and of course, Moses was right. Once Pharaoh saw the storm was over and felt relief, he again went back on his word and refused to let the Israelites go.

God always keeps His promises.

Have you, like Pharaoh, ever made a promise and then failed to make good on it? Promises are easy to make during a difficult situation, but the resolve to fulfill them tends to fade away once relief is felt.

Contrast the promises people make with the promises of God. Unlike humans, God will not go back on His word. He will always do what He says He will do, and He will not waver. Make a list of God's promises and keep it handy. Remind yourself of His promises and draw upon their strength, whether in good times or bad. Take comfort in knowing that, unlike Pharaoh, our God keeps His promises.

God is not a man, so he does not lie.
He is not human, so he does not change his mind.
Has he ever spoken and failed to act?
Has he ever promised and not carried it through?

—Numbers 23:19, NLT

The grass withers and the flowers fade,
but the word of our God stands forever.

—Isaiah 40:8, NLT

Jesus Christ is the same yesterday, today, and forever.

—Hebrews 13:8, NLT

Plague 7—The Terrifying Storm

This storm must have been extraordinary, with a great amount of hail accompanied by thunder and lightning, which some Bible versions describe as fire running along the ground. Exodus 9:23–24 in the King James Version reads like this:

"And Moses stretched forth his rod toward heaven: and the LORD sent thunder and hail, and the fire ran along upon the ground; and the LORD rained hail upon the land of Egypt. So there was hail, and fire mingled with the hail, very grievous, such as there was none like it in all the land of Egypt since it became a nation."

Thoughts to Ponder

How were plague number three (gnats) and plague number six (boils) similar?

_____

_____

_____

Before the onset of plague number seven, the hailstorm, God reveals to Pharaoh His purpose for Pharaoh's life with this powerful discourse: "By now I could have lifted my hand and struck you and your people with a plague to wipe you off the face of the earth. But I have spared you for a purpose—to show you my power and to spread my fame throughout the earth" (Exodus 9:15–16, NLT).

Do you think Pharaoh really believed this statement from God? How do you think being told this affected Pharaoh's future decisions?

_____

_____

_____

In the above-mentioned scripture, God told Pharaoh He could have already killed Pharaoh and his people, but He chose not to. Turn this statement around for a moment and think from Pharaoh's perspective. Pharaoh was one of the most powerful rulers in the world, with great resources at his disposal. Why did he continue to tolerate Moses and Aaron, these Hebrew slaves, standing before him, often ruining his morning routine and making their outrageous demands? Why did he not order them executed immediately?

_____

_____

_____

_____

Chapter 13

Locusts

Exodus 10:1–20, NIV

(1) Then the LORD said to Moses, "Go to Pharaoh, for I have hardened his heart and the hearts of his officials so that I may perform these signs of mine among them (2) that you may tell your children and grandchildren how I dealt harshly with the Egyptians and how I performed my signs among them, and that you may know that I am the LORD."

(3) So Moses and Aaron went to Pharaoh and said to him, "This is what the LORD, the God of the Hebrews, says: 'How long will you refuse to humble yourself before me? Let my people go, so that they may worship me. (4) If you refuse to let them go, I will bring locusts into your country tomorrow. (5) They will cover the face of the ground so that it cannot be seen. They will devour what little you have left after the hail, including every tree that is growing in your fields. (6) They will fill your houses and those of all your officials and all the Egyptians—something neither your parents nor your ancestors have ever seen from the day they settled in this land till now.'" Then Moses turned and left Pharaoh.

(7) Pharaoh's officials said to him, "How long will this man be a snare to us? Let the people go, so that they may worship the LORD their God. Do you not yet realize that Egypt is ruined?"

(8) Then Moses and Aaron were brought back to Pharaoh. "Go, worship the LORD your God," he said. "But tell me who will be going."

(9) Moses answered, "We will go with our young and our old, with our sons and our daughters, and with our flocks and herds, because we are to celebrate a festival to the LORD."

(10) Pharaoh said, "The LORD be with you—if I let you go, along with your women and

children! Clearly you are bent on evil. (11) No! Have only the men go and worship the LORD, since that's what you have been asking for." Then Moses and Aaron were driven out of Pharaoh's presence.

(12) And the LORD said to Moses, "Stretch out your hand over Egypt so that locusts swarm over the land and devour everything growing in the fields, everything left by the hail."

(13) So Moses stretched out his staff over Egypt, and the LORD made an east wind blow across the land all that day and all that night. By morning the wind had brought the locusts; (14) they invaded all Egypt and settled down in every area of the country in great numbers. Never before had there been such a plague of locusts, nor will there ever be again. (15) They covered all the ground until it

was black. They devoured all that was left after the hail—everything growing in the fields and the fruit on the trees. Nothing green remained on tree or plant in all the land of Egypt.

(16) Pharaoh quickly summoned Moses and Aaron and said, "I have sinned against the LORD your God and against you. (17) Now forgive my sin once more and pray to the LORD your God to take this deadly plague away from me."

(18) Moses then left Pharaoh and prayed to the LORD. (19) And the LORD changed the wind to a very strong west wind, which caught up the locusts and carried them into the Red Sea. Not a locust was left anywhere in Egypt. (20) But the LORD hardened Pharaoh's heart, and he would not let the Israelites go.

◇◇◇

Suggested Song

"I Love to Tell the Story" (tinyurl.com/24x7n2ma)

For a moment, it seemed like plague number eight would be different. As Moses and Aaron stood before Pharaoh and his officials, they issued God's warning. Tomorrow locusts would invade the land of Egypt, the likes of which had never been before and never would be again. Pharaoh's officials knew the nation had already endured more than it could bear. At their urging, Pharaoh agreed to let the Israelites go.

His decree, however, was short-lived. When Pharaoh learned that Moses intended to take every Hebrew and every animal that belonged to them, contempt filled his response: "The LORD would have to be with you if I would ever let you and your families go! Look out—you're heading for trouble" (Exodus 10:10,

CSB). In other words, Pharaoh told them—*You've got to be kidding! You'd better watch your step.*[1] With that, he declared that only the men could go and then had Moses and Aaron escorted away.

Each of the preceding plagues had heaped on yet another layer of pain and destruction—to the land, to the animals, and to the people themselves. The fish in the Nile River had died, the hail had killed the livestock, beaten down the crops, stripped the trees bare, and destroyed everything else not under shelter. The people had endured their water being turned to blood, their personal space being invaded by frogs, gnats, and flies, and their bodies being inflicted with festering boils.

Now, with plague number eight, what little was left in Egypt would be destroyed by locusts. Using an east wind, God spread an enormous amount of locusts throughout the land. They covered the ground, infested the people's homes, and devoured any bit of green vegetation that remained in the fields or on the trees. The entire land of Egypt lay decimated.[2]

Desperate for relief, Pharaoh sent for Moses and Aaron. With a level of contrition not seen before, he confessed that he had sinned against God and against them. He pleaded with them to pray to God to take away this deadly plague. Moses complied, and with a strong west wind, God swept every locust into the Red Sea. But, of course, as soon as Pharaoh realized the land had been delivered of its burden, he once again refused to let the Israelites go.

> Desperate for relief, Pharaoh sent for Moses and Aaron.

God's Purpose Behind the Plagues

God could have easily delivered His people. He certainly didn't need Pharaoh's permission. Why, then, did He orchestrate such an elaborate series of plagues? God didn't make His intention a secret. He explicitly revealed His purpose before the plague of

---

1

In some versions of verse 10, Pharaoh accuses Moses of being bent on evil or that he has an evil purpose in mind. Evidently, Pharaoh is telling Moses he is not about to let him get away with this evil plot of robbing him of his slaves. You can read through the various Bible versions of Exodus 10:10 at Biblehub.com (tinyurl.com/4cmsxd9v).

2

The Timeline.com article, "In one year, 12 trillion locusts devastated the Great Plains—and then they went extinct" (tinyurl.com/m5j7wxjh), provides a vivid and compelling description of the great Rocky Mountain locust swarms that occurred during the 1870s. The author states, "The locusts devoured not only crops but gnawed on nearly any organic material, including sawdust, leather, and the very clothes on people's backs. Swarming in numbers perhaps unseen in history, they brought staggering economic ruin to rural communities and, in extreme cases, even death."

hail when, through Moses, God told Pharaoh, "But I have raised you up for this very purpose, that I might show you my power and that my name might be proclaimed in all the earth" (Exodus 9:16, NIV).

By refusing over and over to allow the Hebrews to leave, Pharaoh provided God the opportunity to perform one mighty miracle after another. In a land steeped with gods, mythology, and magic, the power of the one God of the Hebrews far surpassed anything the Egyptians had ever known. Where better for God to exhibit His might than in Egypt, and who better to prevail against than Pharaoh, the ruler of this ancient and powerful nation?

Now, with number eight, the plague of locusts, God told Moses why He had hardened the heart of Pharaoh and his officials: "that you may tell your children and grandchildren how I dealt harshly with the Egyptians and how I performed my signs among them, and that you may know that I am the LORD" (Exodus 10:2, NIV).

God had been silent for several centuries, so far as is recorded in the Bible. Not since the time of Jacob and Joseph do the Scriptures record the Israelites having had communication with God. They had continued to worship God, but their knowledge of God consisted of information passed down to them from their ancestors.

At the same time, the Israelites had been surrounded by Egyptian culture, and they knew of their many false gods. God wanted to make Himself known in a way so powerful there could be no doubt He was the one, the only, the true God. He wanted the account of their deliverance from Egyptian bondage to be compelling, a story for the ages that His people would pass on from generation to generation.

God's story of miraculous deliverance still speaks to His people today.

Just as God, working through Moses, freed the Hebrews from physical bondage in Old Testament times, He later freed mankind from the spiritual bondage of sin and death. He sent to earth His Son, Jesus, who became the perfect sacrifice for the sins of others, once and for all time.

Rather than overcoming an earthly ruler, Jesus prevailed against Satan, the ruler of darkness. Because of Him, death holds no power over those who are faithful. Christians have a beautiful new story of deliverance to tell, the story of Jesus because it is through Him that believers have the hope of eternal life.

> May you be strengthened with all power, according to His glorious might, for all endurance and patience, with joy giving thanks to the Father, who has enabled you to share in the saints' inheritance in the light. He has rescued us from the domain of darkness and transferred us into the kingdom of the Son He loves. We have redemption, the forgiveness of sins, in Him.
>
> —Colossians 1:11–14, HCSB

> For I am not ashamed of the gospel of Christ, for it is the power of God to salvation for everyone who believes, for the Jew first and also for the Greek.
>
> —Romans 1:16, NKJV

What was left in Egypt?

You may have noticed in the reading for the plague of hail, number seven, this statement in Exodus 9:31–32, NLT:

"All the flax and barley were ruined by the hail, because the barley had formed heads and the flax was budding. But the wheat and the emmer wheat were spared, because they had not yet sprouted from the ground."

With all the devastation the Egyptian people had experienced, they at least had the wheat crops, which hadn't yet sprouted. While we are not told the time period between the plague of hail and the plague of locusts, it's likely these crops had at least emerged from the ground by the time the locusts hit. Can you imagine the utter despair of the people to see this food crop also decimated? After the locusts devoured what little was left, Egypt must have looked like a barren wasteland.

Thoughts to Ponder

Why did Pharaoh state that only the men could go worship God?

_____

_____

_____

Go back through all the plagues performed up to this point and try to envision the destruction that had been dealt upon the land, the people, and the animals. What do you think was left after plague eight? What impact do you think the plagues were having upon Moses as he saw God protect His people from the destruction, even while He was revealing Himself in such powerful and undeniable ways?

_____

_____

_____

_____

The Egyptians had a god for almost everything. With the various plagues, God systematically showed His might over their gods. How do you think the people felt with each new plague that was inflicted upon them?

_____

_____

_____

_____

Chapter 14

Darkness and a Final Warning

Exodus 10:21–11:10, NIV

(10:21) Then the LORD said to Moses, "Stretch out your hand toward the sky so that darkness spreads over Egypt—darkness that can be felt." (22) So Moses stretched out his hand toward the sky, and total darkness covered all Egypt for three days. (23) No one could see anyone else or move about for three days. Yet all the Israelites had light in the places where they lived.

(24) Then Pharaoh summoned Moses and said, "Go, worship the LORD. Even your women and children may go with you; only leave your flocks and herds behind."

(25) But Moses said, "You must allow us to have sacrifices and burnt offerings to present to the LORD our God. (26) Our livestock too must go with us; not a hoof is to be left behind. We have to use some of them in worshiping the LORD our God, and until we get there we will not know what we are to use to worship the LORD."

(27) But the LORD hardened Pharaoh's heart, and he was not willing to let them go. (28) Pharaoh said to Moses, "Get out of my sight! Make sure you do not appear before me again! The day you see my face you will die."

(29) "Just as you say," Moses replied. "I will never appear before you again."

(11:1) Now the LORD had said to Moses, "I will bring one more plague on Pharaoh and on Egypt. After that, he will let you go from here, and when he does, he will drive you out completely. (2) Tell the people that men and women alike are to ask their neighbors for articles of silver and gold." (3) (The LORD made the Egyptians favorably disposed toward the people, and Moses himself was highly regarded in Egypt by Pharaoh's officials and by the people.)

(4) So Moses said, "This is what the LORD says: 'About midnight I will go throughout

Egypt. (5) Every firstborn son in Egypt will die, from the firstborn son of Pharaoh, who sits on the throne, to the firstborn son of the female slave, who is at her hand mill, and all the firstborn of the cattle as well. (6) There will be loud wailing throughout Egypt—worse than there has ever been or ever will be again. (7) But among the Israelites not a dog will bark at any person or animal.' Then you will know that the LORD makes a distinction between Egypt and Israel. (8) All these officials of yours will come to me, bowing down before me and saying, 'Go, you and all the people who follow you!' After that I will leave." Then Moses, hot with anger, left Pharaoh.

(9) The LORD had said to Moses, "Pharaoh will refuse to listen to you—so that my wonders may be multiplied in Egypt." (10) Moses and Aaron performed all these wonders before Pharaoh, but the LORD hardened Pharaoh's heart, and he would not let the Israelites go out of his country.

Suggested Song

"Heavenly Sunlight"

tinyurl.com/yeyjydjx)

After all the pain and destruction that had already been inflicted on Egypt, God still had one more miracle to perform before the final plague that would actually set His people free. With no warning to Pharaoh, God sent plague number nine. For three days, a darkness so thick and pervasive the people could not see one another or go anywhere covered the land of Egypt. Only the dwellings of the Israelites had light.

Having witnessed the previous plagues, Pharaoh knew this darkness came from God. He sent for Moses and declared that all the Hebrew people could go worship, but they must leave their flocks and herds behind. Moses again refused Pharaoh's offer and insisted that *all* the animals belonging to the Israelites must go with them—not a hoof could be left behind.

At that point, Pharaoh banished Moses from his sight and, in Exodus 10:28 (NIV), told him to never appear before him again. "The day you see my face," he warned him, "you will die." Pharaoh's level of frustration had obviously reached a boiling point in dealing with these Hebrew slaves and their God. The plagues had kept coming, one after another, and Moses had stubbornly refused to concede to any of his demands.

But that frustration went both ways. Moses, "hot with anger," gave Pharaoh one last warning from God.[1] He revealed to him that the final plague would be death to the firstborn of the Egyptians, not only of the people but also of their animals. He promised that, soon, Pharaoh's officials would be begging him and all of the Hebrews to leave Egypt. And then, Moses assured Pharaoh, "After that I will leave."[2]

Lord over All the Earth

Consider for a moment the previous eight plagues: water into blood, frogs, gnats, flies, death of livestock, boils, hail, and locusts. Each had a physical manifestation and caused some level of destruction. The plague of darkness was different. It was more of a psychological plague. The extreme darkness was frightening and unnatural. It immobilized the country and sent a powerful message—this one God worshiped by the Hebrew slaves is Lord of everything! He controls all the forces of nature, even light itself.

No Egyptian god could do what the God of the Hebrews had done. Even more amazing, He was a God so powerful He could selectively inflict plagues upon the Egyptians while at the same time spare His own people. The livestock of the Israelites had not died, nor had the hail or lightning struck where they lived. Now, while the land of Egypt lay enveloped in deep darkness, this mighty God miraculously provided light for His people.

In our modern world, one of the only places you can experience total darkness is in the depths of a cavern. It can be a frightening sensation, and if you move around, you can easily become disoriented. Three days of darkness must have been terrifying

———— 1 ————

The timeline of the scriptures in Exodus 11:1–3 is a bit confusing. These three verses seem to be parenthetic in nature or information that has been inserted here to provide better clarity. They provide the background for the warning that Moses is about to give Pharaoh concerning the final plague. Evidently, God had revealed this information to Moses earlier or possibly even while he was still in Pharaoh's presence.

———— 2 ————

See Exodus 11:8, (NIV).

> No Egyptian god could do what the God of the Hebrews had done.

The Terrible Darkness

How did God bring about the darkness of plague nine? The Creator of the Universe certainly could have used means that cannot be explained. Or He could have used the elements to do His bidding, such as a dense cloud of fog or, worse, a sandstorm. The "Wind of the Desert," or *khamsin*, can blow across Egypt at various times of the year, bringing clouds of fine sand so thick the light from the sun can be blocked out. If God did choose either dense fog or sand, it's easy to see how the darkness was so thick it could be felt.

The Biblehub.com commentary page for Exodus 10:21 discusses the plague of darkness (tinyurl.com/uduwp8wj).

Brittanica.com provides this definition for "khamsin air current" (tinyurl.com/3p5n5j5b).

for the Egyptian people. No wonder the scriptures often associate Satan and evil with darkness.

God continues to provide light for His people today.

God is the opposite of darkness; in fact, as the Apostle John explained, "God is light and in Him is no darkness at all" (1 John 1:5b, NKJV). God provided light for His people during the plague of darkness, and He continued to provide light for them all during the journey upon which they would soon embark.

Ultimately, God would bring His Son, Jesus, into the world. When Jesus gave His life as the perfect sacrifice for our sins, He conquered the spiritual darkness of the world. He became the light of the world for all time. You can know that no matter the conditions of the physical world, whoever chooses to follow Him will never have to walk in spiritual darkness again.

"I am the light of the world. Anyone who follows Me will never walk in the darkness but will have the light of life."

—John 8:12, HCSB

This is the message which we have heard from Him and declare to you, that God is light and in Him is no darkness at all. If we say that we have fellowship with Him, and walk in darkness, we lie and do not practice the truth. But if we walk in the light as He is in the light, we have fellowship with one another, and the blood of Jesus Christ His Son cleanses us from all sin.

—1 John 1:5–7, NKJV

Thoughts to Ponder

Satan is often associated with darkness and God with light. Do you think the total darkness in Egypt may have symbolized the absence of God, particularly since there was light where the Hebrews lived? Find scriptures in the Bible that talk about darkness. Find scriptures that talk about light. Compare and contrast the darkness with the light.

_____

_____

_____

_____

With each plague, God showed His superiority over various Egyptian gods. Moses and the Israelites were raised in Egyptian culture and knew about these gods. How do you think witnessing the plagues impacted the Israelites and Moses in particular? Exodus 11:3 states Moses was held in high regard by Pharaoh's officials and the people. How would the plagues have bolstered their opinion of Moses?

_____

_____

_____

_____

Why do you think Moses was so angry when he left Pharaoh's presence?

_____

_____

_____

GOD RESCUES HIS CHOSEN PEOPLE

Chapter 15

God Establishes the Passover

Exodus 12:1–28, NLT

(1) While the Israelites were still in the land of Egypt, the LORD gave the following instructions to Moses and Aaron: (2) "From now on, this month will be the first month of the year for you. (3) Announce to the whole community of Israel that on the tenth day of this month each family must choose a lamb or a young goat for a sacrifice, one animal for each household. (4) If a family is too small to eat a whole animal, let them share with another family in the neighborhood. Divide the animal according to the size of each family and how much they can eat. (5) The animal you select must be a one-year-old male, either a sheep or a goat, with no defects.

(6) "Take special care of this chosen animal until the evening of the fourteenth day of this first month. Then the whole assembly of the community of Israel must slaughter their lamb or young goat at twilight. (7) They are to take some of the blood and smear it on the sides and top of the door frames of the houses where they eat the animal. (8) That same night they must roast the meat over a fire and eat it along with bitter salad greens and bread made without yeast. (9) Do not eat any of the meat raw or boiled in water. The whole animal—including the head, legs, and internal organs—must be roasted over a fire. (10) Do not leave any of it until the next morning. Burn whatever is not eaten before morning.

(11) "These are your instructions for eating this meal: Be fully dressed, wear your sandals, and carry your walking stick in your hand. Eat the meal with urgency, for this is the LORD's Passover. (12) On that night I will pass through the land of Egypt and strike down every firstborn son and firstborn male animal in the land of Egypt. I will execute judgment against all the gods of Egypt, for I am the LORD! (13) But the

blood on your doorposts will serve as a sign, marking the houses where you are staying. When I see the blood, I will pass over you. This plague of death will not touch you when I strike the land of Egypt.

(14) "This is a day to remember. Each year, from generation to generation, you must celebrate it as a special festival to the LORD. This is a law for all time. (15) For seven days the bread you eat must be made without yeast. On the first day of the festival, remove every trace of yeast from your homes. Anyone who eats bread made with yeast during the seven days of the festival will be cut off from the community of Israel. (16) On the first day of the festival and again on the seventh day, all the people must observe an official day for holy assembly. No work of any kind may be done on these days except in the preparation of food.

(17) "Celebrate this Festival of Unleavened Bread, for it will remind you that I brought your forces out of the land of Egypt on this very day. This festival will be a permanent law for you; celebrate this day from generation to generation. (18) The bread you eat must be made without yeast from the evening of the fourteenth day of the first month until the evening of the twenty-first day of that month. (19) During those seven days, there must be no trace of yeast in your homes. Anyone who eats anything made with yeast during this week will be cut off from the community of Israel. These regulations apply both to the foreigners living among you and to the native-born Israelites. (20) During those days

you must not eat anything made with yeast. Wherever you live, eat only bread made without yeast."

(21) Then Moses called all the elders of Israel together and said to them, "Go, pick out a lamb or young goat for each of your families, and slaughter the Passover animal. (22) Drain the blood into a basin. Then take a bundle of hyssop branches and dip it into the blood. Brush the hyssop across the top and sides of the doorframes of your houses. And no one may go out through the door until morning. (23) For the LORD will pass through the land to strike down the Egyptians. But when he sees the blood on the top and sides of the doorframe, the LORD will pass over your home. He will not permit his death angel to enter your house and strike you down.

(24) "Remember, these instructions are a permanent law that you and your descendants must observe forever. (25) When you enter the land the LORD has promised to give you, you will continue to observe this ceremony. (26) Then your children will ask, 'What does this ceremony mean?' (27) And you will reply, 'It is the Passover sacrifice to the LORD, for he passed over the houses of the Israelites in Egypt. And though he struck the Egyptians, he spared our families.'" When Moses had finished speaking, all the people bowed down to the ground and worshiped. (28) So the people of Israel did just as the LORD had commanded through Moses and Aaron.

The reading from the last lesson set the scene for the tenth and final plague—the big one, the one that would, at last, compel Pharaoh to relinquish control and allow the Israelites to leave Egypt. Before the timeline continues, however, the author of Exodus (presumably Moses) relays God's instructions on how the Israelites are to partake of the very first Passover.

Observances and celebrations help define a nation, a people, a group, or an organization. This Passover helped mark the beginning of a nation. It provided a unifying ceremony and would soon become one of the defining customs of the Israelite people for all time.

The Passover was so important, in fact, that God used its timing to reset the Hebrew calendar. The month they were in would now be called Abib,[1] and it would become the first month of their year. On the tenth day of this month, families were to select a male lamb or goat that was without blemish and not more than a year old.[2] Then, on the fourteenth day, they were to slaughter this young animal at twilight and roast it whole.

The families were to estimate how much they could eat, sharing with a neighbor if they thought they would have too much for their family alone. Anything left over was to be burned by morning. Along with the lamb, they were to eat bitter salad herbs and bread made without yeast. They were to eat in haste, with their sandals on their feet, staffs in their hands, and the hems of their garments tucked in their belts. In other words, they needed to be prepared to leave at a moment's notice.

Saved by the Blood of a Lamb

This first Passover was much more than an observance or a celebration. First of all, it was a real meal. God knew what an arduous journey lay ahead for His people. The Passover provided the

Suggested Song

"Redeemed by the Blood of the Lamb"

(tinyurl.com/5n8bc9p3)

——— 1 ———
See Exodus 13:4 and Deuteronomy 16:1. Most Bible versions translate the name of this month as *Abib*, although the NIV translates it *Aviv*.

——— 2 ———
Even though either a lamb or goat was acceptable, it seems lambs were traditionally chosen. For more information, see the Biblehub.com commentary page for Exodus 12:3 (tinyurl.com/4fde5s2a).

What is hyssop? As you might expect, scholars disagree as to which specific plant it was. It could have been a species of the herb marjoram, or maybe it was the caper plant, or maybe it was a more general name for a type of plant. It may have had cleansing properties (Psalm 51:7), as it would later be used in various purification rites. In 1 Kings 4:33, it is described as growing out of the walls, so it seems to have been a fairly common plant for the area and readily available. Biblestudytools.com provides this information on "Hyssop" (tinyurl.com/ysj98vt5).

4

This outline provides an overview of God's plan to redeem mankind to Himself: "Redemption from Beginning to End" (tinyurl.com/3rdnvm6b).

sustenance they would surely need as they marched to freedom and escaped the iron grip of Pharaoh forever.

More importantly, the blood from the unblemished lambs saved God's people from death. The people followed the instructions God had given Moses. Using a bundle of hyssop branches, they brushed the blood from the slaughtered lambs across the top and down the sides of the door frames of their homes.[3] Then they went inside and did not come out until morning.

The final plague would be death to every firstborn male in Egypt, whether of the people or their animals. God's people, however, were spared this fate. When the Lord passed through the land that night, He did not allow the death angel to enter those homes whose entrances were marked by the blood of the lamb.

God had planned for the future of His people long before they left Egypt. He had planned how to feed them during this exodus and how to save them from death. He had even planned for them to leave with wealth, with items of clothing and gold and silver willingly given to them by the Egyptians. In establishing the Passover, God revealed His plan for future commemorations for generations to come.

> God had planned for the future of His people long before they left Egypt.

At this same time every year, from the fourteenth day to the twenty-first day of the first month, they were to observe the Feast of the Unleavened Bread. They were to rid their homes of all leavening or yeast and eat nothing containing leavening during this time. In this way, future generations would honor God and commemorate how He had delivered His people from Egyptian slavery.

God has planned for your future as well.

The Passover that God established so long ago helped set the stage for the coming of His Son into the world. Even before the world began, God had a plan to reconcile mankind to Himself.[4] The way He would do it would be through His Son, Jesus, who was with Him from the beginning.

Just as the Israelites were saved from physical death by the blood of a lamb, Christians today are saved from spiritual death by the blood of Jesus. By living a life without sin, Jesus served as the unblemished, sacrificial lamb for all mankind, once and for all time. The blood of *a lamb* saved God's people during that first Passover. The blood of **the Lamb** saves God's people today.

"I am the way, the truth, and the life. No one comes to the Father except through Me."

—John 14:6, NKJV

For you know that it was not with perishable things such as silver or gold that you were redeemed from the empty way of life handed down to you from your ancestors, but with the precious blood of Christ, a lamb without blemish or defect. He was chosen before the creation of the world, but was revealed in these last times for your sake.

—1 Peter 1:18–20, NIV

When people who wore longer garments needed to be able to move unimpeded, such as to work or to run, they often "girded their loins" so they wouldn't get tangled in their robes.

In Exodus 12:11, the Israelites were commanded to be fully dressed while eating the Passover meal. The King James Version and several other versions also state, *with your loins girded*, while the New International Version says, *with your cloak tucked into your belt.*

According to Dictionary. com, the term *gird one's loins* "originally alluded to tucking up the traditional long robe into a girdle (that is, a belt) so it will not hamper physical activity" (tinyurl. com/25eectj7).

An explanation of how to gird one's loins is given in this NazareneIsrael. org article: "Chapter 17: Answering Questions about Garments" (tinyurl.com/2kkdyfpx). Scroll down to find the illustration on "Girding Your Loins."

Thoughts to Ponder

What is the significance of yeast? Why did they need to remove yeast from their homes on the first day of the festival? What would have happened if they had tried to travel with yeast?

_____

_____

_____

_____

_____

How many parallels can you think of between the Passover lamb and Jesus?

_____

_____

_____

_____

What role did hyssop play in the original Passover? What role did hyssop play in John 19:28–30?

_____

_____

_____

_____

_____

Chapter 16

The Final Plague

Exodus 12:29–51, HCSB

(29) Now at midnight the LORD struck every firstborn male in the land of Egypt, from the firstborn of Pharaoh who sat on his throne to the firstborn of the prisoner who was in the dungeon, and every firstborn of the livestock. (30) During the night Pharaoh got up, he along with all his officials and all the Egyptians, and there was a loud wailing throughout Egypt because there wasn't a house without someone dead. (31) He summoned Moses and Aaron during the night and said, "Get up, leave my people, both you and the Israelites, and go, worship Yahweh as you have asked. (32) Take even your flocks and your herds as you asked and leave, and also bless me."

(33) Now the Egyptians pressured the people in order to send them quickly out of the country, for they said, "We're all going to die!" (34) So the people took their dough before it was leavened, with their kneading bowls wrapped up in their clothes on their shoulders.

(35) The Israelites acted on Moses's word and asked the Egyptians for silver and gold jewelry and for clothing. (36) And the LORD gave the people such favor in the Egyptians' sight that they gave them what they requested. In this way they plundered the Egyptians.

(37) The Israelites traveled from Rameses to Succoth, about 600,000 soldiers on foot, besides their families. (38) An ethnically diverse crowd also went up with them, along with a huge number of livestock, both flocks and herds. (39) The people baked the dough they had brought out of Egypt into unleavened loaves, since it had no yeast; for when they had been driven out of Egypt they could not delay and had not prepared any provisions for themselves.

(40) The time that the Israelites lived in Egypt was 430 years. (41) At the end of 430 years, on that same day, all the LORD's divisions went out from the land of Egypt. (42) It was a night of vigil in honor of the LORD, because He would bring them out of the land of Egypt. This same night is in honor of the LORD, a night vigil for all the Israelites throughout their generations.

(43) The LORD said to Moses and Aaron, "This is the statute of the Passover: no foreigner may eat it. (44) But any slave a man has purchased may eat it, after you have circumcised him. (45) A temporary resident or hired hand may not eat the Passover. (46) It is to be eaten in one house. You may not take any of the meat outside the house, and you may not break any of its bones. (47) The whole community of Israel must celebrate it. (48) If a foreigner resides with you and wants to celebrate the LORD's Passover, every male in his household must be circumcised, and then he may participate; he will become like a native of the land. But no uncircumcised person may eat it. (49) The same law will apply to both the native and the foreigner who resides among you."

(50) Then all the Israelites did this; they did just as the LORD had commanded Moses and Aaron. (51) On that same day the LORD brought the Israelites out of the land of Egypt according to their divisions.

◇◇◇

Suggested Song

"The Gospel Is for All"

(tinyurl.com/5b3scne5)

One last plague remained before Pharaoh would release his grip and allow the Israelites to leave Egypt. From mighty Pharaoh to the lowly maidservant, from prisoners in the dungeon to any livestock that remained from the previous plagues, every first-born male would be struck dead.

Pharaoh knew this plague was coming. Moses had warned him. All Pharaoh could do was wait. The only thing he could do to prevent this tragedy from occurring was to let the Israelites leave, and he wasn't going to do that.

Pharaoh's officials and the Egyptian people knew this plague was coming as well. The feeling of dread must have hung in the air as heavy as the darkness during the previous plague. Over and over, they had experienced the power of this mighty God. *Everything* Moses had foretold had come true, so there was no reason for them to hope for a different outcome this time. They awaited the inevitable,

People throughout the land got up in the middle of the night to check on their loved ones. Cries of anguish filled the air as the angel of death struck. Every household not protected by the blood of the lamb suffered the death of their firstborn son, as well as the firstborn males among their animals. For Pharaoh, that likely meant the death of his heir to the kingdom.

Finally, Pharaoh relented. He sent for Moses and Aaron and commanded them to leave. He demanded that they take all their people and all their animals and get out of Egypt. In parting, Pharaoh asked of them in verse 32, "Also bless me."

Think for a moment how the entire chain of events in the Israelites' exodus from Egypt occurred just as God had planned. God had used Pharaoh's obstinance and the plagues to exhibit His great might.[1] He had given the Israelites, and Moses in particular, favor in the sight of the Egyptian people.[2] Rather than leaving as a ragtag group of slaves, they left with great wealth—clothing and items of gold and silver readily given to them by the Egyptians.[3] They also left with flocks and herds of livestock because their animals had been spared the devastating plagues.

Fearful that God might kill them all, the Egyptian people helped the Israelites hurry on out of the country. In fact, some even came along with the Israelites and lived among them. But, rather than making a mad scramble for the border, God had planned for an orderly departure. This massive group of people and animals marched out, organized by their divisions,[4] well fed, with sandals on their feet and staffs in their hands.

A mere seventy souls from Jacob's family had originally entered Egypt, and now, a nation emerged. With His mighty hand, God delivered His people, just as He had promised Abram so long ago.[5]

> Cries of anguish filled the air as the angel of death struck.

1

See Exodus 9:16.

2

See Exodus 11:3.

3

See Exodus 12:35–36.

4

See Exodus 12:51.

5

See Genesis 15:13–16.

Up until the time God established His covenant of circumcision with Abram in Genesis 17, Abraham was called Abram. See Genesis 17:5.

See Genesis 12:1–3, NKJV.

Who accompanied the Israelites out of Egypt?

Exodus 12:38 (HCSB) states that an "ethnically diverse crowd" accompanied the Israelites out of Egypt. Other Bible versions call these people a "mixed multitude," with some even referring to them as "rabble."

Who were these people, and why would they want to accompany the Israelites on this risky venture? Bible commentators suggest that because the Israelites had lived in Egypt for centuries, some had intermarried with Egyptians or with those of other cultures living in Egypt. So it could be that some in this group were spouses or other relatives who did not want to be left behind.

A Night to Honor the Lord

On the night when the angel of death passed over the land of Egypt, the blood sprinkled on the door frames of the homes of the Israelites saved them from the death of all their firstborn males. God commanded that, from that time on, year after year, this night would be a night to remember how God had delivered His people from death and rescued them from bondage. This was to be a night set aside to honor the Lord.

While God established the Passover as a time of remembrance for the Israelites, He made a way for others to participate as well. He instructed the same laws were to apply to everyone. People of other heritages accompanied the Israelites on their exodus out of Egypt. If they wished to keep the Passover, they could, provided they observed the same covenant of circumcision that God had established with Abraham.[6] That meant all the males in a participating person's household had to be circumcised. Just as the exodus from Egypt would not be exclusively for the Israelite people, neither would the Passover.

God's promise to Abram continues to bless our lives today.

Back in Genesis 12, when God called Abram to leave his country and go to the land He would show him, He also promised to bless him and make of him a great nation. Further, the blessings were not for his progeny alone. He also promised Abram that "in you all the families of the earth shall be blessed."[7] Abram would serve as a portal through whom God's blessings would ultimately flow to the whole world. For now, God's blessings were flowing through to all who exited Egypt.

It would be through God's Son, Jesus, that He would fulfill His promise to Abram. Through Jesus, who symbolically served as the Passover lamb once and for all, we have salvation. Through Jesus, the floodgates of blessings were opened to the world. The

Passover and God's deliverance of His people from bondage were integral to God's overall plan of bringing Jesus into the world to provide a way of salvation for us today. May we continually honor God for all He has done to deliver us from the bondage of sin and to reconcile us to Himself.

For I am not ashamed of the gospel, because it is God's power for salvation to everyone who believes, first to the Jew, and also to the Greek.

—Romans 1:16, HCSB

Salvation is found in no one else, for there is no other name under heaven given to mankind by which we must be saved.

—Acts 4:12, NIV

Then Jesus came near and said to them, "All authority has been given to Me in heaven and on earth. Go, therefore, and make disciples of all nations, baptizing them in the name of the Father and of the Son and of the Holy Spirit, teaching them to observe everything I have commanded you. And remember, I am with you always, to the end of the age."

—Matthew 28:18–20, HCSB

It's also possible that because the Egyptians had enslaved the Israelites, they had pressed other groups into servitude as well. Egypt had a store of food during the great famine, while many other countries did not. A wide variety of people may have made their way to Egypt during this time and never left.

This group of people is mentioned again in Numbers 11:4. They began to crave the good food that had been available to them in Egypt. This caused the Israelites to start weeping and wailing—*If only we had meat to eat!* The "mixed multitude" was not a positive influence on the Israelites.

Members of this group were likely low on the social scale and had been assigned menial tasks. Deuteronomy 29:11 states there were foreigners living in their camps who chopped their wood and carried their water.

Whoever this "ethnically diverse" group was, they found their ticket out of Egypt with the Israelites.

Thoughts to Ponder

Why did the Israelites eat unleavened bread the night the death angel passed over? Compare their eating of the bread the last night before they were set free with Jesus eating the bread the last night before His crucifixion.

_____

_____

_____

_____

_____

What was the significance of the way the Passover lamb was to be prepared? Why were they to eat all of the Passover lamb in one house, not taking any outside and not breaking any of its bones? See Exodus 12:8–11, 46 and Numbers 9:12.

_____

_____

_____

_____

_____

After commanding Moses to leave and threatening him with death in Exodus 10:28, why do you suppose Pharaoh later asked Moses to bless him in Exodus 12:32?

_____

_____

_____

_____

_____

Chapter 17

Out of Egypt

Exodus 13:17–14:12, NKJV

(13:17) Then it came to pass, when Pharaoh had let the people go, that God did not lead them by way of the land of the Philistines, although that was near; for God said, "Lest perhaps the people change their minds when they see war, and return to Egypt." (18) So God led the people around by way of the wilderness of the Red Sea. And the children of Israel went up in orderly ranks out of the land of Egypt.

(19) And Moses took the bones of Joseph with him, for he had placed the children of Israel under solemn oath, saying, "God will surely visit you, and you shall carry up my bones from here with you."

(20) So they took their journey from Succoth and camped in Etham at the edge of the wilderness. (21) And the LORD went before them by day in a pillar of cloud to lead the way, and by night in a pillar of fire to give them light, so as to go by day and night. (22) He did not take away the pillar of cloud by day or the pillar of fire by night from before the people.

(14:1) Now the LORD spoke to Moses, saying: (2) "Speak to the children of Israel, that they turn and camp before Pi Hahiroth, between Migdol and the sea, opposite Baal Zephon; you shall camp before it by the sea. (3) For Pharaoh will say of the children of Israel, 'They are bewildered by the land; the wilderness has closed them in.' (4) Then I will harden Pharaoh's heart, so that he will pursue them; and I will gain honor over Pharaoh and over all his army, that the Egyptians may know that I am the LORD." And they did so.

(5) Now it was told the king of Egypt that the people had fled, and the heart of Pharaoh and his servants was turned against the people; and they said, "Why have we done this, that we have let Israel go from serving us?" (6) So he made ready his chariot and took his people with him.

(7) Also, he took six hundred choice chariots, and all the chariots of Egypt with captains over every one of them. (8) And the LORD hardened the heart of Pharaoh king of Egypt, and he pursued the children of Israel; and the children of Israel went out with boldness. (9) So the Egyptians pursued them, all the horses and chariots of Pharaoh, his horsemen and his army, and overtook them camping by the sea beside Pi Hahiroth, before Baal Zephon.

(10) And when Pharaoh drew near, the children of Israel lifted their eyes, and behold, the Egyptians marched after them. So they were very afraid, and the children of Israel cried out to the LORD. (11) Then they said to Moses, "Because there were no graves in Egypt, have you taken us away to die in the wilderness? Why have you so dealt with us, to bring us up out of Egypt? (12) Is this not the word that we told you in Egypt, saying, 'Let us alone that we may serve the Egyptians'? For it would have been better for us to serve the Egyptians than that we should die in the wilderness."

◇◇◇

Suggested Song

"Turn Your Eyes upon Jesus"

(tinyurl.com/3r97df5e)

For centuries, God had been preparing to deliver His people from Egypt. Even while making His covenant with Abram, He had foretold of this great event. Now, the time was at hand, and this generation of Israelites would be the people whom God would bring up out of Egypt.

These Israelites had witnessed firsthand God's mighty power. They had seen the many plagues He had inflicted upon the Egyptians. They knew that, time after time, they had escaped unscathed; their God had protected them.

God knew, however, that their faith was fragile, even tentative. They had lived in servitude for many years, and if they faced war so soon into their journey, they might turn and flee back to Egypt. So rather than lead them by the shorter route through Philistine territory, which would surely be hostile, God directed Moses to take a desolate route toward the Red Sea.[1] This kept them in Egyptian territory, and the path they traveled made it appear that they were lost.

Can you imagine trying to lead and give directions to such a massive group of people and animals? Their escape, as well

--------- 1 ---------

The Bible names specific sites which they passed through, but some of these locations are difficult to verify today. Suffice it to say, they headed south, down the Sinai Peninsula.

as their journey to the Promised Land, depended in large part upon the successful organization of this multitude. Fortunately for Moses, God had planned that part out as well. By means of a special cloud that went before them, God Himself provided guidance. This tall pillar of cloud served as a constant visual reminder to the Israelites of God's presence, and it accompanied them all the way to the Promised Land. At night, it turned into a pillar of fire. This allowed the Israelites the advantage of being able to travel day or night.

Amid the many preparations, Moses faithfully remembered to take Joseph's bones with them out of Egypt. Except for his childhood and his brief trip back to Canaan to bury his father, Joseph had spent most of his life in Egypt. He knew that God, who had been faithful during his life, would certainly keep the promise He had made to his forefathers. Joseph made his family swear an oath to carry his bones with them to the Promised Land when the time came for their deliverance. Moses made sure that happened.

It didn't take long for Pharaoh and his officials to recover from the shock of the death plague. You can almost see their grief turning into anger. Because of these slaves, they had suffered enormously, both personally and economically. Even worse, in a moment of weakness, they had allowed their source of free labor to march out of the country, along with a great amount of livestock and wealth. In short, the most powerful ruler of the most powerful country in the world had been bested by a group of slaves and their one God—and he knew it! Predictably, Pharaoh went back on his word, but this time it would be his last.

Fueled by pride and rage, Pharaoh pursued the Israelites with the full force of his army. It must have been a sight to behold, with 600 choice chariots plus the vast amount of other chariots, horses, and troops. It's no wonder the Israelites were terrified when they looked up and saw this massive Egyptian army thundering toward them, no doubt in a great cloud of dust. They knew they were no match against such a powerful force.

Hemmed in by the sea on one side and the Egyptians on the other, the Israelites were trapped. They knew if they even survived the coming onslaught, they would surely be recaptured and subjected to even greater cruelty than before. They cried out against Moses, declaring they would have been better off had they never left Egypt in the first place! For people who had witnessed all the miracles that God had performed on their behalf, their faith evaporated almost instantly as they faced what they thought would be their inevitable demise.

> Hemmed in by the sea on one side and the Egyptians on the other, the Israelites were trapped.

Guided by God

It's easy when you're looking back on history to marvel at the Israelites' lack of faith. Their grumbling, complaining, and crying out against God and Moses would become a recurring theme as they made their way to the Promised Land. Of all people, they should have known that God would see them through. God had chosen them; He had delivered them, and His presence was right there with them. All they had to do was look up and see the pillar of cloud guiding them.

Yet how many times have God's people today grumbled, complained, and cried out against Him? Like the Israelites, you may feel overwhelmed, even crushed, by the challenges you're facing. It's easy to lash out against others and against God when you're in the midst of a crisis, afraid and hurting.

God will never forsake His people.

No matter what you are facing today, whether it's a speed bump in the road of life or something as formidable as the Egyptian army thundering toward you, know that God's people do not

Joseph, the First Israelite in Egypt

Joseph was the first member of his family to go to Egypt. He was only seventeen years old when his older brothers sold him to the Ishmaelites, who then sold him to Potiphar, one of Pharaoh's officials in Egypt. Several years later, he interpreted Pharaoh's dreams, whereupon Pharaoh placed him in charge of the country. He was second in authority only to Pharaoh himself. This positioned him perfectly to receive and care for his family when the famine became severe in Canaan.

Psalm 105 gives an

walk alone. He provides guidance for us today, just as He did for the Israelites so long ago.

Rather than Moses and a towering cloud, however, we have something even better. We have the Word of God, and it's right here with us. All we have to do is open our Bibles and allow the scriptures to speak to us. As you go about your studies, remember the words of James: "Draw near to God, and He will draw near to you" (James 4:8a, ESV).

Your word is a lamp to my feet and a light to my path.

—Psalm 119:105, NKJV

The LORD is a refuge for the oppressed,
a stronghold in times of trouble.
Those who know your name trust in you,
for you, LORD, have never forsaken those who seek you.

—Psalm 9:9–10, NIV

And I tell you, ask, and it will be given to you; seek, and you will find; knock, and it will be opened to you. For everyone who asks receives, and the one who seeks finds, and to the one who knocks it will be opened.

—Luke 11:9–10, ESV

excellent synopsis of God's promises to His people, including the account of the famine, Joseph being sold as a slave, and the Israelites' deliverance from Egyptian captivity. The story of Joseph begins in Genesis 37. Jacob's death is recorded in Genesis 49:29–33. The account of Joseph taking Jacob's remains back to Canaan is given in Genesis 50.

Joseph made his family take an oath in Genesis 50:25 that when the Israelites finally left Egypt, they would take his bones with them. Centuries later, Moses was faithful to fulfill the promise his ancestors had made. Joseph lived to be 110 years old.

Thoughts to Ponder

In what other instances in the Bible did God's presence dwell within the form of a cloud? (See 1 Kings 8:10–13, 1 Thessalonians 4:17, and Revelation 14:14.)

_____

_____

_____

_____

As Pharaoh and his army drew near to the Israelites, what do you suppose they were thinking when they saw the Israelites near the sea?

_____

_____

_____

_____

How did the route the Israelites took out of Egypt work to their advantage in the end, even better than if they had taken the shorter route through Philistine territory?

_____

_____

_____

_____

_____

Chapter 18

Crossing the Red Sea

Exodus 14:13–31, NKJV

(13) And Moses said to the people, "Do not be afraid. Stand still, and see the salvation of the LORD, which He will accomplish for you today. For the Egyptians whom you see today, you shall see again no more forever. (14) The LORD will fight for you, and you shall hold your peace."

(15) And the LORD said to Moses, "Why do you cry to Me? Tell the children of Israel to go forward. (16) But lift up your rod, and stretch out your hand over the sea and divide it. And the children of Israel shall go on dry ground through the midst of the sea. (17) And I indeed will harden the hearts of the Egyptians, and they shall follow them. So I will gain honor over Pharaoh and over all his army, his chariots, and his horsemen. (18) Then the Egyptians shall know that I am the LORD, when I have gained honor for Myself over Pharaoh, his chariots, and his horsemen."

(19) And the Angel of God, who went before the camp of Israel, moved and went behind them; and the pillar of cloud went from before them and stood behind them. (20) So it came between the camp of the Egyptians and the camp of Israel. Thus it was a cloud and darkness to the one, and it gave light by night to the other, so that the one did not come near the other all that night.

(21) Then Moses stretched out his hand over the sea; and the LORD caused the sea to go back by a strong east wind all that night, and made the sea into dry land, and the waters were divided. (22) So the children of Israel went into the midst of the sea on the dry ground, and the waters were a wall to them on their right hand and on their left. (23) And the Egyptians pursued and went after them into the midst of the sea, all Pharaoh's horses, his chariots, and his horsemen.

(24) Now it came to pass, in the morning watch, that the LORD looked down upon the army of the Egyptians through the pillar of fire and cloud, and He troubled the army of the Egyptians. (25) And He took off their chariot wheels, so that they drove them with difficulty; and the Egyptians said, "Let us flee from the face of Israel, for the LORD fights for them against the Egyptians."

(26) Then the LORD said to Moses, "Stretch out your hand over the sea, that the waters may come back upon the Egyptians, on their chariots, and on their horsemen." (27) And Moses stretched out his hand over the sea; and when the morning appeared, the sea returned to its full depth, while the Egyptians were fleeing into it. So the LORD overthrew the Egyptians in the midst of the sea. (28) Then the waters returned and covered the chariots, the horsemen, and all the army of Pharaoh that came into the sea after them. Not so much as one of them remained. (29) But the children of Israel had walked on dry land in the midst of the sea, and the waters were a wall to them on their right hand and on their left.

(30) So the LORD saved Israel that day out of the hand of the Egyptians, and Israel saw the Egyptians dead on the seashore. (31) Thus Israel saw the great work which the LORD had done in Egypt; so the people feared the LORD, and believed the LORD and His servant Moses.

◇◇◇

Suggested Song

"Be Still and Know That I Am God"

(tinyurl.com/32ku2twd)

———— 1 ————

See Genesis 15:13–14.

Huddled on the shore, with the sea on one side and the Egyptian army thundering toward them on the other, Moses and the Israelites knew the time had come. Events foretold so long ago were quickly becoming a reality right before their eyes.[1] If they were to be delivered, it had to be now or never, and so, in their despair, the people cried out to Moses.

With great confidence, Moses responded to them in verse 13: "Do not be afraid. Stand still, and see the salvation of the LORD, which He will accomplish for you today." What trust coming from the man who had stood before the burning bush begging God to choose someone else! Moses knew the Israelites were no match for the mighty Egyptian army, but he also knew they didn't have to be. Their God, who had worked so many amazing miracles through him and his brother, Aaron, would fight this battle for them.

Yet God may not have told Moses ahead of time exactly *how* their deliverance would occur. In verse 15, even while reassuring the people, Moses apparently cried out to God in some way, perhaps asking Him to save them. With their deliverance being a foregone conclusion, God essentially told him—*Why are you standing here crying out? Get going!*

Finally, at that point, God told Moses what was about to occur. He instructed Moses to take his staff and extend his hand over the water. The waters of the sea would part, and the Israelites would be able to walk on dry ground over to the opposite shore.

With that, Moses and the Israelites now knew their pathway of escape, but it would take time for such a massive group of people and animals to get across. To keep the Egyptians from overrunning them, God caused the pillar of cloud to move from the front of the camp to around behind the Israelites. The cloud covered the Egyptians in darkness, while it provided light for the Israelites at the same time. In this way, God shielded His people from the approaching Egyptians and allowed the Israelites the time they would need to cross safely into Arabia.

By means of a strong east wind, God caused the waters of the sea to part. The wind blew all night long, drying out the bed of the sea and pushing the waters back to create great walls on either side of the pathway. The Israelites were able to walk across the bed of the sea on dry ground.

The cloud followed the Israelites, and as dawn approached, the Egyptians finally gained enough visibility to pursue their prey. If the Egyptians had stopped for a moment to think things through, they would have recalled all the terrible plagues they had experienced back in Egypt at the hand of the Israelites' God. They would have recognized the towering, supernatural cloud that accompanied the Israelites as evidence that their God was still with them. Had they considered those factors, they surely

One gallon of water weighs over eight pounds. It's hard to even estimate how much water rushed back into place when the walls of water collapsed, but the acceleration with which the water moved, combined with the mass of the water, created an enormous force. The Egyptians had virtually no chance of survival.

———— 3 ————

See Exodus 14:13b, NKJV.

The Pillar of Cloud

God guided the Israelites all during their journeys by means of a cloud that rose high in the sky like a pillar (Exodus 13:21–22). During the night, it became a pillar of fire to help illuminate their way and enable them to travel at night if God so directed. You may find various commentaries, which refer to the cloud as the "Shekinah glory." While that specific term does not appear in the Bible, it does refer to God's presence

would not have raced headlong into the bed of a sea with walls of water towering over them on either side.

But rather than pause to acknowledge God's presence or power, the Egyptians charged right in behind the Israelites. The scriptures say in verse 17 that God "hardened" their hearts. He gave them over to their own stubborn pride, which, in turn, led to their destruction.

As the Egyptians pursued the Israelites, God caused confusion among their army. Finally, when the wheels began to come off their chariots, they came to their senses. They realized that God was fighting *for* the Israelites and *against* them, and they tried to turn and run. By then, however, they were past the point of escape.

With the Israelites now safely across, God told Moses to once again stretch his hand over the sea. The waters closed, causing all the Egyptians and their horses to perish. You can imagine the mighty rushing and churning of the waters as the sea returned to its normal levels. Water is heavy, and the crushing force from the walls of water collapsing on the army probably caused them to die almost instantly. It's no wonder there were no survivors.[2]

As the Israelites looked back upon the sea they had just crossed, they witnessed the total annihilation of their aggressors. The words Moses had proclaimed earlier on the opposite shore had proved true: "The Egyptians whom you see today, you shall see again no more forever."[3] All those who had desired to either kill the Israelites or return them to captivity had perished.

Delivered by God

On that day, God accomplished something the Israelites could never have managed by themselves. They could not have outrun the Egyptian army, particularly with their families and herds of livestock. They were ill-equipped to turn and fight such a great military force. If they had taken a land route and somehow managed to get past the borders of Egypt, this powerful army would quite likely have chased them down anyway, regardless of which country they were in. God's plan not only saved the Israelites, but it also eliminated the entire Egyptian army. No one was left to come after them!

God's miraculous plan also made clear to the Israelites that their deliverance was not due to their own abilities. They contributed nothing to their salvation other than walking through the bed of the sea. It was just as Moses had said it would be in verse 14: "The LORD will fight for you, and you shall hold your peace." When the Israelites passed between the great walls of water on either side, they were transformed. They entered as slaves being pursued by the Egyptians, but they emerged a free people.

> They entered as slaves being pursued by the Egyptians, but they emerged a free people.

God continues to save His people today.

Just as God had a plan for saving the Israelites from the Egyptians, He also had a plan to save us from sin and eternal condemnation. Before He created the world, God planned for a way to redeem all those who would believe in His name. That Way would be through His Son, Jesus.

Much like the Israelites, we are incapable of saving ourselves. We cannot live a life that is righteous enough or perform works worthy enough for us to merit our own salvation. Thankfully, we don't have to. Jesus paid the price for us with His own blood. All we have to do is obey His Word and walk the path that God has set before us.

dwelling on earth. This article addresses the topic: "What Is the Shekinah glory?" (tinyurl.com/4zaf493j).

During the Israelites' escape from Egypt, the pillar of cloud went around and behind the Israelites and came between them and the Egyptian army. In that way, it served as a shield by keeping the Egyptians in darkness and away from the Israelites (Exodus 14:19–20). While they were traveling to the Promised Land, it continued to serve as a shield from the elements by helping block some of the desert heat during the day and providing light and possibly a bit of warmth during the cold nights (Psalm 105:39). The cloud accompanied them to the Promised Land and determined not only their pathway but also when they would set out from camp (Numbers 9:15–23).

For the LORD God is a sun and shield;
the LORD bestows favor and honor.
No good thing does he withhold
from those who walk uprightly.

—Psalm 84:11, ESV

Even youths shall faint and be weary,
and young men shall fall exhausted;
but they who wait for the LORD shall renew their
strength;
they shall mount up with wings like eagles;
they shall run and not be weary;
they shall walk and not faint.

—Isaiah 40:30–31, ESV

Therefore, since we are surrounded by so great a cloud of witnesses, let us also lay aside every weight, and sin which clings so closely, and let us run with endurance the race that is set before us, looking to Jesus, the founder and perfecter of our faith, who for the joy that was set before him endured the cross, despising the shame, and is seated at the right hand of the throne of God.

—Hebrews 12:1–2, ESV

Thoughts to Ponder

What does it mean that God hardened Pharaoh's heart and those of his officials? Did they have a choice or not in how they responded to the situation?

_____

_____

_____

_____

In Exodus 14:17b–18 (NKJV), God declared, "So I will gain honor over Pharaoh and over all his army, his chariots, and his horsemen. Then the Egyptians shall know that I am the LORD, when I have gained honor for Myself over Pharaoh, his chariots, and his horsemen." If God's purpose was to free the Israelites from slavery, why was it also important to Him to gain honor over the Egyptians?

_____

_____

_____

_____

The Israelites' deliverance from Egypt became a defining event in their history. God refers to it many times in the Scriptures. In 1 Corinthians 10:1b–2 (NKJV), the Apostle Paul states, "All our fathers were under the cloud, all passed through the sea, all were baptized into Moses in the cloud and in the sea." What did their crossing the sea symbolize?

_____

_____

_____

_____

Chapter 19

A Song of Praise to the Lord

Exodus 14:30–15:21, ESV

(14:30) Thus the LORD saved Israel that day from the hand of the Egyptians, and Israel saw the Egyptians dead on the seashore. (31) Israel saw the great power that the LORD used against the Egyptians, so the people feared the LORD, and they believed in the LORD and in his servant Moses.

(15:1) Then Moses and the people of Israel sang this song to the LORD, saying,
"I will sing to the LORD, for he has triumphed gloriously;
the horse and his rider he has thrown into the sea.

(2) The LORD is my strength and my song,
and he has become my salvation;
this is my God, and I will praise him,
my father's God, and I will exalt him.

(3) The LORD is a man of war;
the LORD is his name.

(4) "Pharaoh's chariots and his host he cast into the sea,

and his chosen officers were sunk in the Red Sea.

(5) The floods covered them;
they went down into the depths like a stone.

(6) Your right hand, O LORD, glorious in power,
your right hand, O LORD, shatters the enemy.

(7) In the greatness of your majesty you overthrow your adversaries;
you send out your fury; it consumes them like stubble.

(8) At the blast of your nostrils the waters piled up;
the floods stood up in a heap;
the deeps congealed in the heart of the sea.

(9) The enemy said, 'I will pursue, I will overtake,
I will divide the spoil, my desire shall have its fill of them.

I will draw my sword; my hand shall destroy them.'

(10) You blew with your wind; the sea covered them;
they sank like lead in the mighty waters.

(11) "Who is like you, O LORD, among the gods?
Who is like you, majestic in holiness,
awesome in glorious deeds, doing wonders?

(12) You stretched out your right hand;
the earth swallowed them.

(13) "You have led in your steadfast love the people whom you have redeemed;
you have guided them by your strength to your holy abode.

(14) The peoples have heard; they tremble;
pangs have seized the inhabitants of Philistia.

(15) Now are the chiefs of Edom dismayed;
trembling seizes the leaders of Moab;
all the inhabitants of Canaan have melted away.

(16) Terror and dread fall upon them;
because of the greatness of your arm, they are still as a stone,

till your people, O LORD, pass by,

till the people pass by whom you have purchased.

(17) You will bring them in and plant them on your own mountain,
the place, O LORD, which you have made for your abode,
the sanctuary, O Lord, which your hands have established.

(18) The LORD will reign forever and ever."

(19) For when the horses of Pharaoh with his chariots and his horsemen went into the sea, the LORD brought back the waters of the sea upon them, but the people of Israel walked on dry ground in the midst of the sea. (20) Then Miriam the prophetess, the sister of Aaron, took a tambourine in her hand, and all the women went out after her with tambourines and dancing. (21) And Miriam sang to them:
"Sing to the LORD, for he has triumphed gloriously;
the horse and his rider he has thrown into the sea."

When God called Moses from within the burning bush and Moses offered every excuse he could think of, did you wonder why God didn't just move on and choose someone more willing? God could have come up with a contingency plan, but He clearly didn't want to do that.

For one thing, God had just spent eighty years preparing Moses for his role as leader of the Israelites. And for another, the time was at hand to fulfill the promise He had made to Abraham so long ago. He needed Moses to go ahead and step into his life's defining role. So God simply refused to take Moses's "no" for an answer.

This lesson's remarkable passage makes it even more clear why God was unwilling to settle for anyone besides Moses. With the Israelite people having lived as slaves in Egypt, who else among them would have been able to compose such lovely verse? Probably no one. While God inspired Moses's writings, consider that Moses was likely among the most highly educated people in the world at that time. With Moses, God had so much ability to work with—ability that it's doubtful anyone else among the Israelites possessed.

This passage, which several versions of the Bible label as "The Song of Moses," is the first song recorded in the Scriptures. Up to this point, the Bible does not mention singing as an element of worship. But when Moses penned these verses of praise to God in response to the Israelites' deliverance from the Egyptians, he changed the tenor of worship for all time. Singing and music became integral parts of worship and remain so to this day. We know, too, that singing will be a part of worship for eternity.

In this song, Moses not only praises God but also tells the story of the Israelites. He tells where they have just been and how their mighty God miraculously saved them by defeating those who sought to destroy them. Then, he tells where they are going,

Suggested Song

"The New Song"
(tinyurl.com/4kvk2deh)

The Songs of Moses

While the song in Exodus 15 is the first song recorded in the Bible, a song also attributed to Moses in Revelation 15:3–4 is one of the last songs recorded in the Bible. The two songs are not the same, but both are songs that praise and glorify God. It's also interesting to note that Moses wrote Psalm 90 and possibly other psalms as well.

At God's direction, Moses penned another song right before his death. God knew the disasters and difficulties that lay ahead for the Israelite people. This song would serve to remind them of their heritage and all that God had done for them. It would also be a song they could pass on to future generations. God gave Moses the instructions for writing this song in Deuteronomy 31:19–22, while the song itself is recorded in Deuteronomy 32.

The Bible contains approximately 185 songs. Most of them are

of the nations and leaders who will melt away as the Lord leads His people to the land He has promised them.

As Moses surely knew, crafting a story into verse makes it much more memorable. (How many times have you gotten a song stuck in your head?) He and the God who inspired his writing wanted the story of the Israelites' deliverance to be remembered not only by those currently living but by future generations as well.

> Moses helped the people celebrate who they were while praising their God.

This song also helped breathe life back into the Hebrew culture. As slaves, the Israelites had been immersed in all things Egyptian. Their own heritage had been suppressed for many years. With this song, Moses helped the people celebrate who they were while praising their God and commemorating the momentous event they had just experienced. His writing set the pattern for future compositions found in Scripture.

Taking the Time to Honor God

Before proceeding on their journey, Moses stopped beside the sea they had so miraculously crossed and wrote this song. He understood the importance of what he and the Israelites had just experienced. He wanted to immediately record the event and honor God while the memories were still fresh and vivid.

By writing this tribute in the form of a verse, he created a way for all of the Israelites, not just him, to participate in offering praise to God for their deliverance. When the Israelites passed through the sea, they were a changed people. They entered as a group of scared slaves, fearing for their lives. They emerged as a nation, freed from their aggressors. Now they would become the ones feared by other nations as they made their way to the land God had promised for their inheritance.

Give praise and thanks to God for all He has done in your life.

With so much emphasis in today's culture on one's own desires and self-fulfillment, it's easy to forget to praise and honor God. Even our prayers are often focused on begging God to grant our wishes. While our gracious Father has encouraged us to cast all our cares on Him, let us not forget to thank Him for this bounteous privilege and praise His glorious name.

Like Moses, take the initiative and make time to offer thanks and praise to God as you travel the path God has set before you. Act upon your intentions now while the fullness of your joy is still in your heart. Remember, God always loves to hear from His children!

in Psalms, which served as the songbook of the Old Testament. The Song of Solomon is a love song, while the book of Lamentations contains songs mourning the destruction of Jerusalem. The remainder of the songs are scattered mostly throughout the Old Testament, with a few being in the book of Revelation in the New Testament.

Jeffrey Kranz identifies many of the songs in the Bible in his article: "All the Songs in the Bible" (tinyurl.com/2wy85jec).

And I saw something like a sea of glass mingled with fire, and those who have the victory over the beast, over his image and over his mark and over the number of his name, standing on the sea of glass, having harps of God. They sing the song of Moses, the servant of God, and the song of the Lamb, saying:

"Great and marvelous are Your works,
Lord God Almighty!
Just and true are Your ways,
O King of the saints!
Who shall not fear You, O Lord, and glorify Your name?
For You alone are holy.
For all nations shall come and worship before You,
For Your judgments have been manifested."

—Revelation 15:2–4, NKJV

Thoughts to Ponder

Moses made an incredible impact on the Scriptures. He is credited for writing the Pentateuch. Originally, this was a single volume that was later divided into what are now the first five books of our Bible. By word count, Moses wrote more than any other single author of the Bible. With this song, he formally introduced the element of singing into worship.

What did worship look like up to this point in history? How did worship change during Moses's time? How did it change during the time of the kings and during the time of Christ?

_____

_____

_____

Various commentators surmise that Miriam and the women repeated the verse in Exodus 15:21 after each of the segments or stanzas of the song, not just at the end. This would mean that the song's format is very similar to many of the hymns sung in worship today, where the refrain or chorus is sung after every verse.

Various versions of the Bible and various commentaries differ on how they divide this Song of Moses into stanzas, with some not indicating divisions. Where would you place the breaks for the stanzas or verses, and why would you place them there? Briefly outline the main thoughts that Moses presented in this song.

_____

_____

_____

What are the physical and mental benefits of singing? How could this Song of Moses have been therapeutic for a group of scared slaves who had just escaped capture or death and now found themselves in a foreign country? How can singing be therapeutic for us today?

_____

_____

_____

GOD PROVIDES
FOR HIS PEOPLE

Chapter 20

The Israelites Grumble

Exodus 15:22–16:8, NLT

(15:22) Then Moses led the people of Israel away from the Red Sea, and they moved out into the desert of Shur. They traveled in this desert for three days without finding any water. (23) When they came to the oasis of Marah, the water was too bitter to drink. So they called the place Marah (which means "bitter").

(24) Then the people complained and turned against Moses. "What are we going to drink?" they demanded. (25) So Moses cried out to the LORD for help, and the LORD showed him a piece of wood. Moses threw it into the water, and this made the water good to drink.

It was there at Marah that the LORD set before them the following decree as a standard to test their faithfulness to him. (26) He said, "If you will listen carefully to the voice of the LORD your God and do what is right in his sight, obeying his commands and keeping all his decrees, then I will not make you suffer any of the diseases I sent on the Egyptians; for I am the LORD who heals you."

(27) After leaving Marah, the Israelites traveled on to the oasis of Elim, where they found twelve springs and seventy palm trees. They camped there beside the water.

(16:1) Then the whole community of Israel set out from Elim and journeyed into the wilderness of Sin, between Elim and Mount Sinai. They arrived there on the fifteenth day of the second month, one month after leaving the land of Egypt. (2) There, too, the whole community of Israel complained about Moses and Aaron.

(3) "If only the LORD had killed us back in Egypt," they moaned. "There we sat around pots filled with meat and ate all the bread we wanted. But now you have brought us into this wilderness to starve us all to death."

(4) Then the LORD said to Moses, "Look, I'm going to rain down food from heaven for you. Each day the people can go out and pick up as much food as they need for that day. I will test them in this to see whether or not they will follow my instructions. (5) On the sixth day they will gather food, and when they prepare it, there will be twice as much as usual."

(6) So Moses and Aaron said to all the people of Israel, "By evening you will realize it was the LORD who brought you out of the land of Egypt. (7) In the morning you will see the glory of the LORD, because he has heard your complaints, which are against him, not against us. What have we done that you should complain about us?" (8) Then Moses added, "The LORD will give you meat to eat in the evening and bread to satisfy you in the morning, for he has heard all your complaints against him. What have we done? Yes, your complaints are against the LORD, not against us."

◇◇◇

Suggested Song

"Trust and Obey"

(tinyurl.com/bdhs66et)

——— 1 ———

See the DistanceCalculator.net (tinyurl.com/5e9wecy7).

With the Israelites safely across the Red Sea and their enemies vanquished, only a few hundred miles now separated them from Canaan, the land God had promised to Abraham long ago. If you look at a map, you can see that the direct distance from modern-day Cairo in Egypt to the city of Jericho, near where the Israelites finally crossed over into the Promised Land, is less than 300 miles.[1]

Why, then, did this journey, which should have taken several months, instead last forty years? The reason begins to become apparent in the passage for this lesson. Actually, a hint surfaced back in Exodus 14, when the Israelites had stood on the opposite shore of the Red Sea and watched Pharaoh and his mighty Egyptian army thunder toward them.

A detrimental pattern of behavior emerged early in the Israelites' journey. Whenever they felt stress or fear, the Israelites would turn on Moses and Aaron—and on God. They would proclaim, usually in a dramatic fashion, that they would have been better off if they had never left Egypt

> A detrimental pattern of behavior emerged early in the Israelites' journey.

than facing whatever circumstance and certain demise now lay before them.

Just three days after leaving the site where they had miraculously crossed the Red Sea on dry ground, the Israelites grumbled against Moses about the water. Having adequate water was a real concern. They could carry only a limited amount, and their supplies were running dangerously low. Then, when they finally found water at Marah, it wasn't drinkable. Distressed, they asked Moses what they were to drink. Moses, in turn, cried out to God, who then showed Moses a certain piece of wood.[2] After he threw the wood into the water, it became good to drink.

There at Marah, God made an ordinance for the Israelites, and it was to serve as a test for them. He promised them that if they would listen to Him, pay attention to His commands, and do what was right in His eyes, He would not bring on them any of the diseases He had inflicted on the Egyptians. Then He declared to them, "I am the LORD who heals you."[3] God wanted them to trust Him, and He wanted them to listen to Him and obey Him. When they didn't, He would indeed inflict certain physical measures upon them as discipline. This test of their faith would prove, time and again, to be difficult for them. God would later refer to them as a "stiff-necked people" because of their stubborn refusal to trust in Him and obey His commands.

It didn't take long for the Israelites to forget this ordinance from God. A little later, as they made their way to the wilderness of Sin,[4] they once again complained to Moses and Aaron. At this point in their journey, it had been only one month since they had left Egypt. The horrors of their slavery and their miraculous delivery should have been fresh on their minds, but instead, they began to reminisce about the good old days back in Egypt. They declared it would have been better for them to have stayed in Egypt, where they had plenty to eat, than to be brought out into the desert to starve to death. Rather than trust in God to provide for them, they fell back into their old pattern of behavior.

—————— 2 ——————
Different versions call the piece of wood a tree or a log.

—————— 3 ——————
See Exodus 15:26 (NLT).

—————— 4 ——————
This desolate region is also called the Desert of Sin. It is not to be confused with the Wilderness of Zin. The word "Sin" refers to the geographical area and is not related to the word "sin" in English. See "Wilderness of Sin" in the *Encyclopedia of the Bible* (tinyurl.com/bdehhpna).

With that, God explained to Moses His plan for feeding this great multitude of people as they journeyed to the Promised Land. Moses then relayed God's message to the Israelites. He also told them that when they complained, they weren't really murmuring against him and Aaron; they were actually murmuring against God. The people would have been wise to have considered this a warning, but, of course, they did not.

Learning to Trust in God and Obey His Word

Up to this point, no group of people in recorded biblical history had ever witnessed more miraculous events than this generation of Israelites. They had seen God's power displayed firsthand when he had inflicted the plagues upon the Egyptians, even while sparing the Israelites from those same plagues. They had crossed through the bed of the Red Sea without getting their feet wet and with towering walls of water on each side. They had just tasted the good water drawn from the bitter pool at Marah.

Yet, at each point of stress along their journey, they quickly turned against Moses and against God. Every time they ran into fear or discomfort, they seemed to forget all they had witnessed and experienced. Learning to trust in God to care for them, no matter what they encountered, would take time. It wasn't the distance that kept the Israelites from reaching the Promised Land in a timely manner; it was their spiritual development that caused God to delay their journey for forty years.

God's people continue to work on their spiritual development today.

When you read historical accounts and already know how the story ends, it's easy to hypothesize what the characters should have done along their journey. It's not so easy when it's your own life happening in real time, and you're faced with difficult situations.

Think about how you handle the challenges that come your way. Do you complain and attempt to blame God or other people, as the Israelites often did? Or do you instead call out to God, as Moses did, seeking His help and guidance?

Complaining and blaming others are behaviors that show a lack of gratitude and an unwillingness to take personal responsibility. Being mindful of your behavior goes a long way in changing how you respond to various situations.

Take the time to express gratitude to God, as Moses did with the song he composed in Exodus 15. Doing so will help you focus on what is good in your life. Ask for God's guidance and help in turning the control over to Him. Trust in His promises, obey His Word, and acknowledge that He loves you and will see you through your own life's journey.

Trust in the LORD with all your heart,
And lean not on your own understanding;
In all your ways acknowledge Him,
And He shall direct your paths.

—Proverbs 3:5–6, NKJV

Trust in the LORD always, for the LORD God is the eternal Rock.

—Isaiah 26:4, NLT

In Exodus 12, as the people were preparing to leave Egypt, God reset their calendar. This new first month of their year was to be called Abib (or Aviv in some versions). On the tenth day of this month, they selected their Passover lamb. They ate the lamb along with the rest of the Passover meal on the evening of the fourteenth day. Shortly afterward, the death angel struck at midnight. The Israelites then left Egypt on the fifteenth day of their new year (Exodus 12:51 and Numbers 33:3).

The Israelites arrived in the wilderness of Sin on the fifteenth day of the second month, making it exactly one month since they had left Egypt.

Thoughts to Ponder

Recall that a "mixed multitude" left Egypt along with the Israelites (Exodus 12:38, Numbers 11:4). How do you think these people influenced the attitudes and behaviors of the Israelites?

_____

_____

_____

_____

_____

When the Israelites were complaining to Moses about the food and water, how were they actually complaining against God?

_____

_____

_____

_____

_____

How do people, in general, and Christians, in particular, murmur against God today? What can you do to change your attitude when you find yourself complaining against God?

_____

_____

_____

_____

_____

Chapter 21

Manna and Quail

Exodus 16:9–36, NLT

(9) Then Moses said to Aaron, "Announce this to the entire community of Israel: 'Present yourselves before the LORD, for he has heard your complaining.'" (10) And as Aaron spoke to the whole community of Israel, they looked out toward the wilderness. There they could see the awesome glory of the LORD in the cloud.

(11) Then the LORD said to Moses, (12) "I have heard the Israelites' complaints. Now tell them, 'In the evening you will have meat to eat, and in the morning you will have all the bread you want. Then you will know that I am the LORD your God.'"

(13) That evening vast numbers of quail flew in and covered the camp. And the next morning the area around the camp was wet with dew. (14) When the dew evaporated, a flaky substance as fine as frost blanketed the ground. (15) The Israelites were puzzled when they saw it.

"What is it?" they asked each other. They had no idea what it was.

And Moses told them, "It is the food the LORD has given you to eat. (16) These are the LORD's instructions: Each household should gather as much as it needs. Pick up two quarts for each person in your tent."

(17) So the people of Israel did as they were told. Some gathered a lot, some only a little. (18) But when they measured it out, everyone had just enough. Those who gathered a lot had nothing left over, and those who gathered only a little had enough. Each family had just what it needed.

(19) Then Moses told them, "Do not keep any of it until morning." (20) But some of them didn't listen and kept some of it until morning. But by then it was full of maggots

and had a terrible smell. Moses was very angry with them.

(21) After this the people gathered the food morning by morning, each family according to its need. And as the sun became hot, the flakes they had not picked up melted and disappeared. (22) On the sixth day, they gathered twice as much as usual—four quarts for each person instead of two. Then all the leaders of the community came and asked Moses for an explanation. (23) He told them, "This is what the LORD commanded: Tomorrow will be a day of complete rest, a holy Sabbath day set apart for the LORD. So bake or boil as much as you want today, and set aside what is left for tomorrow."

(24) So they put some aside until morning, just as Moses had commanded. And in the morning the leftover food was wholesome and good, without maggots or odor. (25) Moses said, "Eat this food today, for today is a Sabbath day dedicated to the LORD. There will be no food on the ground today. (26) You may gather the food for six days, but the seventh day is the Sabbath. There will be no food on the ground that day."

(27) Some of the people went out anyway on the seventh day, but they found no food. (28) The LORD asked Moses, "How long will these people refuse to obey my commands and instructions? (29) They must realize that the Sabbath is the LORD's gift to you. That is why he gives you a two-day supply on the sixth day, so there will be enough for two days. On the Sabbath day you must each stay in your place. Do not go out to pick up food on the seventh day." (30) So the people did not gather any food on the seventh day.

(31) The Israelites called the food manna. It was white like coriander seed, and it tasted like honey wafers.

(32) Then Moses said, "This is what the LORD has commanded: Fill a two-quart container with manna to preserve it for your descendants. Then later generations will be able to see the food I gave you in the wilderness when I set you free from Egypt."

(33) Moses said to Aaron, "Get a jar and fill it with two quarts of manna. Then put it in a sacred place before the LORD to preserve it for all future generations." (34) Aaron did just as the LORD had commanded Moses. He eventually placed it in the Ark of the Covenant—in front of the stone tablets inscribed with the terms of the covenant. (35) So the people of Israel ate manna for forty years until they arrived at the land where they would settle. They ate manna until they came to the border of the land of Canaan.

(36) The container used to measure the manna was an omer, which was one-tenth of an ephah; it held about two quarts.

◇◇◇

Only a few days after God had provided drinking water at Marah, the people were complaining again. This time it was about food. They seemed to have forgotten the many ways God had previously cared for them. Once again, they grumbled against Moses and Aaron because they were hungry.

Did they really believe that the God who had been planning their trip to the Promised Land for hundreds of years had forgotten to think about how to feed them during their journey?

Evidently, they did. With this latest round of complaining, God called a family meeting.

When God charged the Israelites while they were at Marah to listen to Him and obey His statutes, He told them He would take care of them and keep them healthy. Remember, too, that in the pillar of cloud accompanying the Israelites, the presence of the Lord was constantly with them. It's not as if He had led them into this desolate region and forsaken them. God was there with them and had been with them in the cloud since before they crossed the Red Sea. They had a continual sign from heaven in their midst. Even so, God wanted to reassure the people of His presence and reaffirm His might. So, as Aaron was speaking to the assembly, the "glory of the Lord" appeared in the cloud.

God told Moses He had heard the Israelites complaining. Moses was to tell the people they would have meat to eat that evening, and the next morning they would have bread. Then, as they saw God's words come true, they would know for sure that the Lord was their God.

Indeed, the food appeared just as God said it would. The camp was covered with quail that evening, and the next morning, when the dew lifted, small particles covered the ground. The people didn't know what it was, but Moses explained that it was the food God had given them to eat. They were to gather an omer[1] for each person in their tent.

Suggested Song

"He Knows Just What I Need"

(tinyurl.com/2p9c7psa)

1

Note that the New Living Translation used for this lesson translates an omer as two quarts (verses 16, 33 and 36). For an estimate of various weights and measures mentioned in the Bible, see the article "What Are the Modern Equivalents of Biblical Weights and Measures?" (tinyurl.com/3rz7mwvj).

Just as God had tested the people with the bitter water at Marah, he again tested them here in the wilderness of Sin with His instructions concerning the gathering of manna. "Then the LORD said to Moses, 'Behold, I will rain bread from heaven for you. And the people shall go out and gather a certain quota every day, that I may test them, whether they will walk in My law or not. And it shall be on the sixth day that they shall prepare what they bring in, and it shall be twice as much as they gather daily'" (Exodus 16:4–5, NKJV).

God supplied food on a daily basis because He wanted the people to learn to depend on Him.[2] He wanted them to trust that He would do what He said He would do. He made it such that no matter how much or how little they gathered for the day, each person had exactly enough. Then He took it a step further. Those who had gathered more than they needed for the day were not allowed to keep the surplus. Anything left over spoiled by the next morning. Moreover, any ungathered manna left outside on the ground melted away in the heat of the sun each day.

> God supplied food on a daily basis because He wanted the people to learn to depend on Him.

Despite all the miracles they had witnessed and the constant presence of the cloud in their camp, many of the Israelites still had trouble fully trusting in God. Indeed, some kept excess manna overnight, only to awaken to find maggots and an unsavory stench. Their failure to obey God's instructions angered Moses.

Then the sixth and seventh days presented yet another test for the Israelites. On the sixth day of the week, they were to gather twice the usual amount and go ahead and prepare the extra for eating. On the seventh day, they were to rest and not go out to gather manna. On this one day of the week, the extra amount they had prepared from the day before would still be good to

2

The miracle of the manna became a continuous, forty-year-long miracle. God continued to provide manna for the Israelites all during their journey until they actually crossed over into Canaan (Exodus 16:35 and Joshua 5:10–12).

eat. Unfortunately, some of the people still went out seeking to gather manna on the seventh day, despite God's instructions.

God's Provision of Food and Rest

What wonderful gifts God bestowed on the Israelites early in their journey to the Promised Land. By sending them manna, He kept this vast multitude of people nourished, even while passing through places that were often arid and desolate. If they had been forced to slaughter their animals for food, they would have quickly killed off their herds and flocks.

God also gave the Israelites the gift of the Sabbath, a day of rest. This must have been a welcome respite for a people who had previously lived as slaves, driven daily to the point of exhaustion and beyond. So important was this day of rest that observing the Sabbath became one of the Ten Commandments God gave them later at Mt. Sinai.

Trusting in God's care on a daily basis remains a challenge for Christians today.

Even though He no longer drops manna from the sky, God continues to faithfully provide for His people. Yet when His care doesn't happen according to a certain time schedule or doesn't appear in the prescribed manner, it's easy to assume God doesn't care or that He's not listening. As time passes, a whole different scenario may emerge and reveal God's wisdom and plan. How many times have you been so thankful, after the fact, that God did *not* grant you what you asked of Him?

Just as God proved Himself faithful to the Israelites in so many ways, He continues to prove Himself faithful to His people today. And He does it continually, on a daily basis. His charge to us is to study His Word, follow His precepts, and trust Him to work His will in our lives. After all, God has been planning our

The Glory of the Lord

The glory of the Lord must have been manifest with brilliant light or possibly fire. In Exodus 24:15–17, while the Israelites were receiving God's covenant, the glory of the Lord rested on Mt. Sinai. A cloud covered the mountain, shielding the people from the extreme brilliance of God's glory. Exodus 24:17 (NKJV) describes it thus: "The sight of the glory of the LORD was like a consuming fire on the top of the mountain in the eyes of the children of Israel."

Later, Moses asked God in Exodus 33:18–23 to show him His glory. God told him he could not see His face, for no one could see Him and live, but He did somehow let Moses glimpse a portion of His glory. In Exodus 34:5–9, God came down in the cloud and passed in front of Moses. When Moses came down from the mountain after this encounter in Exodus 34:29–35, his face was radiant because he had spoken with God and been in His presence. This brightness frightened the people, so he covered his face with a veil. The Apostle Paul also talked about this in 2 Corinthians 3:7–8, that the Israelites could not look steadily at Moses's face because of the glory of his countenance.

spiritual journey to an eternity with Him for a very long time. He will not fail to nourish us along the way.

I was young and now I am old, yet I have never seen the righteous forsaken or their children begging bread.

—Psalm 37:25, NIV

Keep your lives free from the love of money and be content with what you have, because God has said, "Never will I leave you; never will I forsake you."

—Hebrews 13:5, NIV

Thoughts to Ponder

Although God rested on the seventh day of creation, did those who worshiped Him observe a day of rest on the seventh day prior to His instructions given here in Exodus 16?

_____

_____

_____

_____

What did Moses do with the manna so that future generations would remember God's care for the Israelites during their journey to the Promised Land? Why was it important for him to do this?

_____

_____

_____

_____

At this point, God has not yet given Moses the Law, which He will do later at Mt. Sinai. How has He been introducing the Israelites to various elements that will later be included in the Law?

_____

_____

_____

_____

Chapter 22

Water from a Rock and the Battle at Rephidim

Exodus 17, NIV

(1) The whole Israelite community set out from the Desert of Sin, traveling from place to place as the LORD commanded. They camped at Rephidim, but there was no water for the people to drink. (2) So they quarreled with Moses and said, "Give us water to drink."

Moses replied, "Why do you quarrel with me? Why do you put the LORD to the test?"

(3) But the people were thirsty for water there, and they grumbled against Moses. They said, "Why did you bring us up out of Egypt to make us and our children and livestock die of thirst?"

(4) Then Moses cried out to the LORD, "What am I to do with these people? They are almost ready to stone me."

(5) The LORD answered Moses, "Go out in front of the people. Take with you some of the elders of Israel and take in your hand the staff with which you struck the Nile, and go. (6) I will stand there before you by the rock at Horeb. Strike the rock, and water will come out of it for the people to drink." So Moses did this in the sight of the elders of Israel. (7) And he called the place Massah and Meribah because the Israelites quarreled and because they tested the LORD saying, "Is the LORD among us or not?"

(8) The Amalekites came and attacked the Israelites at Rephidim. (9) Moses said to Joshua, "Choose some of our men and go out to fight the Amalekites. Tomorrow I will stand on top of the hill with the staff of God in my hands."

(10) So Joshua fought the Amalekites as Moses had ordered, and Moses, Aaron and Hur went to the top of the hill. (11) As long

as Moses held up his hands, the Israelites were winning, but whenever he lowered his hands, the Amalekites were winning. (12) When Moses's hands grew tired, they took a stone and put it under him and he sat on it. Aaron and Hur held his hands up—one on one side, one on the other—so that his hands remained steady till sunset. (13) So Joshua overcame the Amalekite army with the sword.

(14) Then the LORD said to Moses, "Write this on a scroll as something to be remembered and make sure that Joshua hears it, because I will completely blot out the name of Amalek from under heaven."

(15) Moses built an altar and called it The LORD is my Banner. (16) He said, "Because hands were lifted up against the throne of the LORD, the LORD will be at war against the Amalekites from generation to generation."

Suggested Song

"God Our Banner"

(tinyurl.com/2hye3auy)

1

Numbers 33 lists the places where the Israelites camped during their journey from Egypt to the Promised Land. Verses 12–14 name their stops between the Desert of Sin and Rephidim.

2

For more information, see "Rephidim" in *Smith's Bible Dictionary* (tinyurl.com/52pjrxth) and in the *International Standard Bible Encyclopedia* (tinyurl.com/htaxcpss).

After the Israelites left the Desert of Sin, they camped at Dophkah and then at Alush before arriving at Rephidim.[1] The huge number of people and livestock traveling through this arid region required a lot of water. Whether these interim places had water is unknown, but it stands to reason they would not be able to go many days without it. They could carry only a limited amount with them.

By the time they reached Rephidim, they were desperate. Here was a place whose very name suggested "rest" or "stay."[2] The Israelites surely expected to find water, but unfortunately, there was none.

The Israelites immediately turned on Moses. Once again, they blamed him for their troubles and demanded that he provide them water. They questioned why they were brought up out of Egypt only to die in the wilderness. Like the water that was supposed to be at Rephidim, their memory of God's provision and protection had evaporated.

Moses reminded the Israelites that when they quarreled with him, they were putting God to the test. Unfortunately, they refused to listen and were ready to kill him for leading them to this place.

Moses appealed to God for intervention, and of course, God came to Moses's rescue. He told Moses to take his staff and some of the elders and go to the rock at Horeb. There, God promised to be with him and to bring water out of the rock. All Moses had to do was strike the rock with his staff.

No matter how unlikely it seemed that water could come from a rock, Moses trusted God and followed His instructions. God responded by providing enough water for all the people. Then Moses aptly named the place "Massah and Meribah." (*Massah* means temptation or testing, and *Meribah* means quarreling, strife, or contention.[3])

With their water problem solved, the Israelites immediately faced an even greater danger. For the first time since the waters of the Red Sea had engulfed the Egyptian army during their escape, they were facing a human enemy. The Amalekites attacked them from behind, hitting their weakest and most vulnerable members. The account in Deuteronomy 25:17–18 (NKJV) provides a few more details of this event: "Remember what Amalek did to you on the way as you were coming out of Egypt, how he met you on the way and attacked your rear ranks, all the stragglers at your rear, when you were tired and weary; and he did not fear God."

So who were the Amalekites, and why would they attack the Israelites? Amalek is listed in Genesis 36:12 as a grandson of Esau, who was the twin brother of Jacob, the father of the Israelites. It's likely the territory the Israelites were passing through had been claimed by the Amalekites. Sites that contained water, which Rephidim supposedly did on occasion, were especially valuable. This vast horde of people and animals, whether they were relatives or not, would have been seen as a threat.

Moses called upon his assistant, Joshua, to lead the Israelites in battle against the Amalekites. The next day, Moses, Aaron,

----

3

In Numbers 20:13, the name Meribah was also given to Kadesh, where the people again strove with God over water. See "Meribah" in *Smith's Bible Dictionary* (tinyurl.com/3mctzmsk).

Jewish tradition identifies Hur as being the husband (or possibly the son) of Miriam, who was Aaron and Moses's older sister. The scriptures do not confirm this, however, nor was the character in the movie, *Ben-Hur*, based on any of the men named Hur in the Bible. For more information, see the articles: "Who Was Hur in the Bible?" (tinyurl. com/2a786ah7) and "Is Ben-Hur in the Bible?" (tinyurl. com/2scwepmy).

In time, the Amalekites indeed appear to have been wiped out. For a more detailed synopsis, see "Exodus 17," particularly verses 8 and 14 in *Ellicott's Commentary* (tinyurl. com/3rbvj5j2).

and Hur[4] went up to the top of a hill that overlooked the battle site. As long as Moses kept his staff and hands lifted toward heaven, the Israelites prevailed, but when he lowered his hands, the Amalekites began winning the battle. When Moses tired, Aaron and Hur brought him a rock to sit on. Then, with one of them on each side of Moses, they literally supported him, propping up his arms—all day long. Joshua fought until the sun went down and, with God's help, defeated the Amalekites.

The Lord Is My Banner

Once again, God presented Moses and the Israelites with a powerful lesson. Only by Moses keeping his hands and staff raised toward heaven that day were they able to win the battle. From the moment they left Egypt, God had been teaching Moses and the Israelites that they had to truly and completely depend on Him—for water, food, and their very lives.

Rephidim should have been just another stop along their journey, but it turned out to be much more. There, God miraculously provided the people with water from the rock at Horeb, and there He saved them from the Amalekites. In response, Moses built an altar and named it *The LORD Is My Banner*. With this altar, Moses proclaimed the Israelites' allegiance to their one God. They were victorious in battle that day because the Lord was on their side. They pledged to march under His banner forever.

> Rephidim should have been just another stop along their journey, but it turned out to be much more.

God wanted the events which happened at Rephidim to be remembered as well. When the Amalekites attacked the Israelites, they not only killed their own kinsmen but also showed their disdain for God Himself. Because they had tried to fight against His authority and throne, God declared He would completely blot out the name of Amalek from under heaven.[5] He instructed

Moses to record His decree against them. Knowing that Joshua was next in line to lead His people, God told Moses to make sure Joshua understood the decree.

The Lord is the banner of His people today.

Christians today unite under the name of Jesus. As God's Son, Jesus came to earth and fought our greatest battle for us. He defeated death, once and for all time. Like the Israelites' battle with the Amalekites, it's not a battle we could have ever won on our own. Because of His victory, all those who believe in Him and obey His teachings have the hope of eternal life.

May we, like Moses, always look to the Lord for our salvation. As the Apostle Peter stated in Acts 4:12 (NKJV): "Nor is there salvation in any other, for there is no other name under heaven given among men by which we must be saved." Let us march under the banner of the Lord forever.

And I, if I be lifted up from the earth, will draw all men unto me.

—John 12:32, KJV

Finally, be strong in the Lord and in the strength of his might. Put on the whole armor of God, that you may be able to stand against the schemes of the devil.

—Ephesians 6:10–11, ESV

While many altars were built during Old Testament times, only a few were given a name. In Genesis 33:19–20, when Jacob finally arrived back safely at Shechem in Canaan with his wives and children and livestock, he built an altar and called it El Elohe Israel. (Depending on how it's translated, this phrase can mean "God, the God of Israel" or "mighty is the God of Israel.") Another altar was named "Witness" by the people of Reuben and Gad in Joshua 22:34. Then, in Judges 6:24, Gideon built an altar and called it "The LORD is Peace."

The Israelites' battle with the Amalekites and their subsequent victory was a momentous occasion. It marked the first time they had fought as a nation against another people. Moses wanted to make sure their victory would be remembered by giving the name, The Lord Is My Banner, to the altar where they worshiped God after the battle.

Thoughts to Ponder

Joshua is mentioned for the first time in Scripture in this chapter. What do you know about Joshua's early life before he became the next leader of the Israelites? Why didn't Moses himself go fight? Why did God specifically direct that Joshua hear and know about what Moses was to write in the scroll or book?

_____

_____

_____

_____

_____

What was the significance of Moses holding up his hands during the battle with the Amalekites? What about his staff?

_____

_____

_____

_____

_____

The Amalekites were kinsmen of the Israelites. Why did God condemn them so harshly?

_____

_____

_____

_____

_____

Chapter 23

The Beginnings of a Judicial System

Exodus 18, NKJV

(1) And Jethro, the priest of Midian, Moses' father-in-law, heard of all that God had done for Moses and for Israel His people—that the LORD had brought Israel out of Egypt. (2) Then Jethro, Moses' father-in-law, took Zipporah, Moses' wife, after he had sent her back, (3) with her two sons, of whom the name of one was Gershom (for he said, "I have been a stranger in a foreign land") (4) and the name of the other was Eliezer (for he said, "The God of my father was my help, and delivered me from the sword of Pharaoh"); (5) and Jethro, Moses' father-in-law, came with his sons and his wife to Moses in the wilderness, where he was encamped at the mountain of God. (6) Now he had said to Moses, "I, your father-in-law Jethro, am coming to you with your wife and her two sons with her."

(7) So Moses went out to meet his father-in-law, bowed down, and kissed him. And they asked each other about their well-being, and they went into the tent. (8) And Moses told his father-in-law all that the LORD had done to Pharaoh and to the Egyptians for Israel's sake, all the hardship that had come upon them on the way, and how the LORD had delivered them. (9) Then Jethro rejoiced for all the good which the LORD had done for Israel, whom He had delivered out of the hand of the Egyptians. (10) And Jethro said, "Blessed be the LORD, who has delivered you out of the hand of the Egyptians and out of hand of Pharaoh, and who has delivered the people from under the hand of the Egyptians. (11) Now I know that the LORD is greater than all the gods; for in the very thing in which they behaved proudly, He was above them." (12) Then Jethro, Moses' father-in-law, took a burnt offering and other sacrifices to offer to God. And Aaron

came with all the elders of Israel to eat bread with Moses' father-in-law before God.

(13) And so it was, on the next day, that Moses sat to judge the people; and the people stood before Moses from morning until evening. (14) So when Moses' father-in-law saw all that he did for the people, he said, "What is this thing that you are doing for the people? Why do you alone sit, and all the people stand before you from morning until evening?"

(15) And Moses said to his father-in-law, "Because the people come to me to inquire of God. (16) When they have a difficulty, they come to me, and I judge between one and another; and I make known the statutes of God and His laws."

(17) So Moses' father-in-law said to him, "The thing that you do is not good. (18) Both you and these people who are with you will surely wear yourselves out. For this thing is too much for you; you are not able to perform it by yourself. (19) Listen now to my voice; I will give you counsel, and God will be with you: Stand before God for the people, so that you may bring the difficulties to God. (20) And you shall teach them the statutes and the laws,

and show them the way in which they must walk and the work they must do. (21) Moreover you shall select from all the people able men, such as fear God, men of truth, hating covetousness; and place such over them to be rulers of thousands, rulers of hundreds, rulers of fifties, and rulers of tens. (22) And let them judge the people at all times. Then it will be that every great matter they shall bring to you, but every small matter they themselves shall judge. So it will be easier for you, for they will bear the burden with you. (23) If you do this thing, and God so commands you, then you will be able to endure, and all this people will also go to their place in peace."

(24) So Moses heeded the voice of his father-in-law and did all that he had said. (25) And Moses chose able men out of all Israel, and made them heads over the people: rulers of thousands, rulers of hundreds, rulers of fifties, and rulers of tens. (26) So they judged the people at all times; the hard cases they brought to Moses, but they judged every small case themselves.

(27) Then Moses let his father-in-law depart, and he went his way to his own land.

News travels fast, no matter what era you live in or how remote the region. By the time the events in this chapter occurred, Jethro, Moses's father-in-law, had already heard the news of God's deliverance of the Israelites out of Egypt. He set out to meet with Moses. This begs the question—how did he know where to go? He may have heard through the wilderness grapevine where they were headed. Or perhaps a group as massive in size as the Israelites, with a pillar of cloud towering over their campsite, was not that difficult to find.

It's more likely, however, that Moses had previously told Jethro all that occurred during his encounter with God and the burning bush. Recall God's promise to Moses in Exodus 3:12 (NKJV): "And this shall be a sign to you that I have sent you: When you have brought the people out of Egypt, you shall serve God on this mountain." If Moses had shared this information, then Jethro would have known Moses would head back to the mountain where it all started.

One of the reasons for Jethro's visit was to return Moses's wife and sons to him. How or why they came to be with Jethro in the first place is not known. The last mention of Moses's family was in Exodus 4:20–26, when Moses put his wife and sons on a donkey and headed to Egypt. Remember that the Lord had stopped Moses and tried to kill him because one of his sons was uncircumcised. We could speculate that contention arose when Zipporah had to use a flint knife to circumcise her son, and this was the reason she and their sons went back to stay with Jethro. Or it could have been that Moses sent them back to keep them out of harm's way during what was certain to be a tumultuous time. The scriptures simply do not tell us.

Jethro seemed eager to hear about all that had transpired during Moses's miraculous journey into and out of Egypt. As the priest of Midian and a fellow descendant of Abraham,[1] Jethro

Suggested Song

"Far and Near the Fields Are Teeming"

(tinyurl.com/56c9syen)

— 1 —

In addition to Ishmael and Isaac, Abraham had six more sons by his wife or concubine, Keturah, of which Midian was one. See Genesis 25:1–6 and 1 Chronicles 1:32–33.

Melchizedek, the Forerunner of Christ

Hebrews 7:1 tells us that Melchizedek was the king of Salem and a priest of the Most High God. He is the first person mentioned in the Scriptures who is called a priest of God (Genesis 14:18). Yet Hebrews 7:3 tells us his origin and genealogy are unknown. For sure, he was a descendant of Noah, as all the other families on earth were wiped out during the flood. It's encouraging to know that amid all the idol worship that had become so prevalent by Abraham's time, there were other descendants of Noah who continued to worship the true and living God.

Hebrews 7:2 goes on to tell us that the name Melchizedek means "king of righteousness," while his title, King of Salem, means "king of peace." How fitting, then, that Jesus Christ, our Messiah, should be named a priest forever after the order of Melchizedek, the king of righteousness and peace. While Jesus physically descended

knew the significance of Israel's deliverance. These happenings affirmed to him that the God he and his people had been worshiping for so many years was indeed the true God. This God had proven Himself to be greater than all other false gods, and Jethro had come prepared to thank Him and worship Him.

The following day, even with Jethro still there as his guest, Moses felt compelled to resume his duty of judging disputes among the Israelites. Jethro watched as people came to Moses all day long with their complaints, squabbles, and questions. Moses explained to Jethro later that evening that he not only served as judge but also provided instructions concerning God's decrees and laws.

It was immediately clear to Jethro that Moses was under too much pressure. The workload was too heavy for him to handle alone. He warned his son-in-law that he would wear himself and the people out if he tried to manage everything on his own. Jethro then proposed a more efficient plan, one that began with teaching the people. Rather than providing instruction on a case-by-case basis after a matter arose, Jethro suggested Moses first teach everyone God's decrees and laws. Remember, these people had lived in Egypt for centuries. They needed to be shown how to live as God's people and given instruction as to what was expected of them. It's likely this step alone significantly reduced the number of cases.

Then, to handle the disputes, Jethro suggested that Moses appoint officials over groups of thousands, hundreds, fifties, and tens. The officials at the lower levels could handle minor disputes. More serious or complicated cases would progress up to the higher levels. Only matters that were too difficult for this system to handle would be presented to Moses.

Scripture says that Moses listened to his father-in-law and did all that he suggested. This speaks to Moses's humility and character. While he may have been God's chosen leader, he willingly listened to Jethro and wisely took his advice. After that, Jethro left and went back to his home. If Moses or his family ever saw him again, it's not recorded.

The Impact of Jethro's Visit

In a relatively short period, Jethro helped Moses establish the structure for a judicial system for the Israelites. He spoke with wisdom and patience and in a way that did not undermine Moses's authority among the people. He also implored Moses to seek God's guidance in following his suggestions and to act in accordance with God's will.

As significant as this was, another remarkable event also occurred during Jethro's visit. It's easy to miss, as only one verse (Exodus 18:12, NKJV) describes it: "Then Jethro, Moses' father-in-law, took a burnt offering and other sacrifices to offer to God. And Aaron came with all the elders of Israel to eat bread with Moses' father-in-law before God."

Jethro's worship of God provides insight for us today.

Before the Law of Moses had been given and before Aaron had been appointed high priest of the Israelites, the priest of Midian offered a burnt offering and other sacrifices to God. Aaron and all the elders of Israel came and attended this worship ceremony, and together they ate bread with Jethro in the presence of God. The leaders of God's chosen people were led in worship and communion by someone outside of the lineage through which Christ would ultimately come. Evidently, well before the time of the Law of Moses, the worship of God was more widespread than is recorded in the Scriptures.

This communion is reminiscent of Abram's communion with Melchizedek in Genesis 14:18–24. Before God ever made his covenant with Abram, Melchizedek was king of Salem[2] and a priest of God Most High. When Abram returned from his battle to retrieve his nephew, Lot, who had been captured, Melchizedek brought out bread and wine and blessed him. In turn, Abram

through Abraham and Isaac, His priesthood existed well before the giving of the Law. Unlike the priesthood of Aaron, which the Law established, His priesthood is permanent because He lives forever.

Moreover, Jesus has become the guarantor of a much better covenant than the Law (Hebrews 7:22). His New Covenant, which He established with the shedding of His blood, offers eternal salvation to all who will follow Him and obey His teachings. As Hebrews 7:25 (NIV) tells us, "Therefore he is able to save completely those who come to God through him, because he always lives to intercede for them." Jesus, then, is both our perfect high priest forever and our King of righteousness and peace.

2

It's likely that Salem is the same place that would later be known as Jerusalem. For more information, see "Salem" in the *Encyclopedia of the Bible* (tinyurl.com/yc7eakce).

3

Psalm 110, a psalm of David, foretold the coming of Christ and, in verse 4b (NKJV), states: "You are a priest forever according to the order of Melchizedek." The book of Hebrews discusses at length the everlasting priesthood of Jesus and in Hebrews 7 likens Him to Melchizedek (especially verses 20–25).

paid homage to Melchizedek by presenting him with a tithe, or a tenth, of all the goods he had brought back from battle.

God's love transcends culture and family lineage.

God later designated Isaac to be the one through whose earthly lineage Jesus, the Son of God, would ultimately enter the world. However, these scriptures concerning Jethro and Melchizedek reveal that the worship of God has never been exclusive to the Israelites. Indeed, Christ is a priest forever, not of the Levitical priesthood after the order of Aaron but after the order of Melchizedek, someone who worshiped God before Abram ever had an heir.[3] Jethro's actions, much like those of Melchizedek, speak to us today and serve as yet another example that the worship of God transcends time, place, and lineage.

> These scriptures concerning Jethro and Melchizedek reveal that the worship of God has never been exclusive to the Israelites.

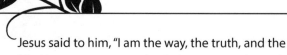

Jesus said to him, "I am the way, the truth, and the life. No one comes to the Father except through Me."

—John 14:6, NKJV

And Jesus came and spoke to them, saying, "All authority has been given to Me in heaven and on earth. Go therefore and make disciples of all nations, baptizing them in the name of the Father and of the Son and of the Holy Spirit, teaching them to observe all things that I have commanded you; and lo, I am with you always, even to the end of the age."

—Matthew 28:18–20, NKJV

Thoughts to Ponder

Review the list of qualifications that Jethro suggested for the lower court judges (Exodus 18:21). Then look at the qualifications given for deacons (Acts 6:1–6 and 1 Timothy 3:8–13). How are their qualifications and appointed duties similar or dissimilar?

_____

_____

_____

Note the interactions between Moses and Jethro. Jethro is probably older than Moses, as he is the father of Moses's wife. He is also recognized as a priest and spiritual leader. Yet Jethro is careful to honor Moses and treats him with great respect, even while he gives him instruction as to how to organize the judicial system. What insights might Jethro have gained concerning Moses's character during the forty years he lived in Midian? Now that the Israelites have been safely brought out of Egypt by God, what does that tell Jethro about Moses?

_____

_____

_____

Up until he met with Moses, it's possible that Jethro may have worshiped or offered sacrifices to more than one god, perhaps to cover all the possible contingencies. He seemed truly delighted to learn all that God had done in delivering the Israelites out of Egypt. This proved to him that the one God of the Israelites was real and truly powerful, unlike other gods made of wood or stone. How do you think Jethro's meeting with Moses helped spread the worship of God, Yahweh, throughout other parts of the known world? (Recall God's promise to Abram in Genesis 12:1–3 that through him, all nations or families of the world would be blessed.)

_____

_____

_____

Chapter 24

God's Covenant with the Israelites

Exodus 19, HCSB

(1) In the third month, on the same day of the month that the Israelites had left the land of Egypt, they entered the Wilderness of Sinai. (2) After they departed from Rephidim, they entered the Wilderness of Sinai and camped in the wilderness, and Israel camped there in front of the mountain.

(3) Moses went up the mountain to God, and the LORD called to him from the mountain: "This is what you must say to the house of Jacob, and explain to the Israelites: (4) 'You have seen what I did to the Egyptians and how I carried you on eagles' wings and brought you to Me. (5) Now if you will listen to Me and carefully keep My covenant, you will be My own possession out of all the peoples, although all the earth is Mine, (6) and you will be My kingdom of priests and My holy nation.' These are the words that you are to say to the Israelites."

(7) After Moses came back, he summoned the elders of the people and set before them all these words that the LORD had commanded him. (8) Then all the people responded together, "We will do all that the LORD has spoken." So Moses brought the people's words back to the LORD.

(9) The LORD said to Moses, "I am going to come to you in a dense cloud, so that the people will hear when I speak with you and will always believe you." Then Moses reported the people's words to the LORD. (10) And the LORD told Moses, "Go to the people and consecrate them today and tomorrow. They must wash their clothes (11) and be prepared by the third day, for on the third day the LORD will come down on Mount Sinai in the sight of all the people. (12) Put boundaries for the people all around the mountain and say: Be careful that you don't go up on the mountain or touch its base. Anyone who touches the

mountain will be put to death. (13) No hand may touch him; instead he will be stoned or shot with arrows. No animal or man will live. When the ram's horn sounds a long blast, they may go up the mountain."

(14) Then Moses came down from the mountain to the people and consecrated them, and they washed their clothes. (15) He said to the people, "Be prepared by the third day. Do not have sexual relations with women."

(16) On the third day, when morning came, there was thunder and lightning, a thick cloud on the mountain, and a loud trumpet sound, so that all the people in the camp shuddered. (17) Then Moses brought the people out of the camp to meet God, and they stood at the foot of the mountain. (18) Mount Sinai was completely enveloped in smoke because the LORD came down on it in fire. Its smoke went up like the smoke of a furnace, and the whole mountain shook violently. (19) As the sound of the trumpet grew louder and louder, Moses spoke and God answered him in the thunder.

(20) The LORD came down on Mount Sinai at the top of the mountain. Then the LORD summoned Moses to the top of the mountain, and he went up. (21) The LORD directed Moses, "Go down and warn the people not to break through to see the LORD; otherwise many of them will die. (22) Even the priests who come near the LORD must purify themselves or the LORD will break out in anger against them."

(23) But Moses responded to the LORD, "The people cannot come up Mount Sinai, since You warned us: Put a boundary around the mountain and consider it holy." (24) And the LORD replied to him, "Go down and come back with Aaron. But the priests and the people must not break through to come up to the LORD, or He will break out in anger against them." (25) So Moses went down to the people and told them.

◇◇◇

By the time the Israelites arrived at the mountain of God, they had already experienced quite a journey. They had observed a multitude of miraculous events in Egypt, walked between walls of water on dry ground as they crossed the sea to freedom, and witnessed the destruction of the mighty Egyptian army. They had miraculously received both food and water and defeated the Amalekites in battle. Now, they would meet God Himself, enter into a covenant with Him, and receive His Law.

As Moses approached the mountain, God's words must have been ringing in his ears. Months earlier, he had stood on this same mountain beside a burning bush. He had made every excuse he could think of, yet God refused to yield. When God called Moses to lead the Israelites out of Egypt, He made him a promise: "I will certainly be with you, and this will be the sign to you that I have sent you: when you bring the people out of Egypt, you will all worship God at this mountain" (Exodus 3:12, HCSB).

God had kept His promise. Moses had returned to this very mountain with the Israelite people in tow.

In the coming verses, God will present His Law to the Israelite people.[1] But it's important to note that He didn't just give it to them and expect them to accept it. He first asked them to make a commitment to Him. *He wanted them to want to be His people.*

God spoke to Moses on the mountain and told him to remind the people of all they had seen Him do to the Egyptians on their behalf. God wanted the people to remember that He had miraculously delivered them and brought them here to Himself. They had witnessed the extraordinary measures God had taken to protect and care for them. Then He made them another promise: If they would obey Him fully and keep His covenant, they would be His treasured possession out of all the nations of the earth. They would be a holy nation, a kingdom of priests.

Moses delivered God's message to the elders. They, in turn, must have presented it to the people because, in verse 8, *all*

——— 1 ———
The Law given in the Old Testament is often referred to as the Mosaic Law or the Law of Moses.

the people responded together: "We will do all that the LORD has spoken." With this, they committed themselves to God.

Moses brought the people's response back to God. Then, for the people's benefit, God told Moses He was going to speak to him from a dense cloud. While He didn't need to do that in order to talk to Moses, He wanted the Israelites to witness Him speaking with Moses. He wanted them to know that He recognized Moses as their leader so they would always believe him and put their trust in Him.

To help the people understand the importance of the moment, God instructed the people to consecrate themselves. They were to wash their clothes and abstain from sexual relations during this time. God also instructed that a boundary be placed around the mountain. No person or animal was to even touch the mountain, or else they had to be killed. Should that occur, they couldn't be killed by laying hands upon them but rather by stoning or shooting them with an arrow. God did not want the people trying to force their way up to see Him and perish. Only when the ram's horn sounded a long blast could they even approach the mountain.

For two days, the people prepared, and on the morning of the third day, God descended upon the mountain in a fire. What an awesome sight it must have been! With thunder and lightning and a deafening trumpet blast, a thick cloud covered the mountain. Understandably, everyone in the camp trembled. Then Moses led the people out of the camp to meet with God. They stood at the foot of the mountain where smoke billowed as from a furnace, and the sound of the trumpet grew louder and louder. The earth shook violently beneath them. It was amid such a scene as this that Moses spoke—and God answered!

The impact of this event on the people must have been tremendous. God responded when Moses called to Him! God then called Moses up to the top of the mountain. There, He told Moses once again to remind the people not to try to force their way up and that He wanted Moses to bring Aaron back up with him after he had delivered that warning. Moses, surely in awe himself, obeyed.

Called to Be God's People

Centuries earlier, God had made a covenant with Abraham, the forefather of this people.[2] His descendants, who now stood before the mountain of God, were the fulfillment of much of what God had promised him. This group, who had lived their entire lives in Egypt as slaves, would be the ones called to accept God's Law and henceforth live as His people. In so doing, they would also be called to make transformative changes in their lives.

This Law, soon to be given to Moses on Mount Sinai, would prove difficult for God's people to keep. It provided them awareness of their sins but not freedom from their sins. Because of their transgressions, precious few souls who stood there on that day would actually be allowed to enter the Promised Land.

God has granted us the right to become His children.

The Law would, however, go on to play an integral part in God's plan to ultimately make salvation available to the world. Today, it is Jesus, rather than Moses, who leads us to the mountain of God. When He came to earth and lived a life without sin, He completely fulfilled the Law and its requirements. Upon His death, burial, and resurrection, He ushered in the New Covenant under which Christians live today. Because of Jesus, we now have true freedom—freedom from the sin which seeks to enslave us. Even better, those who receive Jesus have the right to become not only the people of God but children of God!

───── 2 ─────

God made His covenant with Abram (later called Abraham) in Genesis 15. In Genesis 15:13–21, God foretold what would occur concerning his descendants.

The Holiness of the Mountain

The Israelites were to consider the mountain of God, or Mount Sinai, as holy. The holiness of the mountain stemmed from the fact that the presence of God resided there at the time. As God told Moses later, no one can see His face and live. His command, then—that no human or animal touch the mountain—was for their protection, to keep them from trying to come on up the mountain to see Him (Exodus 19:21). He also wanted the people to learn to obey

Him, something they had trouble doing on occasion.

God commanded that any person or animal who touched the mountain be put to death. Moreover, no hand could touch the transgressor. They had to be stoned or shot with an arrow. Why did God issue such a command? If the executioner touched the transgressor, he would be touching the one who touched the mountain. That, in effect, would make the executioner guilty of touching the mountain as well. As a result, the executioner had to kill the offender without making direct contact.

But as many as received Him, to them He gave the right to become children of God, to those who believe in His name: who were born, not of blood, nor of the will of the flesh, nor of the will of man, but of God.

—John 1:12–13, NKJV

Behold what manner of love the Father has bestowed on us, that we should be called children of God!

—1 John 3:1a, NKJV

Thoughts to Ponder

What was the purpose of the people having to sanctify themselves before their meeting with God? Does God want us to be physically clean today? Was this for the people's benefit or for God's?

_____

_____

_____

_____

_____

What does it mean that the Israelites were to be a "kingdom of priests"?

_____

_____

_____

_____

How did the happenings here at the mountain of God help validate Moses's role as God's chosen leader of the Israelites?

_____

_____

_____

_____

God Reveals His Character and Calls His People to Holiness

Chapter 25

The Ten Commandments

Exodus 20:1–17, HCSB

(1) Then God spoke all these words:

(2) I am the LORD your God, who brought you out of the land of Egypt, out of the place of slavery.

(3) Do not have other gods besides Me.

(4) Do not make an idol for yourself, whether in the shape of anything in the heavens above or on the earth below or in the waters under the earth. (5) You must not bow down to them or worship them; for I, the LORD your God, am a jealous God, punishing the children for the fathers' sin, to the third and fourth generations of those who hate Me, (6) but showing faithful love to a thousand generations of those who love Me and keep My commands.

(7) Do not misuse the name of the LORD your God, because the LORD will not leave anyone unpunished who misuses His name.

(8) Remember the Sabbath day, to keep it holy: (9) You are to labor six days and do all your work, (10) but the seventh day is a Sabbath to the LORD your God. You must not do any work—you, your son or daughter, your male or female slave, your livestock, or the foreigner who is within your gates. (11) For the LORD made the heavens and the earth, the sea, and everything in them in six days; then He rested on the seventh day. Therefore the LORD blessed the Sabbath day and declared it holy.

(12) Honor your father and your mother so that you may have a long life in the land that the LORD your God is giving you.

(13) Do not murder.

(14) Do not commit adultery.

(15) Do not steal.

(16) Do not give false testimony against your neighbor.

(17) Do not covet your neighbor's house. Do not covet your neighbor's wife, his male or female slave, his ox or donkey, or anything that belongs to your neighbor.

Suggested Song

"Amazing Grace"

(tinyurl.com/3dafehpt)

With the people trembling at the base of the mountain, God spoke. This time, it wasn't only Moses that He spoke to. Rather, He spoke directly to the people, the same people who had agreed to obey Him and keep His covenant. He presented to them a code of conduct that would come to be known as the Ten Commandments.[1]

Elegant in their simplicity and clarity, these commandments instructed the people how to behave in virtually every aspect of their lives. They addressed their relationships with God and with one another. God would go on to give them many more commands, but these first ten precepts provided the underlying framework for His more extensive instructions.

God predicated His commands with why His people should honor and obey Him. He had done what no false god could have ever done: He had delivered them out of Egypt from the land of slavery. With His actions, He had shown His unparalleled love and devotion for these people.

His first four commands concerned how the people were to act toward God Himself. They were to have no other gods but Him, nor were they to make an image to worship, nor were they to take His name in vain. Remember that the Israelites had been immersed in the culture of the Egyptians for centuries, where the gods were too numerous to count. Images of these ancient gods still exist today in various forms and drawings. The idea of one living, all-powerful God whose essence could not possibly be contained in a piece of stone or wood or gold ran counter to all they had witnessed in Egypt.

God expounded a bit on the second command. In so doing, He provided insight into His character. He is a jealous God and shares the stage with no one. For us today, the "other" gods and idols may appear in the form of the material possessions we

---

1

Although not called the Ten Commandments here, they are referred to as such in Exodus 34:28, Deuteronomy 4:13, and Deuteronomy 10:4. Literally translated, they are "the Ten Words." Religious leaders later referred to them as the "Decalogue," a term found in various Bible commentaries.

desperately seek to acquire or the positions of power and prestige we strive to attain.

The third command addressed how the people were to speak about God. His name is righteous, and to take His name in vain is particularly offensive to Him. Using the name of God while uttering profanity dishonors Him. Moreover, God is the embodiment of truth, and it is impossible for Him to lie.[2] Swearing falsely or deliberately stating an untruth while invoking the name of God attempts to make Him a liar as well. Misusing the name of God in any way attempts to debase God Himself, something He said would not go unpunished.

With the fourth command, God presented a wonderful gift to His people. While the seventh day of the week, the Sabbath, was to be set aside in reverence toward God, it also gave everyone and their animals rest from their work. For a people who, only a few months earlier, were enslaved and driven beyond exhaustion, God's institution of the Sabbath day of rest must have been a welcome relief for their bodies and souls.

The remaining six commands dealt with how the people were to act toward one another. It's not surprising the first of these addressed how they were to treat their own parents. Notice that God did not command obedience to one's parents, which would apply more to younger children, nor did He command they be cared for, which would apply more when parents are elderly or infirm. Rather, He instructed that parents be honored, a word which applies to every stage of life and embodies not only one's actions but also one's attitude toward their parents. The Apostle Paul would later point out in Ephesians 6:1–3 that this is the first commandment which also holds a promise.

From there, God provided four more commands for how the people were to act toward other people. To turn this group of former slaves into an independent nation and create a civilized and peaceful community, everyone needed to follow the same rules:

—— 2 ——
The writer of Hebrews attests that it is impossible for God to lie in Hebrews 6:18.

- Respect the lives of others—do not murder.

- Respect the marital bonds of others and the sanctity of their households—do not commit adultery.

- Respect the property of others—do not steal.

- Respect the character of others—do not testify falsely about them.

The final command struck at the root of all evil. It dealt with the sins of the heart. Beyond controlling one's spoken words or actual deeds, God expected them to control their thoughts. In so doing, they would be able to choke off evil before it became manifest. Jesus would later stress the importance of the thoughts that people harbor within their hearts: "For out of the abundance of the heart the mouth speaks. A good man out of the good treasure of his heart brings forth good things, and an evil man out of the evil treasure brings forth evil things" (Matthew 12:34b–35, NKJV).

God's Instructions for Life

Never before had God given a comprehensive code of conduct to His people. From the time of Adam, He had communicated with individuals, whether directly or through an angel or in a dream or vision. But with a plan to eventually bring the world to Himself, He chose a group of people for His own. They would be the ones through whose lineage the Messiah would later enter the world.

These people had lived as slaves in a land filled with false gods. What they understood about the true God, Yahweh, consisted of the limited knowledge that had been passed down to them from their ancestors. They needed to encounter God firsthand, and they needed a set of instructions by which to live as God's people. God made that happen by displaying to them His awesome power and presenting to them His Law.

The Ten Commandments form the foundation for the New Covenant.

Jesus expounded upon these laws in His teachings and used many parables to help us better understand their true intent and meanings. If you read through His "Sermon on the Mount" in Matthew 5–7, you will find these commandments embedded in his teachings.

> "Love the Lord your God with all your heart and with all your soul and with all your mind."

Jesus also beautifully condensed these commandments into just two. When asked which was the greatest or most important commandment in the Law, He replied: "'Love the Lord your God with all your heart and with all your soul and with all your mind.' This is the first and greatest commandment. And the second is like it: 'Love your neighbor as yourself.' All the Law and the Prophets hang on these two commandments'" (Matthew 22:37–40, NIV).

God's words, spoken so long ago on Mount Sinai, still speak to us today. We now have a new and better covenant, one that provides redemption from our sins and the promise of eternal life. But the precepts presented back then still form the basis of how we are to behave in our daily lives, both toward God and toward others. They also represent God reaching down to mankind in an effort to bring us closer to Him. May we never forget the importance of these commandments.

The Ten Commandments

As you read through the list of the Ten Commandments, you'll notice that most of them give instructions concerning what *not* to do. Only numbers four and five are stated in the positive. In these commands, the people were instructed what they should do rather than what they should not do.

The fourth command concerns the Sabbath, and it's one of the longest. In it, God told the Israelites to keep the Sabbath holy. Then He told them how they were to accomplish keeping that day holy and why it was important to Him that they do so.

In the fifth command, God instructed the people to honor their parents. The Apostle Paul later quoted this command in Ephesians 6:1–3 (NKJV) as he was giving instructions to the New Testament church on how they were to live. He noted this command was the first commandment with a promise, with the promise being "that it may be well with you and you may live long on the earth."

Most notably, Jesus summarized the intent of all Ten Commandments into just two: "'Love the Lord your God with all your heart and with all your soul and with all your mind.' This is the first and greatest commandment. And the second is like it: 'Love your neighbor as yourself.' All the Law and the Prophets hang on these two commandments" (Matthew 22:37–40, NIV).

These two summary commandments are also stated in the positive and are given in the Old Testament. Deuteronomy 6:5 contains the first one, and Leviticus 19:18 the second. Jesus pulled them out from among all the other instructions and commands of the Mosaic Law and put them together to succinctly summarize the Law and the teachings of the Prophets. These timeless commands remain words for us to live by today.

So in everything, do to others what you would have them do to you, for this sums up the Law and the Prophets.

—Matthew 7:12, NIV

I am not writing you a new command but one we have had from the beginning. I ask that we love one another. And this is love: that we walk in obedience to his commands. As you have heard from the beginning, his command is that you walk in love.

—2 John 1:5–6, NIV

Thoughts to Ponder

Will every person who honors their parents necessarily live long on the earth? What is the deeper meaning of God's statement in the fifth commandment?

The deeper meaning is that parents are wise + have already experienced so many things. Honoring them may naturally lead to a long life. Also, not all parents are good people + hide it to the outside world. If you can honor your parents, good or bad, you probably find it easier to forgive + be kind.

God hates a liar. Which command(s) deal(s) with intentionally making false statements? What other scriptures come to mind about the gravity of telling a lie?

7th - don't misuse God's name

Are Christians commanded to keep the Sabbath today?

Great question

Chapter 26

Moses Intercedes for the Israelites

Exodus 20:18–21; Deuteronomy 5:1–5, 22–33, HCSB

(Ex. 20:18) All the people witnessed the thunder and lightning, the sound of the trumpet, and the mountain surrounded by smoke. When the people saw it they trembled and stood at a distance. (19) "You speak to us, and we will listen," they said to Moses, "but don't let God speak to us, or we will die."

(20) Moses responded to the people, "Don't be afraid, for God has come to test you, so that you will fear Him and will not sin." (21) And the people remained standing at a distance as Moses approached the thick darkness where God was.

[From Exodus 20:22 on through chapter 23, God delivered to Moses additional commands and statutes which would comprise part of the Book of the Covenant.]

◇◇◇

[The book of Deuteronomy served as Moses's farewell to the Israelite people. Before they crossed over into the Promised Land, he summarized their journey and repeated to them God's laws. The following verses parallel the reading from Exodus 20 and provide additional information.]

(Deut. 5:1) Moses summoned all Israel and said to them, "Israel, listen to the statutes and ordinances I am proclaiming as you hear them today. Learn and follow them carefully. (2) The LORD our God made a covenant with us at Horeb. (3) He did not make this covenant with our fathers, but with all of us who are alive here today. (4) The LORD spoke to you face to face from the fire on the mountain. (5) At that time I was standing between the LORD and you to report the word of the LORD to you, because you were afraid of the fire and did not go up the mountain.

[Here in Deuteronomy 5:6–21, Moses repeats the Ten Commandments.]

(5:22) "The LORD spoke these commands in a loud voice to your entire assembly from the fire, cloud, and thick darkness on the mountain; He added nothing more. He wrote them on two stone tablets and gave them to me. (23) All of you approached me with your tribal leaders and elders when you heard the voice from the darkness and while the mountain was blazing with fire. (24) You said, 'Look, the LORD our God has shown us His glory and greatness, and we have heard His voice from the fire. Today we have seen that God speaks with a person, yet he still lives. (25) But now, why should we die? This great fire will consume us and we will die if we hear the voice of the LORD our God any longer. (26) For who out of all mankind has heard the voice of the living God speaking from the fire, as we have, and lived? (27) Go near and listen to everything the LORD our God says. Then you can tell us everything the LORD our God tells you; we will listen and obey.'

(28) "The LORD heard your words when you spoke to me. He said to me, 'I have heard the words that these people have spoken to you. Everything they have said is right. (29) If only they had such a heart to fear Me and keep all My commands always, so that they and their children will prosper forever. (30) Go and tell them: Return to your tents. (31) But you stand here with Me, and I will tell you every command—the statutes and ordinances—you are to teach them, so that they may follow them in the land I am giving them to possess.'

(32) "Be careful to do as the LORD your God has commanded you; you are not to turn aside to the right or the left. (33) Follow the whole instruction the LORD your God has commanded you, so that you may live, prosper, and have a long life in the land you will possess.

◇◇◇

Suggested Song

"The Love of God"
(tinyurl.com/bdhsp6br)

The Law ultimately consisted of much more than the Ten Commandments that God delivered to Moses and Aaron before the people that day on the trembling mountain. But after witnessing God's initial proclamation, the people grew exceedingly fearful. Hearing the voice of God frightened them much more than watching the mountain before them shake violently and billow smoke like a furnace.

The people, along with their tribal leaders and elders, approached Moses and begged him to stand as their intermediary before God. Being so close to God and hearing His voice made them fearful for their lives. They asked that Moses be the one to draw near to God's presence and then come back and tell them all that He had said.

God heard the people's request and agreed. He instructed them to return to their tents while He delivered His statutes and ordinances to Moses. Moses would then come back and teach the people His commands. He cautioned the people to follow His instructions completely, not turning aside to the right or the left, so that they might live and prosper and have a long life in the land they would soon possess.

Moses, Teacher and Intermediary

When God called to Moses from the burning bush, He told him to bring the Israelites out of Egypt (Exodus 3:10). Moses had completed that mission, but the *entire* role God had intended for him to fulfill was far from over. As harrowing as it had been, delivering the people from Pharaoh's grip and out of Egypt was the easy part. Now it was time for Moses to assume the responsibility of teaching the people God's laws and ordinances and acting as their go-between with God—a calling he would serve the rest of his life.

> As harrowing as it had been, delivering the people from Pharaoh's grip and out of Egypt was the easy part.

In the past, the Israelites had based their faith in God upon His interaction with their ancestors. Information about God and worship instructions had been passed down from generation to generation. All that changed when God spoke to this people from the mountain. As Moses pointed out to them in Deuteronomy 5:2–3, God's covenant was with *them*, not their ancestors. When

——— 1 ———
The "mountain of God" is referred to as both Mount Horeb and Mount Sinai in the Scriptures. This article explains more about this mountain where God entered into a covenant with the Israelites and presented His Law to Moses: "What is the significance of Mount Horeb in the Bible?" (tinyurl.com/5xya6xnf).

——— 2 ———
This article explains how the giving of the Law fits into God's overall plan for bringing His Son, the Messiah, into the world: "What Is the Dispensation of Law?" (tinyurl.com/yck7vy5p). Note that the word "dispensation" is not found in the Scriptures. Bible scholars, at their discretion, have used it to denote various time periods and often differ on the number and names of the dispensations.

God presented His Law on Mount Sinai (or Mount Horeb),[1] a new era began.[2]

God had good plans for His people. He told them that if they were faithful to Him alone and kept His commandments, they would live in the Promised Land forever. When the people agreed, God presented the remainder of the Law to Moses, who then relayed God's Word to the people and recorded it in the Book of the Covenant.

Moses went on to directly apply the Law by teaching and admonishing the people, as well as by judging the many disputes that arose among them. And on numerous occasions, Moses stood between God and the people, pleading for their lives and attempting to sway Him from the wrath the unfaithful Israelites repeatedly incurred.

Yes, Moses's role as teacher and intermediary was likely the most challenging of all. But it was also the role for which God had been preparing Moses from the moment he was rescued by Pharaoh's daughter from the Nile. His early life had given him access to education, both academic and cultural, that served him well as a leader and as a scribe. Moses recorded not only the Law but the people's journey and God's interaction with them along the way.

Although Moses initially had to be prodded into the leadership role to which God had called him, once he stepped into that role, he gave it his all. He eventually went on to establish a relationship with God such that God would speak with him face-to-face, as with a friend.[3] And as the leader of the Israelite nation, Moses helped ensure the safety and survival of the lineage that would bring the Messiah into the world.

Jesus is our intermediary.

The Law, which God gave through Moses, was an important step in ultimately making salvation available to the world. When

---

——— 3 ———

This scripture in Exodus 33:11a (NIV) talks about Moses's relationship with God: "The LORD would speak to Moses face-to-face, as one speaks to a friend."

The Book of the Covenant

In addition to the Ten Commandments, which were written on slabs of stone, God gave other commands and instructions to Moses that He expected the Israelites to follow. These additional commands are recorded in Exodus 20:22–23:33 and are referred to collectively as the "Book of the Covenant."

Jesus came to earth and lived a life without sin, He fulfilled all the requirements of this Law, which no one before Him had been able to accomplish. In so doing, He ushered in a new era. He set aside the first to establish a New Covenant and became the perfect sacrifice for sin, once and for all time.

Having done this, Jesus now sits at the right hand of God and acts as our High Priest. As the writer of Hebrews explained, "because Jesus lives forever, he has a permanent priesthood. Therefore he is able to save completely those who come to God through him, because he always lives to intercede for them" (Hebrews 7:24–25, NIV). Not only did Jesus establish the new and better covenant under which we now live, but He also continues to intercede on our behalf. Christians enjoy such unfathomable gifts and privileges because God sent Jesus into the world to save us—and Moses helped prepare His path.

For there is one God, and one mediator between God and men, the man Christ Jesus; who gave himself a ransom for all, to be testified in due time.

—1 Timothy 2:5–6, KJV

Then he said, "Look, I have come to do your will." He cancels the first covenant in order to put the second into effect. For God's will was for us to be made holy by the sacrifice of the body of Jesus Christ, once for all time.

—Hebrews 10:9–10, NLT

After the Israelites heard God speak the Ten Commandments, they grew fearful from being so close to God. They asked if Moses could intermediate for them, and God agreed (Exodus 20:18–21). God then delivered this collection of commands to Moses, who wrote them down. Moses presented them to the people, and they answered as with one voice that they would do all that God had said. Moses then ratified the Israelites' agreement or covenant with God through the sprinkling of blood (Exodus 24:1–8).

These articles provide more information: "What is the Covenant Code or the Book of the Covenant (Exodus 20:22–23:33)?" (tinyurl.com/2p9dsbft); "Book of the Covenant" (tinyurl.com/yc7umftu); and "Covenant, Book of the" (tinyurl.com/2m5zammk).

Thoughts to Ponder

Why were the people so fearful of hearing the voice of God?

_____

_____

_____

_____

_____

How is approaching God different for us today? See Hebrews 12:18–24.

_____

_____

_____

_____

_____

Why did the Israelite people need an intermediary? Why do we need one today?

_____

_____

_____

_____

_____

Chapter 27

Ratifying the Covenant

Exodus 24, NKJV

(1) Now He said to Moses, "Come up to the LORD, you and Aaron, Nadab and Abihu, and seventy of the elders of Israel, and worship from afar. (2) And Moses alone shall come near the LORD, but they shall not come near; nor shall the people go up with him."

(3) So Moses came and told the people all the words of the LORD and all the judgments. And all the people answered with one voice and said, "All the words which the LORD has said we will do." (4) And Moses wrote all the words of the LORD. And he rose early in the morning, and built an altar at the foot of the mountain, and twelve pillars according to the twelve tribes of Israel. (5) Then he sent young men of the children of Israel, who offered burnt offerings and sacrificed peace offerings of oxen to the LORD. (6) And Moses took half the blood and put it in basins, and half the blood he sprinkled on the altar. (7) Then he

took the Book of the Covenant and read in the hearing of the people. And they said, "All that the LORD has said we will do, and be obedient." (8) And Moses took the blood, sprinkled it on the people, and said, "This is the blood of the covenant which the LORD has made with you according to all these words."

(9) Then Moses went up, also Aaron, Nadab, and Abihu, and seventy of the elders of Israel, (10) and they saw the God of Israel. And there was under His feet as it were a paved work of sapphire stone, and it was like the very heavens in its clarity. (11) But on the nobles of the children of Israel He did not lay His hand. So they saw God, and they ate and drank.

(12) Then the LORD said to Moses, "Come up to Me on the mountain and be there; and I will give you tablets of stone, and the law and commandments which I have written, that you may teach them."

(13) So Moses arose with his assistant Joshua, and Moses went up to the mountain of God. (14) And he said to the elders, "Wait here for us until we come back to you. Indeed, Aaron and Hur are with you. If any man has a difficulty, let him go to them." (15) Then Moses went up into the mountain, and a cloud covered the mountain.

(16) Now the glory of the LORD rested on Mount Sinai, and the cloud covered it six days. And on the seventh day He called to Moses out of the midst of the cloud. (17) The sight of the glory of the LORD was like a consuming fire on the top of the mountain in the eyes of the children of Israel. (18) So Moses went into the midst of the cloud and went up into the mountain. And Moses was on the mountain forty days and forty nights.

Suggested Song

"What Can Wash Away My Sin?"

(tinyurl.com/jwevmtys)

As for momentous occasions in the Old Testament, the events recounted in this chapter rank near the top. From previous readings, you know that the Israelites were in the process of entering into a covenant with God. They heard Him speak the Ten Commandments and grew so fearful they asked Moses to be their intermediary. He then ascended the mountain again to receive further commands and instructions from God.

So now, upon Moses's return, he relayed to the Israelites all that God had told him. The people responded as with one voice—they would do all that God had said! They agreed to the terms of this covenant, not only to God's commands and instructions but also to the judgments He set forth for breaking them.

With the verbal agreement in place, Moses proceeded to write down everything God had spoken. This covenant would be binding on God's people for generations to come. It needed to be recorded for posterity, and thankfully Moses had the ability to do that. How amazing to think that what Moses wrote at that time became part of the Scriptures we hold in our hands today!

Moses then made preparations to formalize the Israelites' covenant with God. He arose early in the morning, for it would take some time to accomplish all he had set about to do. He built an altar at the foot of the mountain for worship. He set up twelve stone pillars or large rocks to represent the twelve tribes of Israel who were parties to this covenant. He then sent young men to bring oxen and prepare the sacrificial offerings.[1]

Although God had not yet given specific instructions concerning offerings, two types are mentioned in verse 5. The burnt offering, made as an atonement for sins, was completely burned up.[2] This type of offering had been made by God's people, at least since the time of Noah.[3] Recall also that Jethro, Moses's father-in-law, had presented a burnt offering to God in Exodus 18:12. The other type of offering, a peace offering, was meant to be one of fellowship or communion. It was a shared offering between God and man.

Moses then put the covenant into effect with blood. He divided the blood from the offerings in half, representing the two parties to the covenant—God and the Israelites. He sprinkled half of the blood on the altar. The other half he put in basins or bowls. Then he read the Book of the Covenant to the people, and again, they committed to doing all that God had said. With that, Moses sprinkled the remaining half of the blood onto the people, in effect fully ratifying the covenant.

Then, as God had commanded, Moses, along with Aaron and two of his sons, Nadab and Abihu, and seventy of the elders of Israel ascended the mountain to worship. While they could go only part way up, they were near enough to see God and the beautiful sapphire blue stone under His feet. There in God's presence, they ate and drank.

God then called Moses to come further up the mountain to receive His commands, which He had written on tablets of stone. Moses obeyed, and as he and his assistant, Joshua, began their ascent, he told the elders to wait for them until they returned. Moses put Aaron and Hur in charge of overseeing the Israelite community during his absence.

1

Other versions state young bull calves were used for the offering. Various commentaries suggest young, strong men were needed to deal with the animals.

2

God later gave specific instructions concerning the various types of offerings in Leviticus 1–7.

3

Recall that Cain and Abel made offerings, but Noah's offering after getting off the ark is the first time a "burnt offering" is mentioned. It went up to God as a pleasing aroma (Genesis 8:20–22).

With that, Moses climbed until he reached the place where he was hidden by the cloud that covered the mountain. The glory of the Lord rested on the mountain, and from below, it appeared to the Israelites as if a consuming fire were on top of the mountain. For six days, the cloud covered the mountain, and then on the seventh day, God called to Moses from within the cloud. Moses entered the midst of the cloud and stayed on the mountain for forty days and forty nights.

Being in the Presence of God

Can you imagine being able to enter into God's physical presence? This group of Israelites saw what few people have ever had the privilege of experiencing. They were able to see at least something of God. We know from other comments in Scripture that the full glory of God is too overwhelming for humans to see and experience. Even Moses, with all the interaction he had with God, never experienced the full glory of God. Later in his life, Moses specifically asked God to show him His glory, but God replied, "You cannot see my face, for no one may see me and live" (Exodus 33:20, NIV).[4] Nevertheless, whatever these people saw of God, even if He were somehow shrouded, had to have been awe-inspiring.

> This group of Israelites saw what few people have ever had the privilege of experiencing.

These Israelites had also witnessed the plagues inflicted upon the Egyptians and participated in the exodus. They had walked through the middle of a miracle when they crossed the sea on dry land. Now, in this reading, they were allowed to be in the very presence of God, eating and drinking, partaking of what was likely a type of communion or fellowship ceremony. Their experiences should have been life changing.

Yet, out of this group of people assembled on the mountain that day, only one (that we know about) was allowed to enter the

---

4

The passage in Exodus 33:18–23 tells how Moses was able to partially experience the glory of God.

5

See Numbers 20:9–13 for the account of Moses and Aaron sinning by striking the rock at Meribah.

6

See Leviticus 10:1–3 for the account of the deaths of Nadab and Abihu.

7

Besides Joshua, Caleb was the only other Israelite man (not of the tribe of Levi) age twenty or older who was permitted to enter Canaan. The seventy elders are not named, but it is unlikely that Caleb was among them.

8

The scriptures in Romans 3:20 and 7:7 explain that with the Law came the knowledge of sin. Then in Galatians 3:24, Paul explained that the Law served as a schoolmaster or tutor to bring us to Christ. Through Christ, we are justified by faith rather than by having to keep the requirements of the Law—something no one but Christ was able to do.

Promised Land. Moses and Aaron were forbidden to cross over into Canaan because of striking the rock at Meribah,[5] and Nadab and Abihu were consumed by fire from God.[6] The seventy elders perished in the wilderness, along with all those men who were age twenty or older, when God issued His decree that they would have to wander for forty years. Only Joshua, Moses's aide, was permitted to cross the Jordan River into Canaan, and he would do so as the leader of God's people.[7]

After all they had seen and experienced, they still failed to follow God wholeheartedly. Despite their declaration of commitment, they refused to keep God's commands. Why did they falter? Because they were human, just as we are. And like us, their human nature often prevailed over their commitments, particularly when they experienced stress or temptations. If we were in their place back then, it's doubtful we would do any better than they did. As the Apostle Paul would later remind us in Romans 3:23, we all sin and fall short of the glory of God.

We all need a Savior.

Whether the Israelites knew it yet or not, they needed a Savior. By making them conscious of sin, the Law would bring them to that realization. They would come to understand the holiness of God and that they were unable to fulfill the requirements of the Law.[8] Their Savior would be a Savior not only for the Israelite people but for all the world—a world that also desperately needed a Savior.

With that Savior would come a New Covenant, one that provided a way of salvation and eternal life. Just as Moses sealed the Law God gave him on Mount Sinai with blood, our Savior, Jesus, would seal the New Covenant with blood (Matthew 26:28). That blood would be His own, shed as the perfect sacrifice for the sins of the world, once and for all time.

Fire for the Offerings

Offerings were an important part of the Israelites' worship of God. The various types of offerings they were to make are explained in the first seven chapters of Leviticus.

The large bronze altar that stood in the courtyard just outside the Tabernacle was where these offerings were to be made. This altar also served as the source of the fire needed for the smaller altar of incense, which stood inside the Tabernacle (Leviticus 16:12).

A continuous fire was to be kept burning on the bronze altar (Leviticus 6:12–13). The burnt offering was then placed on top of the wood of this altar, and a continual burnt offering was to be kept going, day and night (Exodus 29:42–46). When other offerings were made, they were offered on top of the burnt offering, all using the same fire.

Leviticus 3 describes the peace offering and states in verse 5 (NKJV): "and Aaron's sons shall burn it on the altar upon the burnt sacrifice, which is on the wood that is on the fire, as an offering made by fire, a sweet aroma to the LORD."

Why was the source of the fire so important? At some point, fire came out from the presence of the Lord and consumed the burnt offering and fat portions that were on the bronze altar (Leviticus 9:24). In so doing, God Himself sanctioned the fire on this altar. When Nadab and Abihu later used fire from a different source for their censers to burn incense, fire went out from the Lord and struck them dead (Leviticus 10:1–2). Attempting to use fire God had not authorized went against His command, and He could not allow them to dishonor Him.

Indeed, under the law almost everything is purified with blood, and without the shedding of blood there is no forgiveness of sins.

—Hebrews 9:22, ESV

But as it is, he has appeared once for all at the end of the ages to put away sin by the sacrifice of himself. And just as it is appointed for man to die once, and after that comes judgment, so Christ, having been offered once to bear the sins of many, will appear a second time, not to deal with sin but to save those who are eagerly waiting for him.

—Hebrews 9:26b–28, ESV

Thoughts to Ponder

How did Moses know what to do in making preparations for ratifying the Israelites' covenant with God? What did each of the steps he took symbolize?

_____

_____

_____

_____

_____

Why did God wait until the seventh day after Moses ascended the mountain to speak to him?

_____

_____

_____

_____

_____

Why was Moses on the mountain for forty days and forty nights? Was Joshua with Moses the entire time God presented His Law on the mountain?

_____

_____

_____

_____

_____

Chapter 28

The Golden Calf

Exodus 31:18–32:14, HCSB

(31:18) When He finished speaking with Moses on Mount Sinai, He gave him the two tablets of the testimony, stone tablets inscribed by the finger of God.

(32:1) When the people saw that Moses delayed in coming down from the mountain, they gathered around Aaron and said to him, "Come, make us a god who will go before us because this Moses, the man who brought us up from the land of Egypt—we don't know what has happened to him!"

(2) Then Aaron replied to them, "Take off the gold rings that are on the ears of your wives, your sons, and your daughters and bring them to me." (3) So all the people took off the gold rings that were on their ears and brought them to Aaron. (4) He took the gold from their hands, fashioned it with an engraving tool, and made it into an image of a calf.

Then they said, "Israel, this is your God, who brought you up from the land of Egypt!"

(5) When Aaron saw this, he built an altar before it; then he made an announcement: "There will be a festival to the LORD tomorrow." (6) Early the next morning they arose, offered burnt offerings, and presented fellowship offerings. The people sat down to eat and drink, then got up to play.

(7) The LORD spoke to Moses: "Go down at once! For your people you brought up from the land of Egypt have acted corruptly. (8) They have quickly turned from the way I commanded them; they have made for themselves an image of a calf. They have bowed down to it, sacrificed to it, and said, 'Israel, this is your God, who brought you up from the land of Egypt.'" (9) The LORD also said to Moses: "I have seen this people, and they are indeed a stiff-necked people. (10) Now leave Me alone, so that My anger can burn against them and I can destroy

them. Then I will make you into a great nation."

(11) But Moses interceded with the LORD his God: "LORD, why does Your anger burn against Your people You brought out of the land of Egypt with great power and a strong hand? (12) Why should the Egyptians say, 'He brought them out with an evil intent to kill them in the mountains and wipe them off the face of the earth'? Turn from Your great anger and relent concerning this disaster planned for Your people. (13) Remember Your servants Abraham, Isaac, and Israel— You swore to them by Your very self and declared, 'I will make your offspring as numerous as the stars of the sky and will give your offspring all this land that I have promised, and they will inherit it forever.'" (14) So the LORD relented concerning the disaster He said He would bring on His people.

◇◇◇

Suggested Song

"Dear Lord and Father of Mankind"

(tinyurl.com/y63fprf5)

If you read Exodus chapters 25 through 31, you can see the incredible amount of detailed information God presented to Moses during the forty days and nights he stayed on the mountain. With these instructions, the Israelites would later be able to establish their priesthood and build and furnish the Tabernacle, where God would dwell among them. The information would serve as a guide as they established the culture that would go on to characterize them as a nation, a people chosen and set apart by God. When God finished providing these instructions, He presented Moses with two stone tablets which He had inscribed with His own finger.[1]

At the very same time that God was preparing a means for the Israelites to draw closer to Him, they were rapidly pulling away from Him down below. The wait time in the camp at the foot of the mountain had proven to be too long. They gave up on Moses and abandoned the God who had performed such miraculous deeds on their behalf.

Turning to Aaron, the people demanded that he make them a god to go before them. Evidently, they planned to leave this place without Moses and desired a visible, tangible idol to carry with

---

1

These tablets evidently were inscribed with the Ten Commandments. Here in Exodus 31:18, the inscription is referred to as the testimony or covenant law. See also Exodus 32:15–16.

them. The cloud, which had gone before them as they left Egypt, now rested atop the mountain, and without Moses's strong leadership, they quickly succumbed to their old tendencies.[2]

Aaron caved to their request. He instructed the people to bring him their gold earrings, personal treasures which were likely part of what they had collected from the Egyptians as they departed the country. He took their jewelry, melted it, and formed it into a golden calf. The people then declared this lifeless, inanimate object to be their god. Even worse, they gave it credit for bringing them out of Egypt!

When Aaron saw the people's response to the golden calf, he built an altar in front of it. Perhaps in an effort to lend legitimacy to the whole situation, he announced the next day would be a festival to the Lord. Everyone arose early in the morning and offered burnt offerings and fellowship offerings.[3] Then they sat down to eat and drink and arose to "play," likely engaging in the basest form of revelry.[4]

God saw the debauchery occurring in the camp below and told Moses he needed to go back down the mountain and stop it. The Israelites had quickly turned from following His commands and were worshiping the image of a calf. Declaring them to be a stiff-necked people,[5] God then made what could have been a tempting proposal to Moses. "Now leave Me alone," He said, "so that My anger can burn against them and I can destroy them. Then I will make you into a great nation" (Exodus 32:10, HCSB).

Moses pleaded with God to turn from His wrath. Destroying the Israelites would bring to naught all that He had done to deliver them. The Egyptians would mock God for bringing the Israelites out of Egypt, only to kill them. But more importantly, if God destroyed these people, He would be abandoning the promise He had made to Abraham, Isaac, and Israel, a promise to which He had sworn by His very self. At Moses's urging, God relented from the

> Moses pleaded with God to turn from His wrath.

2

Later scriptures refer to their idol worship. In Leviticus 17:7, the Israelites were commanded to no longer offer sacrifices to the goat idols or demons to which they had prostituted themselves. Joshua urged them to cast aside the gods their fathers served beyond the Euphrates River and in Egypt and to serve the Lord. See Joshua 24:14–15 for his powerful admonition.

3

The Scriptures do not say whether the offerings were made to God or to the idol, but even if they were made to God, they would not have been acceptable under such defiled circumstances.

4

Other Bible versions of Exodus 32:6 state they indulged in pagan revelry (NLT) or engaged in lewd behavior (NASB). The Amplified Bible states they "got up to play [shamefully—without moral restraint]." Read what various commentaries say about this verse at BibleHub.com (tinyurl.com/4tjzkvh8).

5

A horse or other animal which refuses to respond to rein commands is said to be "stiff-necked."

6

See Exodus 4:27 for the account of God instructing Aaron to go into the wilderness to meet Moses.

grave harm He had threatened upon the Israelites, these people whom He had chosen to be His own.

The Testing of Aaron and Moses

What was Aaron thinking in creating this golden calf? It was upon God's instruction that he had traveled to the mountain of God to meet his brother, Moses, whom he presumably had not seen in forty years.[6] It was by his hand that God had performed many of the miracles in Egypt. It was his voice that God had used to help Moses confront Pharaoh and to instruct and guide the Israelites. More recently, it was he whom God had called up onto the mountain, along with two of his sons and seventy elders, to commune in the very presence of God. And it was he, along with Hur, that Moses had placed in charge during his absence.

7

According to other Jewish literature, Hur did indeed take a strong stand against this situation and was murdered by the people. Fearing for his own life, Aaron then became compliant with their wishes. It was supposedly to honor Hur that God later gifted his grandson, Bezalel, with the knowledge and artistic ability to help build the Tabernacle and other items and furnishings that God instructed (Exodus 31:1–5). The *Jewish Encyclopedia* provides more information in this article, "Hur" (tinyurl.com/ydhm8drw).

Some commentaries suggest that the people came upon him as a mob, surrounding him and overwhelming him with their demands for a god. Perhaps the pagan influences he had been subjected to in Egypt prevailed without the strength of Moses in his life. Whatever his reasoning, nothing could have justified his actions. We learn later in Deuteronomy 9:20 that God was so angry with Aaron for making the golden calf that He wanted to destroy him, but Moses prayed for him, and God spared him.

8

See Exodus 15:20–21 for the part Miriam sang in the Israelite's song of deliverance.

9

See Numbers 12:3 (KJV): "Now the man Moses was very meek, above all the men which were upon the face of the earth." Note that other versions use the word "humble" rather than "meek."

Why did no one step forward during this time, either to support Aaron in the event he had tried to stand against the people or to challenge him in his wrongdoing? His coleader, Hur, should have been the first, yet he is not mentioned in Scriptures past the time Moses appointed him while on the mountain.[7] Certainly, the seventy elders who had gone up on the mountain to see God should have objected. They were respected members of the community and influential within their tribes. Aaron's own sons had also been in God's presence on the mountain, and surely they should have come to their father's side. Likewise, Miriam, the prophetess and older sister—who, not so long ago, had sung a song on the shores of the Red Sea praising God for His deliverance of the Israelites from the Egyptians—could have stepped forward.[8] Yet scriptures do not record anyone trying to stop these sinful, shameful acts.

The situation was so appalling that God was ready to give up on the Israelites and start over. As He informed Moses of the abominable happenings below, He distanced Himself from the people. "For *your* people whom *you* brought out of the land of Egypt have corrupted themselves," God told Moses, seemingly disavowing them as the people He had chosen for Himself (Exodus 32:7, NKJV).

Then, an interesting discourse occurred between God and Moses in Exodus 32:10. Knowing Moses would object, God told Moses to leave Him alone *before* He told him what He planned to do. Moses couldn't do that. Instead, he reasoned with God and interceded for the people. Even God's offer to make Moses himself into a great nation could not dissuade him from pleading for the very lives of the Israelites.

Why didn't Moses accept God's offer?

Moses could have been done with these people who had caused him so much trouble and grief, and his own family could have become God's chosen people. Even if he did consider this offer for a moment, he quickly rejected it. Maybe he knew his family would have their own set of difficulties in following God's commands.

More than likely, however, God had another reason for making this offer. In Numbers 12:3, Moses is referred to as the meekest man on earth,[9] not because he played the part of a doormat but because he totally submitted his own sense of self to God's will. The mantle of leadership, after he had so reluctantly accepted it, was something he never took off. In fulfilling that

God Is Faithful

Do you sense that perhaps God was testing Moses when He offered to destroy the Israelites and make Moses's own family into a great nation? God sometimes teaches us by showing us how powerful our own faith can be and how trustworthy He is. In fact, we may not understand the strength of our own faith until it's put to the test.

Consider what happened back when God asked Abraham to sacrifice his son, Isaac, the one through whom God's promise was to be fulfilled. God was never going to allow Isaac to be killed. Rather, He wanted Abraham to prove his faith, but to whom did God wish for him to prove his faith?

David told Solomon in 1 Chronicles 28:9 that the Lord searches every heart and understands every motive behind a person's thoughts. Why, then, would God need Abraham to prove his faith to Him if He already knew the intent of Abraham's heart? Perhaps God wanted Abraham to prove his faith to himself.

God does not lie, and He does not go back on His promises. Through an oracle that God put in the mouth of Balaam, the soothsayer, He declared in Numbers 23:19 (ESV): "God is not a man, that he should lie, or a son of man, that he should change his mind. Has he said, and will he not do it? Or has he spoken, and will he not fulfill it?"

Moses knew that God could not destroy the Israelites because if He did, He would be going back on the promise He had made to Abraham and then repeated to Isaac and Jacob (or Israel) so long ago. So perhaps God was testing Moses when He proposed to make Moses's progeny into a great nation. By having to reason with God, Moses showed his great faith in God. In so doing, he also strengthened his faith in himself to fulfill the role of intercessor for the Israelite people. Certainly, God knew Moses would need a strong faith in himself for the many trials which lay ahead.

role, he committed to being the mediator for the Israelites, their go-between with God.

Along the way, Moses had developed a deep, personal relationship with God. He knew that God could not and would not break His promise to Abraham, Isaac, and Israel. Moses didn't talk God out of destroying the Israelites and promoting his own family because that wasn't going to happen anyway. What he did was affirm that he was truly the leader and intercessor God had called him to be. Perhaps that was the whole point of this conversation.

So for the one who knows the right thing to do and does not do it, for him it is sin.

—James 4:17, NASB

But Jesus told him, "Anyone who puts a hand to the plow and then looks back is not fit for the Kingdom of God."

—Luke 9:62, NLT

Thoughts to Ponder

A characteristic of God is that He cannot lie. Discuss Titus 1:1–3, Hebrews 6:13–20, and other scriptures which speak to the nature of God.

_____

_____

_____

_____

_____

Which of the Ten Commandments were broken during the incident with the golden calf?

_____

_____

_____

_____

_____

_____

Why was it such an abomination for Aaron to build an altar in front of the golden calf and then declare a festival to the Lord?

_____

_____

_____

_____

_____

Chapter 29

Moses Smashes the Tablets

Exodus 32:15–35, HCSB

(15) Then Moses turned and went down the mountain with the two tablets of the testimony in his hands. They were inscribed on both sides—inscribed front and back. (16) The tablets were the work of God, and the writing was God's writing, engraved on the tablets.

(17) When Joshua heard the sound of the people as they shouted, he said to Moses, "There is a sound of war in the camp."

(18) But Moses replied:

It's not the sound of a victory cry

and not the sound of a cry of defeat;

I hear the sound of singing!

(19) As he approached the camp and saw the calf and the dancing, Moses became enraged and threw the tablets out of his hands, smashing them at the base of the mountain. (20) Then he took the calf they had made, burned it up, and ground it to powder. He scattered the powder over the surface of the water and forced the Israelites to drink the water.

(21) Then Moses asked Aaron, "What did these people do to you that you have led them into such a grave sin?"

(22) "Don't be enraged, my lord," Aaron replied. "You yourself know that the people are intent on evil. (23) They said to me, 'Make us a god who will go before us because this Moses, the man who brought us up from the land of Egypt—we don't know what has happened to him!' (24) So I said to them, 'Whoever has gold, take it off,' and they gave it to me. When I threw it into the fire, out came this calf!"

(25) Moses saw that the people were out of control, for Aaron had let them get out of control, resulting in weakness before their enemies. (26) And Moses stood at the camp's entrance and said, "Whoever is for the LORD, come to me." And all the Levites gathered around him. (27) He told them,

"This is what the LORD, the God of Israel, says, 'Every man fasten his sword to his side; go back and forth through the camp from entrance to entrance, and each of you kill his brother, his friend, and his neighbor.'" (28) The Levites did as Moses commanded, and about 3,000 men fell dead that day among the people. (29) Afterward Moses said, "Today you have been dedicated to the LORD, since each man went against his son and his brother. Therefore you have brought a blessing on yourselves today."

(30) The following day Moses said to the people, "You have committed a grave sin. Now I will go up to the LORD; perhaps I will be able to atone for your sin."

(31) So Moses returned to the LORD and said, "Oh, these people have committed a grave sin; they have made a god of gold for themselves. (32) Now if You would only forgive their sin. But if not, please erase me from the book You have written."

(33) The LORD replied to Moses: "I will erase whoever has sinned against Me from My book. (34) Now go, lead the people to the place I told you about; see, My angel will go before you. But on the day I settle accounts, I will hold them accountable for their sin." (35) And the LORD inflicted a plague on the people for what they did with the calf Aaron had made.

◇◇◇

Suggested Song

"The Great Redeemer"
(tinyurl.com/43m954r9)

Perhaps Joshua did not ascend all the way up the mountain with Moses but stayed some distance away from the presence of God. The scriptures do not tell us, but clearly, he did not hear God tell Moses what was going on below. When Joshua heard the alarming noises coming from the camp, he told Moses it sounded like a war was taking place.

But Moses knew better. It was the sound of riotous singing they heard.

As they came in sight of the camp and Moses saw the golden calf and the revelry that was going on, he became enraged.[1] Throwing down the tablets of stone, he seized the golden calf and burned it up.

Think of the irony of the situation—what had once been the object of the people's adoration became useless powder as he ground up the idol he had just torched. Then, by throwing

---

1

For a bit more insight, read the parallel account Moses gives of this incident with the golden calf in Deuteronomy 9:7–21.

the residue into the camp's water source, Moses forced them to drink tiny pieces of what they had been worshiping. What kind of a god would have ever allowed that?

Moses then turned his attention to Aaron, who, in turn, tried to shift the blame onto the people. Moses had trusted his brother to be in charge during his absence, yet from all appearances, no one was in charge.[2] Moses also knew the news of this occurrence would travel far and wide, even though they were camped out in the middle of nowhere. The Israelites would become a laughing-stock when their enemies heard what had happened.[3]

How heavy Moses's heart must have been as he instructed his fellow Levites to act as executioners. How sad for the Levites to be called upon to kill their own kin. Because of their willingness to obey God that day, even though the cost was so dear, God blessed the Levites.[4]

The next day, Moses went back up the mountain. He confessed the wrongdoing of the Israelites to God and asked for His forgiveness. God assured Moses only those who had sinned against Him would be erased from His book.[5] He told Moses to go ahead with leading the people on to the Promised Land. His angel would go before them, and at the right time, He would punish those who sinned. And with that, God caused a plague to come upon the people for worshiping the golden calf.

> How heavy Moses's heart must have been as he instructed his fellow Levites to act as executioners.

Moses Regains Control and Restores Order

No wonder Moses was so angry as he entered the camp. He had gone from being surrounded by the holy presence of God to finding the Israelites immersed in sinful revelry before an idol. The sense of futility he felt must have been overwhelming. God's delivery of His people from slavery had been an epic event, a

---

2

Most modern versions say the people were out of control or unrestrained. However, Exodus 32:25–26 in the King James Version reads as follows: "And when Moses saw that the people were naked; (for Aaron had made them naked unto their shame among their enemies:) Then Moses stood in the gate of the camp, and said, Who is on the LORD's side? let him come unto me. And all the sons of Levi gathered themselves together unto him."

3

The area where the Israelites were camped had likely already been claimed by others, such as the Amalekites, whom they had battled earlier at Rephidim. There also could have been spies from multiple other groups of people tracking the movement of this massive group of Israelites through the area.

4

The tribe of Levi would later be set apart to serve as priests. See Numbers 3:5–13 and Deuteronomy 10:8–9; 18:1–5.

5

Moses's reference to the "book" seems to indicate he was privy to "inside" information about how God handles things. This stands to reason since he had already spent so much time in God's presence.

In Deuteronomy 9:20 (NKJV), Moses stated: "And the LORD was very angry with Aaron and would have destroyed him; so I prayed for Aaron also at the same time."

7

This article helps explain the role that Christ plays as intercessor for us: "What Is the Purpose of Jesus Interceding for Us in Heaven?" (tinyurl.com/3ph8avxz).

long-anticipated milestone in the fulfillment of the promise He had made to Abraham centuries earlier. Now, in just a few short weeks, the same people who had pledged to do all that God had commanded them had given up on Moses as their leader and forsaken the very God who had chosen them as His own people.

Think of the force it would take to break slabs of stone. Could it be that Moses's shattering of the tablets was not simply a byproduct of his anger but rather a deliberate action on his part? Either way, his smashing the tablets symbolized the damage this pagan worship had done to the people's relationship with God. The people had broken the commands they had so reverently pledged to obey, and in response, Moses broke the tablets on which God Himself had inscribed those commands.

Then there was Aaron. What a disappointment he must have been, both to his brother and to God. Yielding to the people's demand for a god and then creating it for them was shameful enough, but then he managed to degrade himself even further. He attempted to deceive Moses by telling him he had thrown the jewelry into the fire, and out came this calf. No wonder God was so angry with Aaron over this incident that He wanted to kill him.[6]

Were all the people swept up in this pagan worship and revelry? Probably not. The fact that the Levites rallied to Moses's side and were willing to act as executioners on God's behalf would seem to indicate that at least they had not participated. Hopefully, there were others who had also remained faithful to the Lord, although it seems no one had been strong enough to stand against Aaron and the mob.

Moses again interceded for the people. His pleading for God's forgiveness would become a recurrent theme throughout the Israelites' forty-year journey to the Promised Land. Even when he became angry and deeply frustrated with the people, he continued to be their intermediary. So committed was Moses to his role that he was willing to give up his own place in God's book for their sake.

Jesus is our intercessor.

Jesus intercedes today for all those who believe in and follow Him.[7] He willingly took on His role, and in fact, He gave up His life for our sakes. He shed His blood once and for all time so that the sins of all who call upon His name are not counted against them. Christians can know that their names will forever remain in God's book because the blood of Christ continually covers their sins.

When Jesus ascended into heaven, His work for His people was far from over. With all authority in heaven and on earth having been given to Him, Jesus sat down at the right hand of God, where He remains. There, from this highest position of authority, Jesus intercedes for every single person who calls upon His name. Not only was He the perfect sacrifice for our sins, but He continues to be the perfect intercessor for His people. May we never forget to glorify His name—His love for us is simply unfathomable!

The Twelve Tribes of Israel

God blessed the members of the tribe of Levi because they rallied to Moses's side and carried out the Lord's directives during the incident of the golden calf in Exodus 32:25–29. Later, when a census was taken of all the men aged twenty and older who were able to go to war, the Levites were not counted among that number (Numbers 1:49–54). Instead, God called the Levites to be dedicated to His service and charged them with the care of the Tabernacle, all its furnishings, and the ark of the covenant. He also appointed Aaron's lineage to the priesthood. This meant that the tribe of Levi was no longer counted among the twelve tribes of Israel.

In order to continue to have twelve tribes, the descendants of Joseph's two sons, Manasseh and Ephraim, each became a tribe of their own. This arrangement was made possible by a declaration Jacob (or Israel) had made centuries earlier.

Shortly before his death, Jacob claimed Ephraim and Manasseh as his own (Genesis 48:5–6). In this way, Joseph's offspring received a double portion of the inheritance from Jacob.

Jacob likely did this for several reasons. Joseph was his firstborn son by his favored wife, Rachel. Additionally, Jacob had spent many years believing Joseph had been killed when, in reality, his other sons had sold him into slavery (Genesis 37). Joseph, however, by already being in Egypt, was able to move his father and entire family there when the famine became severe. In so doing, Joseph saved his family from starvation. Nevertheless, Jacob's older sons had deceived their father for years. It's no wonder Jacob deemed Joseph worthy of a double portion.

But because Jesus lives forever, his priesthood lasts forever. Therefore he is able, once and forever, to save those who come to God through him. He lives forever to intercede with God on their behalf.

—Hebrews 7:24–25, NLT

Who then will condemn us? No one—for Christ Jesus died for us and was raised to life for us, and he is sitting in the place of honor at God's right hand, pleading for us.

—Romans 8:34, NLT

Thoughts to Ponder

What book does Moses refer to in Exodus 32:32–33?

_____

_____

_____

After all they had witnessed and experienced, why was it so hard for the Israelites to give up pagan worship? How hard has it been for you to give up former practices, beliefs, and behaviors?

_____

_____

_____

_____

Romans 8 is a good chapter to read to gain a better understanding of how both the Holy Spirit (Romans 8:23, 26–27) and Jesus (verses 31–34) intercede on behalf of believers. Nothing can separate us from the love of God and of Christ (verses 35–39). How does this assurance affect your life and worship?

_____

_____

_____

_____

_____

_____

GOD REESTABLISHES
THE RELATIONSHIP

Chapter 30

Moses's Friendship with God

Exodus 33, NIV

(1) Then the LORD said to Moses, "Leave this place, you and the people you brought up out of Egypt, and go up to the land I promised on oath to Abraham, Isaac and Jacob, saying, 'I will give it to your descendants.' (2) I will send an angel before you and drive out the Canaanites, Amorites, Hittites, Perizzites, Hivites and Jebusites. (3) Go up to the land flowing with milk and honey. But I will not go with you, because you are a stiff-necked people and I might destroy you on the way."

(4) When the people heard these distressing words, they began to mourn and no one put on any ornaments.[1] (5) For the LORD had said to Moses, "Tell the Israelites, 'You are a stiff-necked people. If I were to go with you even for a moment, I might destroy you. Now take off your ornaments and I will decide what to do with you.'" (6) So the Israelites stripped off their ornaments at Mount Horeb.

(7) Now Moses used to take a tent and pitch it outside the camp some distance away, calling it the "tent of meeting." Anyone inquiring of the LORD would go to the tent of meeting outside the camp. (8) And whenever Moses went out to the tent, all the people rose and stood at the entrances to their tents, watching Moses until he entered the tent. (9) As Moses went into the tent, the pillar of cloud would come down and stay at the entrance, while the LORD spoke with Moses. (10) Whenever the people saw the pillar of cloud standing at the entrance to the tent, they all stood and worshiped, each at the entrance to their

---

1

The people were likely showing they were in mourning by removing their adornments or ornaments. It could also have been symbolic for the Israelites to go without their ornaments because that's what they had given to Aaron to use in creating the golden calf.

tent. (11) The LORD would speak to Moses face to face, as one speaks to a friend. Then Moses would return to the camp, but his young aide Joshua son of Nun did not leave the tent.

(12) Moses said to the LORD, "You have been telling me, 'Lead these people,' but you have not let me know whom you will send with me. You have said, 'I know you by name and you have found favor with me.' (13) If you are pleased with me, teach me your ways so I may know you and continue to find favor with you. Remember that this nation is your people."

(14) The LORD replied, "My Presence will go with you, and I will give you rest."

(15) Then Moses said to him, "If your Presence does not go with us, do not send us up from here. (16) How will anyone know that you are pleased with me and with your people unless you go with us? What else will distinguish me and your people from all the other people on the face of the earth?"

(17) And the LORD said to Moses, "I will do the very thing you have asked, because I am pleased with you and I know you by name."

(18) Then Moses said, "Now show me your glory."

(19) And the LORD said, "I will cause all my goodness to pass in front of you, and I will proclaim my name, the LORD, in your presence. I will have mercy on whom I will have mercy, and I will have compassion on whom I will have compassion. (20) But," he said, "you cannot see my face, for no one may see me and live."

(21) Then the LORD said, "There is a place near me where you may stand on a rock. (22) When my glory passes by, I will put you in a cleft in the rock and cover you with my hand until I have passed by. (23) Then I will remove my hand and you will see my back; but my face must not be seen."

◇◇◇

Suggested Song

"If Jesus Goes with Me"
(tinyurl.com/yhz8jfry)

The day Moses came down the mountain with the tablets of stone in his hands had to have been one of the best and one of the worst days of his life, all rolled into one. For the first time in human history, God had given a written Law. Moses carried in his arms the Ten Words (or Ten Commandments), which formed the basis for that Law. It should have been a day set aside to honor God, a day of thanksgiving that God had chosen the Israelite people to receive His Law.

Instead, Moses walked into a camp in chaos. When he saw the golden calf, he knew it represented a failure of monumental proportions. The people had failed to keep their solemn oath to follow God and obey His commands. The leadership Moses had left in charge had gone beyond failure to control the people to actually creating the idol they were worshiping. In his anger and frustration, Moses shattered the words which God had written with His own finger against the side of the mountain. Literally, everything seemed to be broken.

Now, in the aftermath of this sad event, it was up to Moses to pick up the pieces. If indeed that could be done, it was something only Moses would be able to do. He turned to God, knowing that God was the only one who could help him. Yet God seemed deeply frustrated with these people as well.

> He turned to God, knowing that God was the only one who could help him.

The Presence of God

While Moses was still on the mountain, God began distancing Himself from the people. As He told Moses what was going on below, He referred to the Israelites as "*your* people, whom *you* brought up out of Egypt . . ." (Exodus 32:7, NIV). Now, as He commanded Moses to take his people and leave, He again referred to them in that manner. They were to depart from His holy presence and strike out on their own to the Promised Land with only an angel to accompany them. God seemed to be totally disavowing Himself of the Israelite people.

Think of how alone Moses must have felt at this time. An angel would be a poor substitute for God's presence, and his coleader, Aaron, had shown himself to be less than dependable. The people had proven themselves difficult to keep on track and challenging to lead. He knew there was no way he wanted to set out across the wilderness to the Promised Land without God Himself accompanying them.

—— 2 ——

Read the account of Jacob wrestling with God in Genesis 32:22–32.

—— 3 ——

The fulfillment of Moses's wish to see God's glory happened later. The account of how it transpired is recorded in the next chapter. See Exodus 34:5–9.

—— 4 ——

Other Bible versions use various words for the Holy Spirit, including Advocate, Counselor, Comforter, and Helper.

Moses retreated to the tent of meeting to be with God. There, he "wrestled" with God, not in the physical sense as Jacob had done centuries earlier,[2] but rather, he verbally reasoned with God. He knew he could talk with God. He knew that he had found favor with God and that God knew him by name. Moses laid out his concerns, and in return, God agreed to his request. His presence would indeed accompany the Israelites to the Promised Land. What a great relief this must have been for Moses.

With this favor granted, Moses again petitioned God. This time, however, He did not ask as the intermediary for the people; rather, he asked for himself. He wanted God to reveal to him His glory, unveiled and unobscured. Moses would later go on to behold what few humans have ever seen. God would indeed show him His glory to the extent that is possible for humans to experience.[3]

God's presence resides in His people today.

As Jesus completed His work on earth, He knew His followers would need God's presence to accompany them on their earthly journey. Shortly before His death, He told His disciples, "I will pray the Father, and He will give you another Helper, that He may abide with you forever—the Spirit of truth, whom the world cannot receive, because it neither sees Him nor knows Him; but you know Him, for He dwells with you and will be in you" (John 14:16–17, NKJV).[4]

What an unbelievable privilege Christians enjoy in the Holy Spirit! He accompanies us on our journey through life. He dwells within us, intercedes for us, and serves as a deposit, a down payment guaranteeing our inheritance in heaven. Because of God's incredible gift of the Holy Spirit, Christians today can know they never have to walk alone.

Do you not know that your bodies are temples of the Holy Spirit, who is in you, whom you have received from God? You are not your own; you were bought at a price. Therefore honor God with your bodies.

—1 Corinthians 6:19–20, NIV

And you also were included in Christ when you heard the message of truth, the gospel of your salvation. When you believed, you were marked in him with a seal, the promised Holy Spirit, who is a deposit guaranteeing our inheritance until the redemption of those who are God's possession—to the praise of his glory.

—Ephesians 1:13–14, NIV

The Tent of Meeting

The tent of meeting served as the precursor to the Tabernacle, which would be built later. God had sanctified the tent of meeting, and an altar stood outside the entrance where offerings were made each morning and each evening.

The tent of meeting served as a place where God could meet with both Moses and the people. With His presence there, God indeed dwelled among the Israelites. See Exodus 29:38–46 for God's instructions concerning the tent of meeting.

Thoughts to Ponder

How was the establishment of the tent of meeting an important step in the Israelites' developing their own relationship with God? See Exodus 29:38–46 for God's instructions concerning the continual offerings and the sanctification of the tent of meeting. See also Exodus 33:7–11.

_____

_____

_____

_____

_____

When Moses asked to see God's glory, he asked this favor for himself. What other personal requests, not associated with being an intermediary for the Israelites, did Moses make of God during his lifetime that are recorded in Scripture? Why did God not immediately grant Moses's request to see His glory?

_____

_____

_____

_____

_____

What are the characteristics of the Holy Spirit? How does He function in the lives of Christians today?

_____

_____

_____

_____

Chapter 31

The New Tablets

Exodus 34:1–11, 27–35, NIV

(1) The LORD said to Moses, "Chisel out two stone tablets like the first ones, and I will write on them the words that were on the first tablets, which you broke. (2) Be ready in the morning, and then come up on Mount Sinai. Present yourself to me there on top of the mountain. (3) No one is to come with you or be seen anywhere on the mountain; not even the flocks and herds may graze in front of the mountain."

(4) So Moses chiseled out two stone tablets like the first ones and went up Mount Sinai early in the morning, as the LORD had commanded him; and he carried the two stone tablets in his hands. (5) Then the LORD came down in the cloud and stood there with him and proclaimed his name, the LORD. (6) And he passed in front of Moses, proclaiming, "The LORD, the LORD, the compassionate and gracious God, slow to anger, abounding in love and faithfulness, (7) maintaining love to thousands,

and forgiving wickedness, rebellion and sin. Yet he does not leave the guilty unpunished; he punishes the children and their children for the sin of the parents to the third and fourth generation."

(8) Moses bowed to the ground at once and worshiped. (9) "Lord," he said, "if I have found favor in your eyes, then let the Lord go with us. Although this is a stiff-necked people, forgive our wickedness and our sin, and take us as your inheritance."

(10) Then the LORD said: "I am making a covenant with you. Before all your people I will do wonders never before done in any nation in all the world. The people you live among will see how awesome is the work that I, the LORD, will do for you. (11) Obey what I command you today. I will drive out before you the Amorites, Canaanites, Hittites, Perizzites, Hivites and Jebusites.

[Verses 12–26 list various commands and instructions God gave to Moses.]

(27) Then the LORD said to Moses, "Write down these words, for in accordance with these words I have made a covenant with you and with Israel." (28) Moses was there with the LORD forty days and forty nights without eating bread or drinking water. And he wrote on the tablets the words of the covenant—the Ten Commandments.

(29) When Moses came down from Mount Sinai with the two tablets of the covenant law in his hands, he was not aware that his face was radiant because he had spoken with the LORD. (30) When Aaron and all the Israelites saw Moses, his face was radiant, and they were afraid to come near him. (31) But Moses called to them; so Aaron and all the leaders of the community came back to him, and he spoke to them. (32) Afterward all the Israelites came near him, and he gave them all the commands the LORD had given him on Mount Sinai.

(33) When Moses finished speaking to them, he put a veil over his face. (34) But whenever he entered the LORD's presence to speak with him, he removed the veil until he came out. And when he came out and told the Israelites what he had been commanded, (35) they saw that his face was radiant. Then Moses would put the veil back over his face until he went in to speak with the LORD.

Suggested Song

"Nearer, Still Nearer"

(tinyurl.com/5zey3zxn)

Imagine the relief and gratitude Moses felt when God instructed him to chisel out the new stone tablets. He knew what that meant: God was about to reissue His Law, and the Israelites were getting a second chance! He also knew that God had promised him His presence would accompany them on to Canaan.

Early the next morning, Moses climbed the mountain one more time. He carried in his arms the freshly hewn slabs of stone. Although the weight he carried was heavy, his heart had to have been lighter than it was the last time he had ascended the mountain. Then, he had come to beg God's forgiveness for the Israelites' grievous sins; now, he came to receive His Law and talk with God.

> The Israelites were getting a second chance!

Drawing Closer to God

Each time Moses interacted with God, he learned more of His character and became closer to God. Moses wanted that closeness. He had told God on his last trip up the mountain, "If you are pleased with me, teach me your ways so I may know you and continue to find favor with you" (Exodus 33:13, NIV). God heard his plea, and this time, He had something special planned for Moses.

High on the mountaintop with no other humans or livestock near, God granted the request Moses had made previously—He showed Moses His glory![1] While standing near Moses, He proclaimed His name. Unlike humans, who are named after the family into which they are born, God is eternal. Without beginning and without end, He is the Great Creator of all that exists. So rather than stating a name by which He called Himself, He instead described His attributes.

Immediately, Moses bowed down and worshiped. Again, he begged God's forgiveness and asked once more that He go with them and take this people as His inheritance.

In response, God declared He would make a covenant with Moses and the people. He would perform wonders that had never before been done in all the world. If they obeyed His commands, He would drive out the inhabitants of the Promised Land before them. Then, God instructed Moses to write down His commands and the instructions He had given him. This would be His covenant with Moses and with Israel.

Moses's face reflected the glory of God.

Although Moses had spoken with God on numerous occasions, this time was different. God revealed more of Himself to Moses than He had before to any other human that's recorded in Scripture, with the possible exception of Adam and Eve when they lived in the Garden of Eden. Not only did God allow Moses

—————— 1 ——————

Upon Moses's request, God had agreed to show him a portion of His glory in Exodus 33:18–23. He didn't do it at that time, however, as Moses was meeting with God at the tent of meeting outside the encampment. To protect other people and livestock from being killed, God had him ascend high up the mountaintop by himself. There, God protected Moses while allowing him a glimpse of His glory.

Hebrews 10:1 (NLT)—"The old system under the law of Moses was only a shadow, a dim preview of the good things to come, not the good things themselves. The sacrifices under that system were repeated again and again, year after year, but they were never able to provide perfect cleansing for those who came to worship."

3

Hebrews 10:8–10 (NLT)—"First, Christ said, 'You did not want animal sacrifices or sin offerings or burnt offerings or other offerings for sin, nor were you pleased with them' (though they are required by the law of Moses). Then he said, 'Look, I have come to do your will.' He cancels the first covenant in order to put the second into effect. For God's will was for us to be made holy by the sacrifice of the body of Jesus Christ, once for all time."
Hebrews 10:14 (NLT)—"For by that one offering he forever made perfect those who are being made holy."
This sermon outline provides a study entitled: "The Purpose of the Old Law" (tinyurl.com/2smfbvfw).

into close proximity of His being, but He also disclosed to him His personal characteristics. God treated Moses as a friend. When Moses descended the mountain, not only did he carry in his hands the new stone tablets now inscribed with the Ten Commandments, but his face also shone from having been so near to God.

While the radiance of Moses's face initially frightened the people, it served as unmistakable evidence of his contact with the divine. The commands and instructions he received and passed on to the people were undoubtedly from God. It also served to bolster his authority, which would be tested severely during the long journey ahead.

Centuries later, the Apostle Paul, in 2 Corinthians 3:13–18, spoke of Moses's radiance and the veil he placed over his face. While the veil shielded others from the brilliance, it also obscured the full effect of God's glory. Paul then used that image of the veil in reference to the Law, which hinted at better things but did not reveal them fully. Rather, it presented the shadow of what was to come.[2] The Law could not save the people fully, but it prepared the way for one who could: Jesus, the Messiah, who would usher in a new and perfect covenant.[3]

When Christ came, He fulfilled all the requirements of the Law. In so doing, He removed the veil and made clear the Way for eternal salvation. We now live under the New Covenant, and Christians today can enjoy a close and personal relationship with God. We can know God by spending time with Him—in prayer, in studying His Word, and in fellowship with other Christians.

Just as God did with Moses so long ago, when we draw near to Him, He draws near to us. And when we draw near to Him, we reflect His glory—not with a physical brilliance as Moses did, but with our very being. How incredible to think that Christians are able to reflect the glory of God!

So humble yourselves before God. Resist the devil, and he will flee from you. Come close to God, and God will come close to you.

—James 4:7–8a, NLT

So all of us who have had that veil removed can see and reflect the glory of the Lord. And the Lord—who is the Spirit—makes us more and more like him as we are changed into his glorious image.

—2 Corinthians 3:18, NLT

Forty Days and Forty Nights

You may have noticed that several times when Moses ascended the mountain of God, he stayed for forty days and forty nights without consuming food or water.

When Moses received the first pair of stone tablets and the additional instructions from God, he was on the mountain forty days and forty nights (Exodus 24:18). The parallel account in Deuteronomy 9:9 states he ate no bread and drank no water during this time.

After the incident with the golden calf, Moses went back up the mountain and begged God's forgiveness. While Exodus 32:30–34 gives a brief summary of Moses's discourse with God, the account in Deuteronomy 9:18–21 goes into more detail. There, Moses states he once again fell prostrate before the Lord (presumably back on the mountaintop) for forty days and forty nights and ate no bread and drank no water during this time.

When Moses received the second set of tablets,

he again ascended the mountain and stayed forty days and forty nights. In Exodus 34:28, it states he consumed no food or water during this time.

How could Moses go so long without sustenance and evidently suffer no ill effect? Quite simply, God sustained him during these times. Moses trusted God to take care of him, and He did.

Our Lord trusted God to take care of Him as well. In Matthew 4:2, Jesus fasted for forty days and forty nights, after which He was tempted by Satan. He knew the human body could not go that long in and of itself, but He, like Moses, trusted God to sustain Him. With confidence, He could tell Satan, "Man does not live on bread alone, but on every word that comes from the mouth of God" (Matthew 4:4, NIV).

During times of trial, remember how God sustained Moses and later how He sustained Jesus. Your trials may last much longer than forty days and forty nights, and some may never be over until your death. Trust in God and know that He will feed your soul.

Thoughts to Ponder

From what other people did God promise to make a great nation of their descendants? What makes the lineage through Abraham, Isaac, and Jacob so special?

_____

_____

_____

_____

God listed some of His characteristics when proclaiming His name to Moses. Discuss the meaning of these characteristics. How did they come into play during His dealings with the Israelites? See Nahum 1:1–8 for a further description of God's characteristics.

_____

_____

_____

_____

Have you ever met someone whose joy in the Lord was evident from the way they spoke and acted? How can Christians live so as to reflect God's glory? Discuss Ephesians 4:17–32.

_____

_____

_____

_____

Chapter 32

Becoming a Nation

Numbers 9:1–5, 15–23; 10:1–28, NLT

(9:1) A year after Israel's departure from Egypt, the LORD spoke to Moses in the wilderness of Sinai. In the first month of that year he said, (2) "Tell the Israelites to celebrate the Passover at the prescribed time, (3) at twilight on the fourteenth day of the first month. Be sure to follow all my decrees and regulations concerning this celebration."

(4) So Moses told the people to celebrate the Passover (5) in the wilderness of Sinai as twilight fell on the fourteenth day of the month. And they celebrated the festival there, just as the LORD had commanded Moses.

[In verses 6–14, God gave special instructions, including how those who were unclean during the time of Passover could partake of it at a later date.]

(9:15) On the day the Tabernacle was set up, the cloud covered it. But from evening until morning the cloud over the Tabernacle looked like a pillar of fire. (16) This was the regular pattern—at night the cloud that covered the Tabernacle had the appearance of fire. (17) Whenever the cloud lifted from over the sacred tent, the people of Israel would break camp and follow it. And wherever the cloud settled, the people of Israel would set up camp. (18) In this way, they traveled and camped at the LORD's command wherever he told them to go. Then they remained in their camp as long as the cloud stayed over the Tabernacle. (19) If the cloud remained over the Tabernacle for a long time, the Israelites stayed and performed their duty to the LORD. (20) Sometimes the cloud would stay over the Tabernacle for only a few days, so the people would stay for only a few days, as the LORD commanded. Then at the LORD's command they would break camp and move on. (21) Sometimes the cloud stayed only overnight and lifted the next morning. But day or night, when the cloud lifted, the people broke camp and moved on. (22) Whether the cloud stayed above the Tabernacle for two days, a month, or a year, the people of Israel stayed in camp and did not move on. But as soon as it lifted, they broke camp and moved on. (23) So they camped or traveled at the LORD's command, and they did whatever the LORD told them through Moses.

(10:1) Now the LORD said to Moses, (2) "Make two trumpets of hammered silver for calling the community to assemble and for signaling the breaking of camp. (3) When both trumpets are blown, everyone must gather before you at the entrance of the Tabernacle. (4) But if only one trumpet is blown, then only the leaders—the heads of the clans of Israel—must present themselves to you.

(5) "When you sound the signal to move on, the tribes camped on the east side of the Tabernacle must break camp and move forward. (6) When you sound the signal a second time, the tribes camped on the south will follow. You must sound short blasts as the signal for moving on. (7) But when you call the people to an assembly, blow the trumpets with a different signal. (8) Only the priests, Aaron's descendants, are allowed to blow the trumpets. This is a permanent law for you, to be observed from generation to generation.

(9) "When you arrive in your own land and go to war against your enemies who attack you, sound the alarm with the trumpets. Then the LORD your God will remember you and rescue you from your enemies. (10) Blow the trumpets in times of gladness, too, sounding them at your annual festivals and at the beginning of each month. And blow the trumpets over your burnt offerings and peace offerings. The trumpets will remind your God of his covenant with you. I am the LORD your God."

(11) In the second year after Israel's departure from Egypt—on the twentieth day of the second month—the cloud lifted from the Tabernacle of the Covenant. (12) So the Israelites set out from the wilderness of Sinai and traveled on from place to place until the cloud stopped in the wilderness of Paran.

(13) When the people set out for the first time, following the instructions the LORD had given through Moses, (14) Judah's troops led the way. They marched behind their banner, and their leader was Nahshon son of Amminadab. (15) They were joined by the troops of the tribe of Issachar, led by Nethanel son of Zuar, (16) and the troops of the tribe of Zebulun, led by Eliab son of Helon.

(17) Then the Tabernacle was taken down, and the Gershonite and Merarite divisions of the Levites were next in the line of march, carrying the Tabernacle

with them. (18) Reuben's troops went next, marching behind their banner. Their leader was Elizur son of Shedeur. (19) They were joined by the troops of the tribe of Simeon, led by Shelumiel son of Zurishaddai, (20) and the troops of the tribe of Gad, led by Eliasaph son of Deuel.

(21) Next came the Kohathite division of the Levites, carrying the sacred objects from the Tabernacle. Before they arrived at the next camp, the Tabernacle would already be set up at its new location. (22) Ephraim's troops went next, marching behind their banner. Their leader was Elishama son of Ammihud. (23) They were joined by the troops of the tribe of Manasseh, led by Gamaliel son of Pedahzur, (24) and the troops of the tribe of Benjamin, led by Abidan son of Gideoni.

(25) Dan's troops went last, marching behind their banner and serving as the rear guard for all the tribal camps. Their leader was Ahiezer son of Ammishaddai. (26) They were joined by the troops of the tribe of Asher, led by Pagiel son of Ocran, (27) and the troops of the tribe of Naphtali, led by Ahira son of Enan.

(28) This was the order in which the Israelites marched, division by division.

◇◇◇

Quite a few scriptures occur in the Bible between the readings from our last lesson and this one. Here are a few of the highlights from those passages:

In Exodus 35–40, God gave Moses instructions concerning the Tabernacle and the items that were to go in it, the ark of the covenant, and the clothing for the priests. When all the work on the Tabernacle was done, Moses inspected it and blessed the people for completing it just as the Lord had instructed.[1] Then, at God's command, the Tabernacle was set up on the first day of the first month of the second year after they had left Egypt.[2] The presence of God within the cloud hovered over the Tabernacle and the Israelites throughout their journey.

> The presence of God within the cloud hovered over the Tabernacle and the Israelites throughout their journey.

Suggested Song

"Lamb of God"
(tinyurl.com/2p9xn8vc)

——— 1 ———

Exodus 39:32–43 gives an account of Moses inspecting the Tabernacle. Everything was completed just as the Lord had commanded.

——— 2 ———

The description of setting up the Tabernacle is given in Exodus 40. Exodus 40:17 states it was set up on the first day of the first month in the second year. Exodus 40:34–38 describes how the glory of the Lord covered the tent of meeting and filled the Tabernacle. By lifting up from or settling down above the Tabernacle, the cloud determined when the Israelites would travel.

─────── 3 ───────

God commanded a census be taken of the Levites a little later in Numbers 3:14–39. For this tribe, all the males one month old or over were counted. The Levites belonged to the Lord and were taken in place of all the firstborn males of Israel. The livestock of the Levites were also taken in place of the firstborn of all the livestock of Israel. See Numbers 3:40–51 for this account.

─────── 4 ───────

See Numbers 1:45–46.

─────── 5 ───────

See Numbers 2 for a description of how the camp was to be arranged.

─────── 6 ───────

The tribe of Levi was further subdivided according to the three sons of Levi: Gershon, Kohath, and Merari. They camped around the tent of meeting, with the Gershonites camping on the west behind the Tabernacle. The descendants of Kohath camped to the south and those of Merari to the north. Moses, Aaron, and Aaron's sons were separated out from the descendants of Kohath. They were to camp east of the Tabernacle, in front of the

In the first part of the book of Leviticus, God gave commands concerning the various offerings and the ordination of Aaron and his sons as priests. In chapter 10:1–11, the account is given of the dramatic deaths of Aaron's sons, Nadab and Abihu, for offering unauthorized fire before the Lord. These were the same two sons who had accompanied Moses, Aaron, and the seventy elders partway up the mountain to commune with God in Exodus 24. In the remainder of Leviticus, God provided the Israelites with additional instructions and commands concerning many aspects of their lives.

The book of Numbers begins with God commanding a census be taken of the Israelite community. All the men aged twenty or older who were able to serve in the army were counted according to their families and clans. The tribe of Levi was not included in this count, as they were to serve as priests and be responsible for everything concerning the Tabernacle.[3]

It is unknown how many people in total were part of the Israelite encampment. The men counted in the census who were age twenty or older and able to serve in the army numbered 603,550.[4] If you add in those men who were unable to serve (i.e., too old, too young, disabled, or infirm), the tribe of Levi, all the women and children, as well as the non-Israelites who accompanied them out of Egypt, the total had to have included several million people. Then when you consider their livestock, you can understand how their encampment must have been enormous.

A Year of Preparation

The reading for this lesson explains several important means God provided to help Moses more effectively lead such a massive group. First and foremost, He used the pillar of cloud to indicate when they would travel and the direction they were to take. He also instructed two silver trumpets be made for the priests. Different blasts were used to signal various commands.

Think how much these trumpets must have aided in communicating with such a large group of people.

God also provided an efficient plan for organizing and mobilizing the Israelites. They were to camp by their tribes in a given order around the Levites and the tent of meeting or Tabernacle.[5] When it was time for them to move on, they were to march out in essentially the same order as they camped, with the Levites divided into two groups and inserted into the mix at certain intervals.[6,7]

The Israelites spent almost a year encamped before the mountain of God.[8] Recall that God had told Moses in Exodus 33:1 to take his people and leave after the incident with the golden calf. Fortunately, Moses interceded for the Israelites and begged God's forgiveness, and He allowed them to remain. They needed that time to receive, absorb, and implement God's numerous commands and instructions. In so doing, they began to develop a culture that would define them as a people—a people set apart and chosen by God.

How fitting that while here, they were able to observe their first Passover since leaving Egypt. Before continuing on to the Promised Land, they celebrated this time of remembrance for all that God had done for them in delivering them from slavery. The Passover would become one of their most important observances.

Christians today celebrate a special time of remembrance.

Communion, or the Lord's Supper, commemorates Christ's death, burial, and resurrection.[9] He served as our Lamb when He sacrificed His life, taking away the sin of the world. He died so that we could be delivered from the bondage of death—Christ died so that we could have eternal life! There could be no greater

tent of meeting. The census of the tribe of Levi, along with a description of their duties, is given in Numbers 3:14–39 and in Numbers 4.

──────── 7 ────────

By having the carriers of the Tabernacle set out earlier than those who carried the holy things, the Tabernacle would already be set up and ready to receive the holy things when their carriers arrived in camp later. See Numbers 10:11–28 for the order in which the Israelites set out from camp.

──────── 8 ────────

The Israelites arrived at their encampment at the mountain of God at least two months after their departure from Egypt (Exodus 19:1). Some Bible versions state they arrived after two full months, while others say they arrived on the first day of the third month or in the third month. They departed on the twentieth day of the second month of the second year after they had left Egypt (Numbers 10:11).

──────── 9 ────────

This article explains more about this special time of remembrance: "What Is the Importance of the Lord's Supper/Christian Communion?" (tinyurl. com/5k5m7a9b).

The Camp of the Israelites

It's hard to envision how large the Israelites' camp was, but it had to have been spread out over many acres of land. The Tabernacle or tent of meeting stood in the center of the camp, with the members of the tribe of Levi camped around it. The towering pillar of cloud hovered over the Tabernacle and turned into a pillar of fire at night.

Then encircling this core of the camp were the other twelve tribes. They were not camped tightly together, as God commanded the tribes to camp some distance away from the Tabernacle (Numbers 2:2). The herds and flocks of animals required a great deal of space as well.

In short, the Israelites' encampment must have been enormous. The trumpets God instructed to be made must have been a great help in aiding communications.

For more information, see the article "Encampment of the Tribes of Israel in the Wilderness" (tinyurl.com/52hhyupt). Scroll down to see a diagram of the layout of the camp.

gift. May we ever praise His name and remember what He has done for us.

The next day John saw Jesus coming toward him and said, "Look! The Lamb of God who takes away the sin of the world! He is the one I was talking about when I said, 'A man is coming after me who is far greater than I am, for he existed long before me.'"

—John 1:29–30, NLT

He took some bread and gave thanks to God for it. Then he broke it in pieces and gave it to the disciples, saying, "This is my body, which is given for you. Do this in remembrance of me." After supper he took another cup of wine and said, "This cup is the new covenant between God and his people— an agreement confirmed with my blood, which is poured out as a sacrifice for you."

—Luke 22:19–20, NLT

Thoughts to Ponder

How were the Israelites able to construct the Tabernacle, the ark of the covenant, all the items that accompanied the Tabernacle, and construct the priestly garments while camped for a year at the mountain of God?

_____

_____

_____

_____

In what situations were the trumpets to be sounded (Numbers 10:1–10)? Find other Old Testament references to the trumpets and how they were used.

_____

_____

_____

_____

How is our Communion or Lord's Supper today similar to the Passover? How does it differ?

_____

_____

_____

_____

Chapter 33

Leaving the Mountain of God

Numbers 10:33–36, 11:1–35, NKJV

(10:33) So they departed from the mountain of the LORD on a journey of three days; and the ark of the covenant of the LORD went before them for the three days' journey, to search out a resting place for them. (34) And the cloud of the LORD was above them by day when they went out from the camp.

(35) So it was, whenever the ark set out, that Moses said:

"Rise up, O LORD! Let Your enemies be scattered, And let those who hate You flee before You."

(36) And when it rested, he said: "Return, O LORD, To the many thousands of Israel."

(11:1) Now when the people complained, it displeased the LORD; for the LORD heard it, and His anger was aroused. So the fire of the LORD burned among them, and consumed some in the outskirts of the camp. (2) Then the people cried out to Moses,

and when Moses prayed to the LORD, the fire was quenched. (3) So he called the name of the place Taberah, because the fire of the LORD had burned among them.

(4) Now the mixed multitude who were among them yielded to intense craving; so the children of Israel also wept again and said: "Who will give us meat to eat? (5) We remember the fish which we ate freely in Egypt, the cucumbers, the melons, the leeks, the onions, and the garlic; (6) but now our whole being is dried up; there is nothing at all except this manna before our eyes!"

(7) Now the manna was like coriander seed, and its color like the color of bdellium. (8) The people went about and gathered it, ground it on millstones or beat it in the mortar, cooked it in pans, and made cakes of it; and its taste was like the taste of pastry prepared with oil. (9) And when

the dew fell on the camp in the night, the manna fell on it.

(10) Then Moses heard the people weeping throughout their families, everyone at the door of his tent; and the anger of the LORD was greatly aroused; Moses also was displeased. (11) So Moses said to the LORD, "Why have You afflicted Your servant? And why have I not found favor in Your sight, that You have laid the burden of all these people on me? (12) Did I conceive all these people? Did I beget them, that You should say to me, 'Carry them in your bosom, as a guardian carries a nursing child,' to the land which You swore to their fathers? (13) Where am I to get meat to give to all these people? For they weep all over me, saying, 'Give us meat, that we may eat.' (14) I am not able to bear all these people alone, because the burden is too heavy for me. (15) If You treat me like this, please kill me here and now—if I have found favor in Your sight—and do not let me see my wretchedness!"

(16) So the LORD said to Moses: "Gather to Me seventy men of the elders of Israel, whom you know to be the elders of the people and officers over them; bring them to the tabernacle of meeting, that they may stand there with you. (17) Then I will come down and talk with you there. I will take of the Spirit that is upon you and will put the same upon them; and they shall bear the burden of the people with you, that you may not bear it yourself alone. (18) Then you shall say to the people, 'Consecrate yourselves for tomorrow, and you shall eat meat; for you have wept in the hearing of the LORD, saying, "Who will give us meat to eat? For it was well with us in Egypt." Therefore the LORD will give you meat, and you shall eat. (19) You shall eat, not one day, nor two days, nor five days, nor ten days, nor twenty days, (20) but for a whole month, until it comes out of your nostrils and becomes loathsome to you, because you have despised the LORD who is among you, and have wept before Him, saying, "Why did we ever come up out of Egypt?"'"

(21) And Moses said, "The people whom I am among are six hundred thousand men on foot; yet You have said, 'I will give them meat, that they may eat for a whole month.' (22) Shall flocks and herds be slaughtered for them, to provide enough for them? Or shall all the fish of the sea be gathered together for them, to provide enough for them?"

(23) And the LORD said to Moses, "Has the LORD's arm been shortened? Now you shall see whether what I say will happen to you or not."

(24) So Moses went out and told the people the words of the LORD, and he gathered the seventy men of the elders of the people and placed them around the tabernacle. (25) Then the LORD came down in the cloud, and spoke to him, and took of the Spirit that was upon him,

and placed the same upon the seventy elders; and it happened, when the Spirit rested upon them, that they prophesied, although they never did so again.

(26) But two men had remained in the camp: the name of one was Eldad, and the name of the other Medad. And the Spirit rested upon them. Now they were among those listed, but who had not gone out to the tabernacle; yet they prophesied in the camp. (27) And a young man ran and told Moses, and said, "Eldad and Medad are prophesying in the camp."

(28) So Joshua the son of Nun, Moses's assistant, one of his choice men, answered and said, "Moses my lord, forbid them!"

(29) Then Moses said to him, "Are you zealous for my sake? Oh, that all the LORD's people were prophets and that the LORD would put His Spirit upon them!" (30) And Moses returned to the camp, he and the elders of Israel.

(31) Now a wind went out from the LORD, and it brought quail from the sea and left them fluttering near the camp, about a day's journey on this side and about a day's journey on the other side, all around the camp, and about two cubits above the surface of the ground. (32) And the people stayed up all that day, all night, and all the next day, and gathered the quail (he who gathered least gathered ten homers); and they spread them out for themselves all around the camp. (33) But while the meat was still between their teeth, before it was chewed, the wrath of the LORD was aroused against the people, and the LORD struck the people with a very great plague. (34) So he called the name of that place Kibroth Hattaavah, because there they buried the people who had yielded to craving.

(35) From Kibroth Hattaavah the people moved to Hazeroth, and camped at Hazeroth.

Finally, they were off! With the ark of the covenant going before them and the presence of God in the cloud to guide them, the Israelites departed from the mountain of God.[1] Their circumstances were difficult,[2] but the Israelites had only a relatively short distance left to travel.[3] They had already endured so much while living in slavery and then escaping from Egypt. Surely, with God's guidance, they could make it just a little longer.

Unfortunately, that was not to be. Only a short way into what should have been the final portion of their journey, the people

Suggested Song

"Does Jesus Care?" (tinyurl.com/ywvj5rbw)

———— 1 ————

From the instructions God gave in Numbers 10:11–28 concerning how the Israelites were to march, it sounds like the ark should be traveling in the middle of the group.

The presence of God hovered over the ark, however, and this cloud was to guide the Israelites in their travel. So it would seem that the ark itself needed to be in front. We are told that when the Israelites finally crossed the Jordan River into the Promised Land, the ark went before the people at that time (Joshua 3).

--------- 2 ---------

From the account in Deuteronomy 1:19 (NIV), the area they traveled through must have been most inhospitable: "Then, as the LORD our God commanded us, we set out from Horeb and went toward the hill country of the Amorites through all that vast and dreadful wilderness that you have seen, and so we reached Kadesh Barnea."

--------- 3 ---------

So near were they to the Promised Land that Moses stated in Deuteronomy 1:2 (NKJV), "It is eleven days' journey from Horeb by way of Mount Seir to Kadesh Barnea."

--------- 4 ---------

Taberah means burning or a place of burning. See "Taberah" in the *Encyclopedia of the Bible* (tinyurl.com/2hpjhw2b). The scriptures do not state what was destroyed in this fire, but it is probable some of the people lost their lives as well as their possessions. In Deuteronomy 9:22, Moses lists both Taberah and

began to complain about their hardships. This displeased God so much that He caused fire to burn among them along the outskirts of the camp. The people cried out to Moses, who in turn prayed to God, and the fire subsided.

Complaining (Again)

Then came the complaints about the food. Feeding several million people in the wilderness for even a few days would have been almost impossible without divine intervention. If the Israelites had slaughtered their own animals for food, they would have quickly depleted their herds and flocks. The manna, which God readily supplied, should have served as yet another reminder of His constant care. Instead, they spoke with contempt against that which sustained their very lives.

The "mixed multitude" began the complaining, and the Israelites joined right in. The whole camp seemed to be weeping and wailing at the entrances of their tents because they had no meat or vegetables. Moses asked God why such a great burden had been placed upon him in dealing with these people, a burden he was not able to carry alone. In his distress, he even asked to be put to death immediately if this was the way things were going to be.

God responded to Moses by having him assemble seventy men who were elders and leaders at the tent of meeting. He placed His Spirit upon them so they could help Moses in managing the needs of the people. He then told Moses to instruct the people to consecrate themselves—for tomorrow, they would have meat to eat. In fact, they would eat meat for a month, and they would come to loathe it because they had rejected the Lord.

Moses then asked God how so much meat could possibly be provided for so many people. God replied with His own question—*Is My arm too short?* In other words, did Moses think this feat was really out of God's reach? Then God told Moses to stand back and watch.

God did what He said He would do and brought in a vast amount of quail. But while the meat was still between the people's teeth, God struck them with a severe plague. That place was named Kibroth Hattaavah, which means graves of craving, lust, or desire[4] because there they buried the people who had craved other foods.

They were so near and yet so far! What an inauspicious beginning for what should have been a momentous occasion—the start of the last leg of their journey to the Promised Land. This group of Israelites stood on the cusp of witnessing the culmination of the promise God had made centuries earlier to Abraham, Isaac, and Jacob. Yet most of them would never enter Canaan. They allowed their present challenges to cause them to lose sight of their ultimate goal.

> They were so near and yet so far!

How many times do we lose sight of our goals?

When we allow our time and energy to be absorbed by immediate concerns, we stop focusing on Jesus. Such concerns, however, are not something that will ever go away. As long as we are alive, it's a given we will face difficult and trying situations.

Think about what Moses did during all the trials he faced while leading the Israelites. He turned to God. He prayed to God. He cried out to God. His words often lacked elegance, and they may have been uttered in sheer desperation. But no matter what, God heard him, and He responded. He'll do the same for you. Pray to God, ask for His help and guidance, and He will respond, even if He has to say no. This life will soon be over. Don't miss eternity with God because you allowed the cares of this world to divert your focus away from Him.

Kibroth Hattaavah among the sites where the Israelites provoked the Lord to wrath. See "Kibroth Hataavah" in the *Encyclopedia of the Bible* (tinyurl.com/28k49x53).

What Was a Day's Journey?

Moses stated in Deuteronomy 1:2 that it was an eleven-day journey from Horeb (or Sinai) by way of Mount Seir to Kadesh Barnea.

Kadesh Barnea was the site where the Israelites were originally set to go in and take the land God had promised them. So when the Israelites left the Mount Sinai region, they were not far from Canaan.

Unfortunately, when they reached Canaan, they failed to trust in God. Instead, they believed the negative reports given by ten of the twelve men sent to spy out the land. Rather than claiming the land which God had promised to Abraham, they were sentenced to wander in the wilderness for forty years. (See Deuteronomy 1:19–40 and Deuteronomy 9:23.)

Distances were often measured in the length of

time needed to travel to a destination. Depending on the circumstances and terrain, a typical "day's journey" would usually be about 20 miles a day, perhaps a little more. That would make the distance from Sinai to Kadesh Barnea about 220 miles.

For more information on what constituted a day's journey, see "Journey" in *Easton's Bible Dictionary* (tinyurl.com/3xdzarzt).

"So do not worry, saying, 'What shall we eat?' or 'What shall we drink?' or 'What shall we wear?' For the pagans run after all these things, and your heavenly Father knows that you need them. But seek first his kingdom and his righteousness, and all these things will be given to you as well."

—Matthew 6:31–33, NIV

The eyes of the LORD are on the righteous, and his ears are attentive to their cry.

—Psalm 34:15, NIV

Thoughts to Ponder

How does the Bible describe "this manna" that the Israelites spoke against in this reading? In addition to today's reading, see also Psalm 78:21–25 and 1 Corinthians 10:1–5.

_____

_____

_____

_____

The people's complaints against their hardships and food were only a symptom of what underlying problem? (The entire chapter of Psalm 78 gives a brief history of Israel. See verses 18–25 and verses 32–33 in particular.)

_____

_____

_____

_____

For whatever reason, two of the seventy elders remained in the camp when God placed His Spirit upon those who had been chosen to help Moses. (It's interesting to note their names were recorded, Eldad and Medad, while those of the other sixty-eight were not.) Why was Joshua upset when he heard they were prophesying in the camp? What did Moses mean by his reply to Joshua?

_____

_____

_____

_____

Chapter 34

Miriam and Aaron Criticize Moses

Numbers 12, NLT

(1) While they were at Hazeroth, Miriam and Aaron criticized Moses because he had married a Cushite woman. (2) They said, "Has the LORD spoken only through Moses? Hasn't he spoken through us, too?" But the LORD heard them. (3) (Now Moses was very humble—more humble than any other person on earth.)

(4) So immediately the LORD called to Moses, Aaron, and Miriam and said, "Go out to the Tabernacle, all three of you!" So the three of them went to the Tabernacle. (5) Then the LORD descended in the pillar of cloud and stood at the entrance of the Tabernacle. "Aaron and Miriam!" he called, and they stepped forward. (6) And the LORD said to them, "Now listen to what I say:

"If there were prophets among you,

I, the LORD, would reveal myself in visions.

I would speak to them in dreams.

(7) But not with my servant Moses.

Of all my house, he is the one I trust.

(8) I speak to him face to face,

clearly, and not in riddles!

He sees the LORD as he is.

So why were you not afraid

to criticize my servant Moses?"

(9) The LORD was very angry with them, and he departed. (10) As the cloud moved from above the Tabernacle, there stood Miriam, her skin as white as snow from leprosy. When Aaron saw what had happened to her, (11) he cried out to Moses, "Oh, my master! Please don't punish us for this sin we have so foolishly committed. (12) Don't let her be like a stillborn baby, already decayed at birth."

(13) So Moses cried out to the LORD, "O God, I beg you, please heal her!"

——————— 1 ———————

The eldest son typically assumed the role of family leadership once his father passed away. Later, in Deuteronomy 21:15–17, God specifically stated that the rights of the firstborn son included a double portion of his father's property.

——————— 2 ———————

While God instructed the Israelites in Exodus 34:12–16 and Deuteronomy 7:1–4 not to make covenants or intermarry with the inhabitants of the land which He was giving them to possess, he had not given that instruction concerning residents of other countries. Even so, if the wife referred to in this reading was Zipporah, Moses had married her years earlier, well before God had given these marriage instructions. It's very likely that others of the Israelite community had intermarried while living in Egypt as well.

——————— 3 ———————

God worked or spoke through Aaron on numerous occasions, particularly while performing miracles in Egypt. Moreover, God had designated Aaron to be Moses's mouthpiece in Exodus

(14) But the LORD said to Moses, "If her father had done nothing more than spit in her face, wouldn't she be defiled for seven days? So keep her outside the camp for seven days, and after that she may be accepted back."

(15) So Miriam was kept outside the camp for seven days, and the people waited until she was brought back before they traveled again. (16) Then they left Hazeroth and camped in the wilderness of Paran.

◇◇◇

Squabbles frequently occur among siblings, and Moses's family was no exception. Aaron, as the firstborn son of the family, may have felt overshadowed or diminished by Moses.[1] Miriam, as the oldest of the siblings, presumably wielded a certain amount of influence over her brothers. She also played a large part in preserving Moses's life as an infant, making it possible for their own mother to care for him. Yet it was Moses, the youngest of the three, whom God had called to be the leader of the Israelite people.

The catalyst for this event was the fact that Moses had married someone of foreign descent.[2] That complaint, however, was merely superficial. Miriam and Aaron's criticism of Moses ran much deeper. They were of exactly the same lineage as Moses and wanted recognition because the Lord had also spoken through them at various times.[3] They thought they deserved some sort of praise or acknowledgment. In short, they were envious of Moses.

God heard their grumbling and immediately called all three siblings out to the Tabernacle or tent of meeting. As He descended in the pillar of cloud before the entrance of the Tabernacle, He called Miriam and Aaron to step forward. If they weren't trembling with fear, they should have been, for God was very angry with them.

What followed was God's wholehearted endorsement of Moses. He explained that, unlike other prophets with whom He communicated by means of visions or dreams, He spoke directly with Moses and not in riddles or sayings. Moreover, He spoke with Moses face-to-face and allowed him to see His unobscured form, the actual manifestation of His being. Why then, God asked, were they not afraid to criticize His servant Moses?

As God departed and the cloud lifted, there stood Miriam, white as snow, beset with leprosy. When Aaron saw her condition, he cried out to Moses, calling him "my lord" (or master), a term of respect showing his deference to Moses. He confessed to the foolishness of their sin and begged for Miriam to be healed from this terrible disease.

Moses didn't gloat or stop to consider whether Miriam deserved to be healed. He didn't pause to expound first on how his siblings had hurt his feelings and derided his wife. Instead, he immediately cried out to God and asked that He heal his sister. His personal pride never came into play.

While Moses may have been quick to forgive, God decided the siblings needed a bit more time to consider their behavior. He instructed that Miriam be shut out of the camp for seven days, the same punishment that would have been ordered had her father shamed her by spitting in her face. During that time, the travels of the Israelites came to a halt while they waited for Miriam to be able to rejoin them. It's likely everyone in the community knew Miriam had been disciplined by God. She is not mentioned again in Scripture until her death at Kadesh in Numbers 20:1.

The Humility of Moses

The words God spoke here in Numbers 12:6–8 concerning Moses are remarkable for several reasons. The scriptures record God speaking directly to people at various times, but He usually did so to provide instructions, guidance, or warnings. Rarely did

4:14–16. As for Miriam, she is referred to as a prophetess in Exodus 15:20 when the Israelites sang praises to the Lord for delivering them from Pharaoh.

— 4 —

Jesus comes to mind, both after His baptism in Matthew 3:16–17 and again at His transfiguration in Matthew 17:1–6. God testified that Jesus was His beloved Son and instructed others to listen to Him.

— 5. —

See James 2:23.

— 6 —

See 1 Samuel 13:14. See also Acts 13:22, where the Apostle Paul gave a brief history of the Jewish people and the events leading up to the coming of Christ.

— 7 —

See Daniel 9:22–23 and 10:11. Rather than "highly esteemed," other versions may use terms such as *greatly beloved, very precious*, or *treasured by God*.

— 8 —

See Acts 9:15–16.

He endorse one person while in the presence of others.[4] Here in this passage, however, God praises Moses's character.

Certainly, other people mentioned in the Bible have been noted favorably by God. Abraham was called the "friend of God"[5] and David "a man after God's own heart."[6] Daniel was esteemed by God.[7] Saul of Tarsus was a chosen vessel for God.[8] Yet the passage here in Numbers indicates that God and Moses had developed a deep personal relationship.

How did that relationship develop? Once Moses accepted the role to which God had called him, he worked to fulfill it with all his being. God had entrusted him to lead and oversee His "house," or the household of Israel, and Moses proved himself faithful in doing so. He depended on God and not on his own understanding or that of other people. He did not allow his own pride or ego to get in the way of what he had been called to do and sought no glory for himself. These characteristics, signs of his humility, enabled him to develop a deep relationship with God.

Moses also truly wanted to know God. Recall earlier when he had asked to see God's glory in Exodus 33:18–23. By that point in his life, Moses had interacted many times with God. God had performed numerous miracles through him and had spoken to him many times while delivering instructions or presenting His commands to the Israelites. Yet Moses sought to see God in His fullness and not just hear His voice or see His form obscured by the veil of a cloud.

We then read in Exodus 34:5–7, where God complied with Moses's request to the extent that was possible for humans to experience His presence. As God passed by in all His glory while shielding Moses from harm, He proclaimed His characteristics, much like we humans do when we are getting acquainted with others. With the exception of Jesus, who knew Him from the beginning of the world, God has allowed very few people the privilege of knowing Him the way Moses did.

God also revealed something of Himself to Miriam and Aaron in the narrative recorded in this reading. He described how He interacted with other prophets and compared this to His interaction with Moses. He told them these things, not because they sought to know Him, but because God wanted them to understand how special Moses was to Him. God wanted them to know He treated Moses as a friend.

> God wanted them to know He treated Moses as a friend.

It's possible for you to know God.

Because we live in the age in which we do, we have ready access to the Scriptures translated into a language we can understand. This remarkable privilege has been available to English-speaking people for only a little over 400 years. Think of the millions who came before us who were not so fortunate!

When Christ came, He not only ushered in a New Covenant, but He also left a precious gift for His followers. After His death, He sent the Comforter, the Holy Spirit, to dwell within Christians. This priceless gift is now available for **all** who believe and obey His teachings, regardless of their gender, nationality, or position of power.

The avenue of prayer provides yet another way for us to come to know God and to draw near to Him. Through the ages, people have called on His name, and the Bible cites numerous examples of how He heard and answered their prayers. The prayer line is always open to God, and He delights in hearing from His children.

When we, like Moses, seek to know God, He will reveal Himself to us. Every page of Scripture tells us something about God. Pray for a receptive heart to understand His will for you, and ask the Holy Spirit to guide you. Practice the type of

Leprosy

Leprosy is a skin disease caused by bacteria. It has existed since ancient times, and people still become infected with it today. Fortunately, an antibiotic treatment now exists that can cure leprosy.

God gave the Israelites specific instructions concerning leprosy and other skin infections in Leviticus 13–14. Anyone thought to have leprosy was to be brought to the priest to be examined. If the priest pronounced that person unclean, they had to wear torn clothes, let their hair remain unkempt, cover the lower part of their face, and cry out, "Unclean! Unclean!" They remained unclean as long as they had the infection. This meant if they truly had leprosy, they would likely never be clean again. They had to live alone outside the camp (Leviticus 13:45–46). You can understand why it was such a dreaded disease for centuries and why it was such a serious punishment for God to make Miriam leprous.

These sites provide more information concerning leprosy: "Leprosy (Hansen's Disease)" (tinyurl.com/2p9xjdaw) and "Leprosy in the Bible" (tinyurl.com/35e9z6t9).

humility Moses exemplified, and aspire to become someone whom God Himself would willingly endorse.

Humble yourselves in the sight of the Lord, and He will lift you up.

—James 4:10, NKJV

Surely He scorns the scornful, But gives grace to the humble.

—Proverbs 3:34, NKJV

Thoughts to Ponder

Why was only Miriam punished by God and not Aaron also?

_____

_____

_____

_____

_____

What comes to mind when you hear someone referred to as meek or humble? Think of Moses's life and consider the many times he spoke with resolve or acted decisively and powerfully. How did his words or actions exemplify real humility?

_____

_____

_____

_____

_____

In Hebrews 3:1–6, the writer compares Moses to Jesus. How are they similar? How is Jesus superior to Moses?

_____

_____

_____

_____

GOD NEVER LEAVES
HIS PEOPLE

Chapter 35

Exploring the Promised Land

Numbers 13, NIV

(1) The LORD said to Moses, (2) "Send some men to explore the land of Canaan, which I am giving to the Israelites. From each ancestral tribe send one of its leaders."

(3) So at the LORD's command Moses sent them out from the Desert of Paran. All of them were leaders of the Israelites. (4) These are their names:

from the tribe of Reuben, Shammua son of Zakkur;

(5) from the tribe of Simeon, Shaphat son of Hori;

(6) from the tribe of Judah, Caleb son of Jephunneh;

(7) from the tribe of Issachar, Igal son of Joseph;

(8) from the tribe of Ephraim, Hoshea son of Nun;

(9) from the tribe of Benjamin, Palti son of Raphu;

(10) from the tribe of Zebulun, Gaddiel son of Sodi;

(11) from the tribe of Manasseh (a tribe of Joseph), Gaddi son of Susi;

(12) from the tribe of Dan, Ammiel son of Gemalli;

(13) from the tribe of Asher, Sethur son of Michael;

(14) from the tribe of Naphtali, Nahbi son of Vophsi;

(15) from the tribe of Gad, Geuel son of Maki.

(16) These are the names of the men Moses sent to explore the land. (Moses gave Hoshea son of Nun the name Joshua.)

(17) When Moses sent them to explore Canaan, he said, "Go up through the Negev and on into the hill country. (18) See what the land is like and whether the people who live there are strong or weak, few or

many. (19) What kind of land do they live in? Is it good or bad? What kind of towns do they live in? Are they unwalled or fortified? (20) How is the soil? Is it fertile or poor? Are there trees in it or not? Do your best to bring back some of the fruit of the land." (It was the season for the first ripe grapes.)

(21) So they went up and explored the land from the Desert of Zin as far as Rehob, toward Lebo Hamath. (22) They went up through the Negev and came to Hebron, where Ahiman, Sheshai and Talmai, the descendants of Anak, lived. (Hebron had been built seven years before Zoan in Egypt.) (23) When they reached the Valley of Eshkol, they cut off a branch bearing a single cluster of grapes. Two of them carried it on a pole between them, along with some pomegranates and figs. (24) That place was called the Valley of Eshkol because of the cluster of grapes the Israelites cut off there. (25) At the end of forty days they returned from exploring the land.

(26) They came back to Moses and Aaron and the whole Israelite community at Kadesh in the Desert of Paran. There they reported to them and to the whole assembly and showed them the fruit of the land. (27) They gave Moses this account: "We went into the land to which you sent us, and it does flow with milk and honey! Here is its fruit. (28) But the people who live there are powerful, and the cities are fortified and very large. We even saw descendants of Anak there. (29) The Amalekites live in the Negev; the Hittites, Jebusites and Amorites live in the hill country; and the Canaanites live near the sea and along the Jordan."

(30) Then Caleb silenced the people before Moses and said, "We should go up and take possession of the land, for we can certainly do it."

(31) But the men who had gone up with him said, "We can't attack those people; they are stronger than we are." (32) And they spread among the Israelites a bad report about the land they had explored. They said, "The land we explored devours those living in it. All the people we saw there are of great size. (33) We saw the Nephilim there (the descendants of Anak come from the Nephilim). We seemed like grasshoppers in our own eyes, and we looked the same to them."

Finally, the Israelites had arrived at the border of the Promised Land! They had been through so much—a treacherous escape from Egypt, a year's stay at the mountain of God, and an arduous journey through inhospitable territory. Now, as they stood poised to receive the land God had promised centuries earlier to Abraham, Isaac, and Jacob, Moses told them, "You have reached the hill country of the Amorites, which the LORD our God is giving us. See, the LORD your God has given you the land. Go up and take possession of it as the LORD, the God of your ancestors, told you. Do not be afraid; do not be discouraged" (Deuteronomy 1:20–21, NIV).

Suggested Song

"Jesus, Savior, Pilot Me" (tinyurl.com/4k3u442w)

> The Promised Land was right in front of them, and it was theirs for the taking.

The Promised Land was right in front of them, and it was theirs for the taking. Only, they weren't quite ready. Instead of trusting God to see them through, they hesitated. They decided they wanted to know what they were getting into before taking the land. In Deuteronomy 1:22 (NLT), Moses stated: "But you all came to me and said, 'First, let's send out scouts to explore the land for us. They will advise us on the best route to take and which towns we should enter.'" This scripture reveals that it was the people who initiated this action, while the Numbers 13:1–2 reading indicates God sanctioned the process and directed them as to how they were to proceed.

Twelve men who were leaders in their respective tribes were selected, and they spied out the land.[1] After forty days, they returned and presented their report along with a sampling of the figs, pomegranates, and grapes they had found. The land, they said, truly flowed with milk and honey, meaning the land was fertile and readily supported an abundance of food-producing plants and animals. They also reported that the people

---

1

Note that no one was selected from the tribe of Levi. This tribe had been chosen by God to serve Him. They had not been among the men counted to serve in the Israelite army, and they would not receive a physical inheritance in the Promised Land. Therefore, no Levite was sent out as a spy. Rather, Joseph's descendants became two tribes named after his two sons, Ephraim and Manasseh. In this way, there remained twelve tribes.

who lived there were strong and dwelled in large, fortified cities. They were men of great stature, with some being descendants of Anak, a people so large the spies seemed like grasshoppers in comparison.

Caleb, the spy from the tribe of Judah, was undaunted by the size of the people or the fortification of their cities. After quieting the people, he urged them to take possession of the land. "We can certainly do it," he assured them in verse 30. He knew the inhabitants of the land were no match for the God who had delivered the Israelites out of Egypt.

The other spies, however, opposed Caleb. Convinced the inhabitants of the land would overpower them, they gave a negative report. They even went so far as to claim the land devoured its inhabitants! Obviously, they wanted the people to believe that taking possession of the Promised Land would be an extremely dangerous venture, one that would be impossible to achieve.

The Turning Point

God had inflicted great plagues and defeated the Egyptian army. He had led the Israelites on dry ground across the Red Sea and miraculously guided them through the wilderness with the pillar of cloud. He had empowered them to defeat the Amalekites in battle. And He had led them to the edge of the Promised Land— the place of rest their people had looked forward to entering for centuries.

Could not God have also protected them as they moved into the Promised Land?

How different this story might have been if the spies had never been sent out in the first place. If the Israelites had simply crossed over in faith, they could have witnessed God taking care of things for them. Instead, they allowed the testimony of ten men to supersede all that they knew of God.

Yes, the people of the land were strong and their cities fortified. Taking possession of the Promised Land would have been difficult and perhaps even impossible—if the task had depended solely upon the strength of the Israelites. But it didn't. Their God, who had performed so many miracles on their behalf, was right there, ready and willing to clear the path for them.

Once again, the Israelites rejected God. This time, however, His patience was spent. This generation stood to gain everything: freedom from slavery, possession of the Promised Land, and fulfillment of God's promise to their ancestors. Instead, the very fate they had feared for so long was set to become their reality. They were now destined to die in the wilderness.

Trusting in the Lord is always the right thing to do.

The compelling arguments presented by the ten spies failed to factor in God's unlimited power. Caleb, on the other hand, knew that with God on their side, the concerns presented by the other spies would be nonissues. He trusted God to continue in the future to come through for them in the same manner as He had so many times in the past.

Trust always involves the future, doesn't it? The past is done and over, written in the annals of history. The future is unknown and unwritten. Our human nature tries to tell us that the only one with whom we can trust our future is ourselves. It's a compelling but false narrative. While we attempt to set things in motion now in an effort to create the future we desire, what actually occurs may differ substantially from what we expected.

God is the only constant in the future, and that is something Caleb understood.

Follow God's guidance and instruction, no matter how much the circumstances appear to dictate otherwise. Know that God is faithful; He will always see you through.

Caleb and Joshua

Caleb from the tribe of Judah and Joshua (or Hoshea) from the tribe of Ephraim were two of the twelve spies sent to scout out the land of Canaan. The reports given by the other ten spies made the people fearful of entering Canaan. Caleb, however, encouraged the people to go ahead and take possession.

When the Israelites decided to return to Egypt in Numbers 14:1–10, both Caleb and Joshua tore their clothes and tried to convince the people not to rebel against the Lord. For taking this stance, the congregation actually wanted to stone them! Fortunately, the glory of the Lord appeared at the tent of meeting there before all the Israelites, effectively intervening on behalf of these two men.

Of the twelve spies, only Caleb and Joshua were permitted to enter the Promised Land (Numbers 14:30). The other ten men were struck down and died of a plague before the Lord (Numbers 14:36–38).

There is a way that appears to be right, but in the end it leads to death.

—Proverbs 14:12, NIV

Ah, Sovereign LORD, you have made the heavens and the earth by your great power and outstretched arm. Nothing is too hard for you.

—Jeremiah 32:17, NIV

Thoughts to Ponder

Where else are giants (or Nephilim or descendants of Anakim) mentioned in the Bible? Did the Israelites have to go against them later when they finally were able to enter the Promised Land?

_____

_____

_____

In the Deuteronomy account of this incident, the report given by the ten spies was so discouraging that it caused the people to lose heart or melted their hearts in fear (Deuteronomy 1:28). When have you lost heart only to later realize the conditions were not actually as dire as they had originally appeared? What did you learn from your experience?

_____

_____

_____

After the Israelites heard this negative report of the ten spies, they retreated to their tents and allowed their discontent and discouragement to fester even further. "Because the LORD hates us," they said, "He has brought us out of the land of Egypt to deliver us into the hand of the Amorites, to destroy us" (Deuteronomy 1:27, NKJV).

While God sought to bring them safely into the Promised Land, the people allowed their thinking to twist His intent around to the polar opposite. What caused them to get this so wrong? Do you think their upbringing in Egypt impacted their thinking? Read Psalm 1 and think about from whom you should accept counsel.

_____

_____

_____

_____

Chapter 36

Forty Years of Wandering!

Numbers 14, NIV

(1) That night all the members of the community raised their voices and wept aloud. (2) All the Israelites grumbled against Moses and Aaron, and the whole assembly said to them, "If only we had died in Egypt! Or in this wilderness! (3) Why is the LORD bringing us to this land only to let us fall by the sword? Our wives and children will be taken as plunder. Wouldn't it be better for us to go back to Egypt?" (4) And they said to each other, "We should choose a leader and go back to Egypt."

(5) Then Moses and Aaron fell facedown in front of the whole Israelite assembly gathered there. (6) Joshua son of Nun and Caleb son of Jephunneh, who were among those who had explored the land, tore their clothes (7) and said to the entire Israelite assembly, "The land we passed through and explored is exceedingly good. (8) If the LORD is pleased with us, he will lead us into that land, a land flowing with milk and honey, and will give it to us. (9) Only do not rebel against the LORD. And do not be afraid of the people of the land, because we will devour them. Their protection is gone, but the LORD is with us. Do not be afraid of them."

(10) But the whole assembly talked about stoning them. Then the glory of the LORD appeared at the tent of meeting to all the Israelites. (11) The LORD said to Moses, "How long will these people treat me with contempt? How long will they refuse to believe in me, in spite of all the signs I have performed among them? (12) I will strike them down with a plague and destroy them, but I will make you into a nation greater and stronger than they."

(13) Moses said to the LORD, "Then the Egyptians will hear about it! By your power you brought these people up from among them. (14) And they will tell the inhabitants of this land about it. They have already

heard that you, LORD, are with these people and that you, LORD, have been seen face to face, that your cloud stays over them, and that you go before them in a pillar of cloud by day and a pillar of fire by night. (15) If you put all these people to death, leaving none alive, the nations who have heard this report about you will say, (16) 'The LORD was not able to bring these people into the land he promised them on oath, so he slaughtered them in the wilderness.'

(17) "Now may the LORD's strength be displayed, just as you have declared: (18) 'The LORD is slow to anger, abounding in love and forgiving sin and rebellion. Yet he does not leave the guilty unpunished; he punishes the children for the sin of the parents to the third and fourth generation.' (19) In accordance with your great love, forgive the sin of these people, just as you have pardoned them from the time they left Egypt until now."

(20) The LORD replied, "I have forgiven them, as you asked. (21) Nevertheless, as surely as I live and as surely as the glory of the LORD fills the whole earth, (22) not one of those who saw my glory and the signs I performed in Egypt and in the wilderness but who disobeyed me and tested me ten times—(23) not one of them will ever see the land I promised on oath to their ancestors. No one who has treated me with contempt will ever see it. (24) But because my servant Caleb has a different spirit and follows me wholeheartedly, I will bring him into the land he went to, and his descendants will inherit it. (25) Since the Amalekites and the Canaanites are living in the valleys, turn back tomorrow and set out toward the desert along the route to the Red Sea."

(26) The LORD said to Moses and Aaron: (27) "How long will this wicked community grumble against me? I have heard the complaints of these grumbling Israelites. (28) So tell them, 'As surely as I live, declares the LORD, I will do to you the very thing I heard you say: (29) In this wilderness your bodies will fall—every one of you twenty years old or more who was counted in the census and who has grumbled against me. (30) Not one of you will enter the land I swore with uplifted hand to make your home, except Caleb son of Jephunneh and Joshua son of Nun. (31) As for your children that you said would be taken as plunder, I will bring them in to enjoy the land you have rejected. (32) But as for you, your bodies will fall in this wilderness. (33) Your children will be shepherds here for forty years, suffering for your unfaithfulness, until the last of your bodies lies in the wilderness. (34) For forty years—one year for each of the forty days you explored the land—you will suffer for your sins and know what it is like to have me against you.' (35) I, the LORD, have spoken, and I will surely do these things to this whole wicked community, which has banded together against me. They will meet their end in this wilderness; here they will die."

(36) So the men Moses had sent to explore the land, who returned and made the whole community grumble against him by spreading a

bad report about it—(37) these men who were responsible for spreading the bad report about the land were struck down and died of a plague before the LORD. (38) Of the men who went to explore the land, only Joshua son of Nun and Caleb son of Jephunneh survived.

(39) When Moses reported this to all the Israelites, they mourned bitterly. (40) Early the next morning they set out for the highest point in the hill country, saying, "Now we are ready to go up to the land the LORD promised. Surely we have sinned!"

(41) But Moses said, "Why are you disobeying the LORD's command? This will not succeed! (42) Do not go up, because the LORD is not with you. You will be defeated by your enemies, (43) for the Amalekites and the Canaanites will face you there. Because you have turned away from the LORD, he will not be with you and you will fall by the sword."

(44) Nevertheless, in their presumption they went up toward the highest point in the hill country, though neither Moses nor the ark of the LORD's covenant moved from the camp. (45) Then the Amalekites and the Canaanites who lived in that hill country came down and attacked them and beat them down all the way to Hormah.

Once again, the Israelites cried inconsolably. The negative report given by the ten spies had convinced them they could not possibly take possession of the Promised Land. They were sure they would be killed if they tried and that their wives and children would be taken into slavery as plunder. They murmured against Moses and Aaron, and they once again wailed out their same tired refrain: *If only we had died in Egypt, if only we had died in the wilderness.*

This time, however, the people took their complaining too far. They decided to choose a leader and return to Egypt, back into the land of slavery from which God had so miraculously delivered them. What a total rejection of all that God had done for them! Upon hearing this, Moses and Aaron fell prostrate, perhaps in despair at the people's obstinance or in fear of the Lord's reaction to the people's repeated rejection—or both. Caleb and Joshua tore their clothes and tried to reason with the people. If the Lord delighted in them, they said, then He would lead them into this good land and give it to them.[1]

Desperate to bolster the people's faith, Caleb and Joshua assured the people of the truth: There was no reason to fear the current inhabitants because they—as strong and as imposing as they seemed—did not have God's protection. The Israelites did! The people's fearful refusal to enter the land was an act of rebellion against the One who had delivered them from Egypt and protected them for the past year.

The people refused to listen. They even went so far as to talk of stoning Caleb and Joshua!

God had finally had enough. His glory, in the form of the cloud, intervened by appearing at the tent of meeting, effectively stopping the riotous moment and protecting the two men from the mob.

This generation of Israelites had rejected God for the last time. Once again, Moses pleaded with God, begging Him not to utterly destroy the people. God relented, pardoning their great sin at Moses's request, but He made this pronouncement: All those who had murmured against Him, age twenty and above, who had been counted in the census, would never set foot in the Promised Land. Instead, they would wander in the wilderness for forty years—one year for each of the forty days the spies had explored the land. They were now destined to perish in the wilderness. The ten spies who had stirred up such dissension with their fearful report didn't have to wait for their demise. God struck those ten men with a plague, and they died right then and there.

> This generation of Israelites had rejected God for the last time.

Realizing the gravity of God's pronouncement, the Israelites mourned greatly. Then, they took it upon themselves to try to rectify their situation. They arose early the next morning and went up the mountain in an effort to take possession of the

---

1

Caleb and Joshua's statement to the Israelites sounds quite similar in nature to the words spoken centuries later by the Apostle Paul in Romans 8:31b (NLT): "If God is for us, who can ever be against us?"

2

The account of this incident in Deuteronomy 1:42–45 (NIV) provides a bit more insight: "But the LORD said to me, 'Tell them, "Do not go up and fight, because I will not be with you. You will be defeated by your enemies."' So I told you, but you would not listen. You rebelled against the LORD's command and in your arrogance you marched up into the hill country. The Amorites who lived in those hills came out against you; they chased you like a swarm of bees and beat you down from Seir all the way to Hormah. You came back and wept before the LORD, but he paid no attention to your weeping and turned a deaf ear to you."

3

What are God's limits? In Numbers 14:22, He stated the Israelites had put Him to the test ten times and had not heeded His voice. While He could have been speaking figuratively, certainly they tested Him on numerous occasions.

Promised Land. Moses warned them the Lord would not be with them and that they would be defeated, but again, they refused to listen. The inhabitants of the land came down, attacking them and driving them back.[2]

Death in the Wilderness

What a sad chapter this was in the history of the Israelite people. The only thing the adults among them had to look forward to now was a long, drawn-out road to death. The younger ones, although they had the Promised Land ahead of them, still had to trudge alongside their elders for the next forty years, witnessing their deaths in the wilderness. God is patient, but in this rebellious encounter with Him, the Israelites learned that He has His limits.[3]

The Israelite people had a hard time developing their faith in God. They had been raised as slaves in a land rife with the worship of false gods. Until Moses reappeared in Egypt, their knowledge of the one true God had been secondhand, passed down to them by their ancestors. Despite all that they had witnessed of God, few of them were ever able to fully overcome the influences from their former life.

Trusting God requires a change in mindset—a change they were unable or unwilling to make. Their lack of faith revealed their disrespect for God. As a result, the Israelites would experience what it meant to have God against them.

Be intentional about developing your faith in God.

How can we today develop a stronger faith in God? A good place to start is by reading the Bible, the inspired Word of God. The Israelites only heard God's Word when it was delivered to them by Moses or read to them later after Moses had written it down.

Forty Years in the Wilderness

When God condemned the Israelites to wander in the wilderness for forty years, to whom did His pronouncement apply? He was speaking to the men who had been counted by Moses and Aaron in the first census who were age twenty and above and able to fight in war (Numbers 1:2–3; 14:28–30). Certainly, every person who grumbled against Him displeased Him, but this group of men would have been the ones who bore the responsibility to enter the Promised Land and take it as God had instructed, and they were the ones who failed to do so. Deuteronomy 2:14–18 also states the hand of the Lord was against the "men of war," or "fighting men."

The men from the tribe of Levi were not counted in the general census and were not subject to this pronouncement. (The Levites were counted separately. See Numbers 1:47–54, 3:15, 3:39, and 26:62.) Their tribe had been set apart to serve God, so their men were not part of the army of Israel, nor was a spy sent out from their tribe.

Moses and Aaron were from the tribe of Levi and should not have been subject to God's pronouncement, but as it turned out, neither of them was allowed to enter the Promised Land. They sinned later while bringing water from the rock at Meribah because they failed to trust God enough to honor Him as holy. As a result, God handed them the same fate as He had the fighting men (Numbers 20:9–13).

How fortunate we are today to have ready access to this fascinating literary collection.

When you read your Bible, ask God to guide you in your studies and open your heart to His Word. As He would later tell the Israelites living in Babylonian exile, "You will seek me and find me when you seek me with all your heart" (Jeremiah 29:13, NIV).

Each page of the Bible reveals something of God's character. The more you read and study your Bible, the more you will come to know God, and your faith will deepen. His great love will become evident, and you will see how He planned for your salvation by sending His Son, Jesus, to earth. You will also see how God has always kept His promises to His people. You can know, with certainty, that He is the same—yesterday, today, and forever—and that He will continue to keep His promises, no matter what.

Know therefore that the LORD your God is God; he is the faithful God, keeping his covenant of love to a thousand generations of those who love him and keep his commandments.

—Deuteronomy 7:9, NIV

The Lord is not slow in keeping his promise, as some understand slowness. Instead he is patient with you, not wanting anyone to perish, but everyone to come to repentance.

—2 Peter 3:9, NIV

Thoughts to Ponder

God once again threatened to destroy the Israelites and make Moses and his lineage a great nation instead. What arguments did Moses present to God to preserve these people?

_____

_____

_____

_____

_____

While "murmuring" usually doesn't involve taking overt action against someone or something, it can create a very powerful force. When the Israelites murmured against Aaron and Moses, what were the deeper implications?

_____

_____

_____

_____

How does this reading show that the "sins of the fathers" can affect their children and future generations? What other examples can you think of where this has happened, in either Bible times or modern day? How can the good things people do impact their children and future generations?

_____

_____

_____

_____

Chapter 37

Korah's Rebellion

Numbers 16:1–35, ESV

(1) Now Korah the son of Izhar, son of Kohath, son of Levi, and Dathan and Abiram the sons of Eliab, and On the son of Peleth, sons of Reuben, took men. (2) And they rose up before Moses, with a number of the people of Israel, 250 chiefs of the congregation, chosen from the assembly, well-known men. (3) They assembled themselves together against Moses and against Aaron and said to them, "You have gone too far! For all in the congregation are holy, every one of them, and the LORD is among them. Why then do you exalt yourselves above the assembly of the LORD?" (4) When Moses heard it, he fell on his face, (5) and he said to Korah and all his company, "In the morning the LORD will show who is his, and who is holy, and will bring him near to him. The one whom he chooses he will bring near to him. (6) Do this: take censers, Korah and all his company; (7) put fire in them and put incense on them before the LORD tomorrow, and the man whom the LORD chooses shall be the holy one. You have gone too far, sons of Levi!" (8) And Moses said to Korah, "Hear now, you sons of Levi: (9) is it too small a thing for you that the God of Israel has separated you from the congregation of Israel, to bring you near to himself, to do service in the tabernacle of the LORD and to stand before the congregation to minister to them, (10) and that he has brought you near him, and all your brothers the sons of Levi with you? And would you seek the priesthood also? (11) Therefore it is against the LORD that you and all your company have gathered together. What is Aaron that you grumble against him?"

(12) And Moses sent to call Dathan and Abiram the sons of Eliab, and they said, "We will not come up. (13) Is it a small thing that you have brought us up out of a land flowing with milk and honey, to kill

us in the wilderness, that you must also make yourself a prince over us? (14) Moreover, you have not brought us into a land flowing with milk and honey, nor given us inheritance of fields and vineyards. Will you put out the eyes of these men? We will not come up." (15) And Moses was very angry and said to the LORD, "Do not respect their offering. I have not taken one donkey from them, and I have not harmed one of them."

(16) And Moses said to Korah, "Be present, you and all your company, before the LORD, you and they, and Aaron, tomorrow. (17) And let every one of you take his censer and put incense on it, and every one of you bring before the LORD his censer, 250 censers; you also, and Aaron, each his censer." (18) So every man took his censer and put fire in them and laid incense on them and stood at the entrance of the tent of meeting with Moses and Aaron. (19) Then Korah assembled all the congregation against them at the entrance of the tent of meeting. And the glory of the LORD appeared to all the congregation.

(20) And the LORD spoke to Moses and to Aaron, saying, (21) "Separate yourselves from among this congregation, that I may consume them in a moment." (22) And they fell on their faces and said, "O God, the God of the spirits of all flesh, shall one man sin, and will you be angry with all the congregation?" (23) And the LORD spoke to Moses, saying, (24) "Say to the congregation, Get away from the dwelling of Korah, Dathan, and Abiram."

(25) Then Moses rose and went to Dathan and Abiram, and the elders of Israel followed him. (26) And he spoke to the congregation, saying, "Depart, please, from the tents of these wicked men, and touch nothing of theirs, lest you be swept away with all their sins." (27) So they got away from the dwelling of Korah, Dathan, and Abiram. And Dathan and Abiram came out and stood at the door of their tents, together with their wives, their sons, and their little ones. (28) And Moses said, "Hereby you shall know that the LORD has sent me to do all these works, and that it has not been of my own accord. (29) If these men die as all men die, or if they are visited by the fate of all mankind, then the LORD has not sent me. (30) But if the LORD creates something new, and the ground opens its mouth and swallows them up with all that belongs to them, and they go down alive into Sheol, then you shall know that these men have despised the LORD."

(31) And as soon as he had finished speaking all these words, the ground under them split apart. (32) And the earth opened its mouth and swallowed them up, with their households and all the people who belonged to Korah and all their goods. (33) So they and all that belonged to them went down alive into Sheol, and the earth closed over them, and they perished from the midst of the assembly. (34) And all Israel who were around them fled at their cry, for they said, "Lest the earth swallow us up!" (35) And fire came out from the LORD and consumed the 250 men offering the incense.

◇◇◇

Korah was a first cousin to Moses and Aaron.[1] (See Moses's Family Tree on page xvi.) The Kohathite family, of which Korah was a member, was part of the tribe of Levi and held a special position in the Israelite community. They were in charge of the most holy things in the Tabernacle.[2]

Korah's scheming for this insurrection must have been in the works for a while for it to involve so many people. He had gathered support from 250 of the community leaders, some of whom were fellow Levites.[3] They contended that the whole Levite community was holy, and the Lord was with them all. Then they accused Moses and Aaron of acting as if they were greater than everyone else. Perhaps they didn't like being under Moses and Aaron's oversight, or maybe they wanted to be honored or recognized more publicly for their position and responsibilities.

When Moses heard this, he fell on his face. He understood the gravity of this challenge. He held his leadership position not because he had desired it but because God had placed him there. Moses acted in accordance with God's instructions, and he knew that Korah and his followers were, in fact, challenging God.

> When Moses heard this, he fell on his face.

Addressing the Levites in the group, Moses reminded them that God had chosen them for the privileged position they held. He had brought them near to Himself to care for the Lord's Tabernacle and to stand before the community and minister to them. Wasn't this distinction enough, Moses asked, or did they now desire the priesthood as well?

Then Moses turned his attention toward Dathan and Abiram, who evidently were not present.[4] When Moses sent for them, they refused to come. In fact, their defiance leaps off the page in this account.[5] You can hear their contempt for Moses when they declared he had taken them *out* of a land flowing with milk

Suggested Song

"As the Deer" (tinyurl. com/y83kpkxe)

(This song is based on Psalm 42, which is credited to the sons of Korah.)

———— 1 ————

Korah's father, Izhar, and Amram, the father of Moses and Aaron, were brothers. They were both sons of Kohath, who was a son of Levi, the third-born son of Jacob, or Israel. Genesis 29:31–35 gives the account of the births of Jacob's first four sons, who were by Leah. Levi's descendants are given in Exodus 6:16–25, including Korah in verse 21 and Korah's sons in verse 24.

———— 2 ————

The tribe of Levi did not receive a physical inheritance like the other tribes. Rather, God had set them apart to serve Him (Numbers 3:11–13). He placed them under the oversight of Aaron and his sons, whom God had chosen to be the priests for the Israelites (Numbers 3:5–10). The descendants of each of the three sons of Levi—Gershon, Kohath, and Merari—had been assigned specific duties. The Kohathites were responsible for the care of the sanctuary itself, which included the ark, table, lampstand, altars, curtain, and all the other items set apart for ministering before the Lord. These were the most holy things, and special care had to be taken in handling them. A brief description of the duties of each of these descendants of Levi is given in Numbers 3:21–37, while Numbers 4 provides more of the details.

——————— 3 ———————

Moses specifically admonished the Levites who rebelled in Numbers 16:7b–11.

——————— 4 ———————

These two men were brothers and the sons of Eliab, who was the son of Pallu, who was the son of Reuben. Like Moses, Aaron, and Korah, their great-grandfathers had been among the original twelve sons of Jacob. Their lineage is given in Numbers 26:4–11, along with a brief summary of Korah's rebellion.

Notice that On, the son of Peleth, is mentioned only in Numbers 16:1. He is not mentioned when Moses goes to find Dathan and Abiram, nor is he or his father mentioned anywhere else in the whole Bible.

——————— 5 ———————

On multiple occasions, God referred to the Israelite community as a "stiff-necked people." Stubborn and unwilling to accept instructions, they often expressed their discontent by grumbling against Moses and Aaron, who were simply following through on God's instructions. All of the insurrectionists exemplified this character trait.

and honey, meaning Egypt, to kill them in the wilderness! In reality, the only thing for them in Egypt had been slavery, back-breaking work, and misery. God had *rescued* them and *preserved* their lives in the wilderness by guiding them with His presence, providing them with food and water, and helping them defeat their attackers.

Rather than showing gratitude, Dathan and Abiram accused Moses of acting like a prince, lording his position over them. Then, to rub salt in the wound, they claimed Moses had not delivered on his promise to bring them into a land flowing with milk and honey, nor had he provided them with an inheritance of fields and vineyards. (In truth, it had been the *Israelites* who refused to cross over and take the Promised Land when given the opportunity.) With a final inflammatory insult, they ended by asking if Moses and Aaron were also going to gouge out the eyes of these men.[6]

Rather than defend himself to his accusers, Moses let God make it clear whom He had chosen as holy or set apart for His purposes. Moses instructed each of the Levites to bring censers[7] in the morning to offer incense before the Lord. It would be up to God to decide who was holy. But after the diatribe from Dathan and Abiram, Moses was angry. He had never wronged any of them nor taken as much as a donkey from them,[8] something God, of course, already knew. Wounded by their words, Moses asked God not to accept Dathan and Abiram's offering, presumably referring to the offering of incense that was to occur in the morning.

The next morning, Korah and his followers and Moses and Aaron gathered before the Tabernacle, or tent of meeting. God was ready to put an end to the rebellion and told Moses and Aaron to get away from the others. Had not Moses and Aaron fallen facedown and begged for the very ones who stood against them, God would have destroyed them right there.

God then told Moses to instruct everyone to move away from the tents of Korah, Dathan, and Abiram.[9] Defiant to the end, Dathan and Abiram, along with their wives and children, came out and stood at the entrances of their tents. In one of the most dramatic scenes in the Bible, the earth split apart under the tents belonging to these three men and swallowed them alive, along with all who were with them and their possessions. As the earth closed back up, the Israelites who were there fled for fear of being swallowed up as well. Then, adding to the drama of the moment, fire from the Lord consumed the 250 men who were offering incense!

Defiance toward God

What motivated these people to rise up against Moses and Aaron? With Korah and the other Levites, it seems to have been a power struggle. The Levites had been set apart by God for His service, and Korah came from the same family of Levites as Moses and Aaron. They saw themselves as being just as good and just as holy as Moses and Aaron. In fact, their argument sounded very similar to that presented by Miriam and Aaron when they had spoken against Moses earlier in Numbers 12.

Dathan and Abiram, as members of the tribe of Reuben, had no connection to the priesthood. Recall that Reuben was the oldest of Jacob's sons, and his descendants should have enjoyed the privileges afforded to the firstborn. Jacob, however, in his final blessing, essentially denied Reuben that status.[10] Whether Dathan and Abiram felt their tribe had been cheated out of their birthright or they simply got swept up in the discontent Korah incited is unknown. Their sins, however, were so egregious in God's sight that He destroyed not only these men but also their families and possessions. Interestingly, Korah's children were spared.[11]

───── 6 ─────

The cruel and merciless act of gouging out someone's eyes was occasionally done in Bible times when a conqueror overcame an enemy, permanently handicapping them. Examples include Samson, whose eyes the Philistines gouged out after finally capturing him (Judges 16:21), and King Zedekiah of Judah, whose eyes King Nebuchadnezzar of Babylon had gouged out after being made to watch all his sons be killed before him (Jeremiah 52:8–11). It is unclear what Dathan and Abiram actually meant by this statement.

───── 7 ─────

A censer was a bowl-shaped utensil with a handle that was used to carry hot coals from the altar. Incense could also be placed on top of the coals and burned in the censer. A description of how it was used on the Day of Atonement is given in Leviticus 16:12–13.

───── 8 ─────

The donkey or ass was likely considered one of the least valuable animals in their livestock herds. It was not a "clean" animal and, therefore, was not to be eaten (clean and unclean animals are described in Leviticus 11). Neither could a donkey be used as a sacrifice. When Moses said he had not taken so much as a donkey from them, he was stating he had not defrauded these men of anything, not even something of so little value.

——— 9 ———
Even though Korah was a Kohathite from the tribe of Levi, and Dathan and Abiram were from the tribe of Reuben, it just happened that they all camped on the south side of the Tabernacle. Their tents were likely fairly close to one another. A diagram of the layout of the Israelite camp is presented in this article: "Encampment of the Tribes of Israel in the Wilderness" (tinyurl.com/52hhyupt). Scroll down to see the diagram of the camp.

——— 10 ———

Jacob denied Reuben the blessing normally afforded the oldest son because he had slept with his concubine, Bilhah, who was Rachel's servant and the mother of his sons, Dan and Naphtali. This incident is recorded in Genesis 35:22. Jacob gave his blessing to his sons in Genesis 49, with Reuben's being given in verses 3–4.

——— 11 ———

When the second census was taken, those from the tribe of Reuben are mentioned in Numbers 26:5–11. Verses 9–10 talk about the rebellion of Dathan, Abiram, and Korah, and verse 11 (NKJV) states: "Nevertheless the children of Korah did not die." Korah's sons are named in Exodus 6:24.

——— 12 ———

"It is a fearful thing to fall into the hands of the living God" (Hebrews 10:31, NKJV).

Acting in defiance of God never works.

How could people who had witnessed firsthand God's power and might on multiple occasions think they could succeed in standing against the leaders God had chosen and the organizational structure He had put in place? Korah, no matter how many followers he gathered, could not have succeeded. Dathan and Abiram severely twisted the truth and then assaulted Moses with their distorted facts. Their defiance of Moses defied God's authority. God is patient, but as this incident again illustrates, He has His limits.

People today continue to act in defiance of God. Even though we live under the New Covenant and Jesus has paid the price for our sins, individuals must take it upon themselves to accept Him as their Savior in order to ultimately be saved. There *will* come a day of reckoning, and as these men all found out, it is a fearful thing to fall into the hands of the living God.[12]

Woe to him who strives with his Maker!

—Isaiah 45:9a, NKJV

There is no wisdom, no insight, no plan that can succeed against the LORD.

—Proverbs 21:30, NIV

Thoughts to Ponder

When Moses fell facedown, what did it signify? Toward whom was this action directed? What do you think he was thinking or speaking while he lay on the ground? Although this action is not customarily done today, how can you apply the meaning of Moses's response to handling challenges in your own life?

_____

_____

_____

_____

Why do you think God spared Korah's sons but destroyed the entire families of Dathan and Abiram? Who were some of the descendants of Korah? (See 1 Chronicles 6:33–38.) Psalm 42 is among the eleven psalms credited to the sons of Korah. This article provides more information on the sons of Korah: "Who Were the Sons of Korah in the Old Testament?" (tinyurl.com/59as3xfx).

_____

_____

_____

_____

Galatians 6:7 (NKJV) states: "Do not be deceived, God is not mocked; for whatever a man sows, that he will also reap." What does this scripture mean? Discuss it in light of today's lesson. This article provides a good discussion of the topic: "What Does It Mean That God Is Not Mocked?" (tinyurl.com/2p937afb).

_____

_____

_____

Chapter 38

God Reaffirms His Leaders

Numbers 16:36–17:13, ESV

(16:36) Then the LORD spoke to Moses, saying, (37) "Tell Eleazar the son of Aaron the priest to take up the censers out of the blaze. Then scatter the fire far and wide, for they have become holy. (38) As for the censers of these men who have sinned at the cost of their lives, let them be made into hammered plates as a covering for the altar, for they offered them before the LORD, and they became holy. Thus they shall be a sign to the people of Israel." (39) So Eleazar the priest took the bronze censers, which those who were burned had offered, and they were hammered out as a covering for the altar, (40) to be a reminder to the people of Israel, so that no outsider, who is not of the descendants of Aaron, should draw near to burn incense before the LORD, lest he become like Korah and his company—as the LORD said to him through Moses.

(41) But on the next day all the congregation of the people of Israel grumbled against Moses and against Aaron, saying, "You have killed the people of the LORD." (42) And when the congregation had assembled against Moses and against Aaron, they turned toward the tent of meeting. And behold, the cloud covered it, and the glory of the LORD appeared. (43) And Moses and Aaron came to the front of the tent of meeting, (44) and the LORD spoke to Moses, saying, (45) "Get away from the midst of this congregation, that I may consume them in a moment." And they fell on their faces. (46) And Moses said to Aaron, "Take your censer, and put fire on it from off the altar and lay incense on it and carry it quickly to the congregation and make atonement for them, for wrath has gone out from the LORD; the plague has begun." (47) So Aaron took it as Moses said and ran into the midst of the assembly. And behold, the plague had already begun among the people. And he put on the incense and made atonement for the

people. (48) And he stood between the dead and the living, and the plague was stopped. (49) Now those who died in the plague were 14,700, besides those who died in the affair of Korah. (50) And Aaron returned to Moses at the entrance of the tent of meeting, when the plague was stopped.

(17:1) The LORD spoke to Moses, saying, (2) "Speak to the people of Israel, and get from them staffs, one for each fathers' house, from all their chiefs according to their fathers' houses, twelve staffs. Write each man's name on his staff, (3) and write Aaron's name on the staff of Levi. For there shall be one staff for the head of each fathers' house. (4) Then you shall deposit them in the tent of meeting before the testimony, where I meet with you. (5) And the staff of the man whom I choose shall sprout. Thus I will make to cease from me the grumblings of the people of Israel, which they grumble against you." (6) Moses spoke to the people of Israel. And all their chiefs gave him staffs, one for each chief, according to their fathers' houses, twelve staffs. And the staff of Aaron was among their staffs. (7) And Moses deposited the staffs before the LORD in the tent of the testimony.

(8) On the next day Moses went into the tent of the testimony, and behold, the staff of Aaron for the house of Levi had sprouted and put forth buds and produced blossoms, and it bore ripe almonds. (9) Then Moses brought out all the staffs from before the LORD to all the people of Israel. And they looked, and each man took his staff. (10) And the LORD said to Moses, "Put back the staff of Aaron before the testimony, to be kept as a sign for the rebels, that you may make an end of their grumblings against me, lest they die." (11) Thus did Moses; as the LORD commanded him, so he did.

(12) And the people of Israel said to Moses, "Behold, we perish, we are undone, we are all undone. (13) Everyone who comes near, who comes near to the tabernacle of the LORD, shall die. Are we all to perish?"

◇◇◇

Suggested Song

"Holy, Holy, Holy! Lord God Almighty"

(tinyurl.com/27x9asn3)

Disastrous events had just occurred in the Israelite camp. The earth had split open, swallowing tents and entire families. Then fire had consumed the rebellious Levites. Those who witnessed these happenings fled the scene, fearful for their lives.

In the aftermath of this tragedy, God instructed Moses to have Eleazar, Aaron's son, pick up the censers of the men who had died.[1] These items had been presented to the Lord and, as such, were holy.[2] After scattering their contents some distance away, Eleazar was to hammer them flat and create a bronze plate to use as a covering for the altar. This covering would then serve as a reminder to the Israelites that no one except the descendants of Aaron should come near to offer incense before the Lord, or else they would become like Korah and his followers.

> This great show of God's might should have made a lasting impression on the whole camp.

This great show of God's might should have made a lasting impression on the whole camp. But instead, *the very next day*, the Israelites murmured against Moses and Aaron and accused them of killing God's people. Their grumblings turned into a gathering, and as they stood in opposition to Moses and Aaron, the cloud suddenly covered the Tabernacle. As the glory of the Lord appeared, Moses and Aaron approached the front of the Tabernacle. Once again, God told Moses to move away from the assembly so He could consume these people. Just as they had done before, Moses and Aaron fell facedown. Moses pleaded for the people, begging God not to destroy them.

This time, however, God would not yield. When Moses realized what was happening, he told Aaron to take a censer, fill it with fire from the altar, and place incense on it. Then he told him to hurry to the assembly to make atonement for the people. Aaron did as Moses instructed and ran into the midst of the people with the burning incense. The wrath of God had gone out among them, and a deadly plague had already begun. As Aaron stood between the living and the dead, he presented the offering of incense to God to make atonement for the sins of the people. With that, the plague was stopped.

In a matter of two days, approximately 15,000 people had paid the ultimate price for challenging God's authority—14,700 people died in this plague, while 250 had been consumed the day before in Korah's rebellion, along with the households of Dathan

---

1

Eleazar was Aaron's third-born son; however, he was now the oldest surviving son after the deaths of Nadab and Abihu, who were killed for offering unauthorized fire before the Lord (Leviticus 10:1–2). Eleazar was chief over the leaders of the Levites, overseeing those who took care of the sanctuary (Numbers 3:32). Specifically, his duties included the oil for the lamp, the sweet incense, the daily grain offering, and the anointing oil. He was also to oversee the Tabernacle and everything in it, including the sanctuary and its furnishings (Numbers 4:16).

2

Evidently, the censers the 250 men brought were their own (i.e., not belonging to the Tabernacle furnishings), but because they had been presented before the Lord, albeit with unauthorized fire and incense, they had become holy. Leviticus 27:28 (NKJV) bears this out: "Nevertheless no devoted offering that a man may devote to the LORD of all that he has, both man and beast, or the field of his possession, shall be sold or redeemed; every devoted offering is most holy to the LORD." Because of the specific priestly duties to which he had been appointed, Eleazar would have been authorized to handle these censers, which were now deemed holy to the Lord.

──── 3 ────

The writer of Hebrews describes the Tabernacle and how it was arranged in Hebrews 9:1–5. In verse 4, the contents of the ark of the covenant are listed.

──── 4 ────

A fire pan or censer was used to bring coals of fire from the bronze altar to use on the altar of incense. Leviticus 16:11–14 describes how Aaron was to enter the Most Holy Place to make atonement once a year. He was to first light the incense so that the cloud of incense could cover or shroud the mercy seat where the presence of God resided, lest he die.

So important was the source of fire that Nadab and Abihu, Aaron's oldest two sons, were struck dead for using foreign or profane fire before the Lord (Leviticus 10:1; Numbers 3:4).

──── 5 ────

The directions God gave Moses concerning the composition of the incense are given in Exodus 30:34–38. This special mixture was holy and was to be used only for worshiping God.

──── 6 ────

God's instructions concerning the burning of incense on the altar of incense are given in Exodus 30:7–10. This altar was not to be used for a burnt offering, a meal offering, or a drink offering, and only the special mixture of holy incense was to be used.

and Abiram, who had been swallowed by the earth. What tragedy had befallen the Israelites! But finally, God had quelled the rebellion.

To make certain the Israelites understood without question whom God had chosen for the priesthood, He ordered a further demonstration. Twelve rods were to be brought, one from each of the leaders of the twelve tribes. God would indicate whom He had chosen by causing that tribe's rod to blossom. The rods were to be inscribed with each man's name. Aaron's name was to be written on the rod of Levi and placed among the rods. When this was done, Moses placed all the rods in the Tabernacle.

The next day, when Moses returned to the Tabernacle, only one rod had blossomed. It was Aaron's rod, and it had sprouted, budded, blossomed, and even produced ripe almonds! It was as if the dead stick had once again become a living branch. Moses brought the rods out, and each leader took back his own. God then instructed Aaron's rod to be kept in the Tabernacle as a sign to the rebellious. By reaffirming His choice of Aaron as high priest in such a dramatic and decisive way, He sought to put an end to their grumblings so no more would die.

Atonement for the People

Under the Law, the offering of incense played an important role in worshiping God. Priests burned the fragrant incense on a small altar overlaid with gold that stood inside the Tabernacle before the opening to the Most Holy Place. Inside the Most Holy Place was the ark of the covenant, which contained the tablets of the covenant, a jar of manna, and soon to be added, Aaron's rod, which budded and bore almonds.[3] Atop the ark was a covering called the mercy seat or atonement cover. This covering featured two cherubim, and it was above the mercy seat between the cherubim that the presence of God resided. It was here, in the Most Holy Place, that God would meet with Moses. The aroma of the incense that burned just outside the thick curtain that separated the Most Holy Place from the rest of the Tabernacle permeated the entire area, making a sweet smell before the Lord.

The fire for the altar of incense was to come from the larger bronze altar used for sacrifices which stood outside the Tabernacle in the courtyard.[4] Only incense made according to God's specific directions could be burned on the altar of incense,[5] and no other type of offering could be made on this particular altar.[6] Aaron was to burn incense on this altar every morning when he tended the lamps and again at twilight. This corresponded to the times when the sacrifices were made on the bronze altar outside.

As soon as it became apparent that the plague had started, Moses knew an offering was needed. By having Aaron, God's appointed high priest, bring out the censer with fire from the altar and use it to burn the holy incense, Moses was having him replicate what usually occurred inside the Tabernacle on the altar of incense. In this manner, Aaron was able to bring an acceptable offering into the midst of the people and thereby make atonement for their sins. For those who witnessed this intercession, there could be no doubt Aaron was, indeed, God's chosen high priest. By standing among the people with his offering of incense, Aaron's actions encouraged God to stop the plague.

Jesus is our offering.

The offering Jesus presented was Himself, the perfect sacrifice for the sins of the world. With His resurrection, He defeated death *forever* and broke the curse that sin held over the world. As Christians, we can view the physical death we will someday experience as only a temporary threshold, one that we gladly step over into the welcoming arms of Jesus and the eternal presence of God.

Aaron, as high priest, offered to God the sweetest sacrifice he had available. Let the striking image presented in these

The Tabernacle and Its Altars

There were two altars associated with the Tabernacle. The altar of burnt offerings was overlaid with bronze and stood in the courtyard outside the door to the Tabernacle. It was used to make animal, grain, and drink offerings. How the bronze altar was to be used and the offerings that were to be made on it are given in Exodus 29:38–46.

The altar of incense was smaller and overlaid with gold. It stood inside the Tabernacle, in front of the Most Holy Place (or Holy of Holies), where the ark of the covenant was kept behind the curtain. This altar was for the burning of incense and not for making the other types of sacrificial offerings. How the golden altar of incense was to be made and used is described in Exodus 30:1–10.

The mercy seat was the covering for the ark of the covenant, which was kept inside the Most Holy Place. It was there that the presence of God in the cloud would hover

(Leviticus 16:2). How the mercy seat was to be made is given in Exodus 25:17–22. In verse 22, God told Moses He would meet with him there and speak with him.

God presented Moses with plans for the Tabernacle in Exodus 25:8–Exodus 27. It was a temporary structure that the Israelites used for worship during their wilderness wanderings and up until when Solomon built the temple in Jerusalem. The temple was built with the same floor plan as the Tabernacle.

This article contains several depictions of the layout of the Tabernacle: "What Is the Holy of Holies?" (tinyurl.com/2cshmjkr).

scriptures—of Aaron going out among the people with his offering of incense—remind us of the perfect offering Jesus made in order to save us from eternal death. Let us also remember that Jesus has never stopped working on our behalf. When He fulfilled His role on earth, He ascended into heaven, where He now sits at the right hand of God. He became our High Priest for all time. And unlike Aaron and his descendants, Jesus will never falter. He lives to intercede for those who come to God through Him.

There were many priests under the old system, for death prevented them from remaining in office. But because Jesus lives forever, his priesthood lasts forever. Therefore he is able, once and forever, to save those who come to God through him. He lives forever to intercede with God on their behalf.

—Hebrews 7:23–25, NLT

Unlike those other high priests, he does not need to offer sacrifices every day. They did this for their own sins first and then for the sins of the people. But Jesus did this once for all when he offered himself as the sacrifice for the people's sins. The law appointed high priests who were limited by human weakness. But after the law was given, God appointed his Son with an oath, and his Son has been made the perfect High Priest forever.

—Hebrews 7:27–28, NLT

Thoughts to Ponder

After witnessing these catastrophes, how did the people respond? (See Numbers 16:34 and Numbers 17:12–13.) For children of God, what would have been a better response? What can we learn from these people?

_____

_____

_____

_____

_____

What was the purpose of the incense offering? What is incense sometimes symbolic of in the Scriptures? (See Psalm 141:2, Revelation 5:8, and Revelation 8:3–4.) This article talks about the symbolism of incense: "Signs & Symbols of the Bible (Incense)" (tinyurl.com/3r58e35n).

_____

_____

_____

_____

_____

Why are Christians no longer required to offer sacrifices on altars? Rather, what is your sacrifice or offering to be?

_____

_____

_____

_____

Chapter 39

Moses Strikes the Rock

Numbers 20:1–13, 22–29, NLT

(1) In the first month of the year, the whole community of Israel arrived in the wilderness of Zin and camped at Kadesh. While they were there, Miriam died and was buried.

(2) There was no water for the people to drink at that place, so they rebelled against Moses and Aaron. (3) The people blamed Moses and said, "If only we had died in the LORD's presence with our brothers! (4) Why have you brought the congregation of the LORD's people into this wilderness to die, along with all our livestock? (5) Why did you make us leave Egypt and bring us here to this terrible place? This land has no grain, no figs, no grapes, no pomegranates, and no water to drink!"

(6) Moses and Aaron turned away from the people and went to the entrance of the Tabernacle, where they fell face down on the ground. Then the glorious presence of the LORD appeared to them, (7) and the LORD said to Moses, (8) "You and Aaron must take the staff and assemble the entire community. As the people watch, speak to the rock over there, and it will pour out its water. You will provide enough water from the rock to satisfy the whole community and their livestock."

(9) So Moses did as he was told. He took the staff from the place where it was kept before the LORD. (10) Then he and Aaron summoned the people to come and gather at the rock. "Listen, you rebels!" he shouted. "Must we bring you water from this rock?" (11) Then Moses raised his hand and struck the rock twice with the staff, and water gushed out. So the entire community and their livestock drank their fill.

(12) But the LORD said to Moses and Aaron, "Because you did not trust me enough to demonstrate my holiness to the people of Israel, you will not lead them into the land I am giving them!" (13) This place was

known as the waters of Meribah (which means "arguing") because there the people of Israel argued with the LORD, and there he demonstrated his holiness among them.

[Verses 14–21 give the account of Edom refusing to let the Israelites pass through their territory.]

(22) The whole community of Israel left Kadesh and arrived at Mount Hor. (23) There, on the border of the land of Edom, the LORD said to Moses and Aaron, (24) "The time has come for Aaron to join his ancestors in death. He will not enter the land I am giving the people of Israel, because the two of you rebelled against my instructions concerning the water at Meribah. (25) Now take Aaron and his son Eleazar up Mount Hor. (26) There you will remove Aaron's priestly garments and put them on Eleazar, his son. Aaron will die there and join his ancestors."

(27) So Moses did as the LORD commanded. The three of them went up Mount Hor together as the whole community watched. (28) At the summit, Moses removed the priestly garments from Aaron and put them on Eleazar, Aaron's son. Then Aaron died there on top of the mountain, and Moses and Eleazar went back down. (29) When the people realized that Aaron had died, all Israel mourned for him thirty days.

Suggested Song

"Lord Speak to Me"

(tinyurl.com/244dumzk)

By the time the events in this chapter occur, the Israelites are close to the end of their forty years of wandering in the wilderness. Scriptures record only a few highlights of those interim years, such as Korah's rebellion, but Moses did provide a listing of their encampment sites in Numbers 33. Because the phrase, *the whole Israelite community* (or *congregation*), is used here in Numbers 20:1 and also in verse 22, some commentators feel many of the people had been dispersed throughout the region during the intervening years and were called back together as the end of the forty years drew near. Regardless, they are all together now when this chapter begins with the death and burial of Miriam, the older sister of Moses and Aaron.

Once again, with all of them gathered in one location, there is no water. As the people contend with Moses, they offer up their same old arguments. You're probably thinking—don't they know by now that God will take care of them? Obviously not, but remember, years have passed since their last recorded water crisis. The people who are now grumbling were likely younger than twenty when God sentenced the Israelites to wander in the wilderness for forty years. But, while the older generation must be close to extinction by this point in time, they seem to have taught the younger ones their grievances against Moses.

What pain this stunning lack of faith must have caused Moses! These people would soon enter the Promised Land in fulfillment of God's centuries-old promise to Abraham, and yet, they were unable to see beyond their temporary conditions. Moses and Aaron turned away from them and went toward the Tabernacle, where they fell facedown before the entrance. The glory of the Lord appeared to them there, and God told Moses to take his staff and his brother and assemble the people. He was to speak to the rock, and it would bring forth water sufficient for both the people and their animals.

> What pain this stunning lack of faith must have caused Moses!

On previous occasions, God had commanded Moses to strike with his rod or staff in performing miracles. In the first plague upon the Egyptians, the waters in the river turned to blood upon being struck with his rod.[1] When God supplied the Israelites with water at Rephidim, He told Moses to strike the rock at Horeb.[2] This time, however, God instructed Moses to take his staff but to only speak to the rock. How much more impressive it would have been to speak water into existence without taking an accompanying action. Undeniably, such a feat could only have been performed by the divine will of God. But Moses did not do that.

Instead, Moses struck the rock—not once, but twice. Even worse, he failed to credit God for the miracle. For almost forty years, Moses had led these people in an effort to deliver them to a reward for which they seemingly had little appreciation. Time and again, he had endured their contending with him,

[1] See Exodus 7:17–20 for the account of the river being turned into blood.

[2] See Exodus 17:5–7 for the account of water coming from the rock at Horeb.

3

As Paul wrote in Romans 3:4 (HCSB): "God must be true, even if everyone is a liar."

4

In Numbers 27:12–14, God explained that both Moses and Aaron disobeyed his command to honor him as holy before the eyes of the community when they rebelled at the waters in the Desert of Zin.

5

From the ages given for Moses (80) and Aaron (83) in Exodus 7:7 when they spoke to Pharaoh, we know that Moses was three years younger than Aaron. That made him approximately 120 at the time of Aaron's death. Deuteronomy 34:7 states Moses was 120 when he died, so we know that the events in this chapter occurred shortly before Moses's own death.

6

"The gifts and sacrifices being offered were not able to clear the conscience of the worshiper. They are only a matter of food and drink and various ceremonial washings—external regulations applying until the time of the new order" (Hebrews 9:9b–10, NIV).

sometimes to the point of fearing for his life. Multiple times, he had interceded for these people, begging God to spare them from His wrath. Now, the Promised Land was so near, and the older generation was almost gone. How Moses's heart must have sunk to hear the same faithless refrain coming from the lips of the very ones who were set to cross over and claim the inheritance promised by God.

Moses sinned with his actions and his words, yet God was faithful. The Almighty provided the water as He had promised. Man is fallible, but God is holy; He cannot lie or falter on His promises.[3] Yet, by the same token, He could not allow this sin to go unpunished. The consequence of Moses's sin was that neither Moses nor Aaron would be allowed to enter the Promised Land.[4]

The Failings of Man

Once he finally accepted God's calling, Moses had proved himself faithful in all that God had asked him to do. Yet he was human, and this time he fell short. He had been the intermediator on so many occasions for the Israelites, begging on their behalf for God's forgiveness. Now, when he, the intermediator, sinned, who was there to intercede for him? Unfortunately, no one.

Then there was Aaron. He was not the one who struck the rock or took credit for providing the water, so why did God punish him as well? God had sent both Moses and Aaron to perform this miracle. As God's chosen high priest, Aaron could have stopped Moses and, in fact, should have stopped him from taking the credit that was due to God alone.

Yet, as with the incident of the golden calf, Aaron lacked the strength of character to confront the sinner and thereby possibly prevent further sin from occurring. Aaron was complicit in the sin Moses committed, and as James would later state, "So whoever knows the right thing to do and fails to do it, for him it is sin" (James 4:17, ESV).

With the forty years of wandering drawing to a close, it was not long after this incident that God determined it was time for Aaron to die. Near the border of Edom, God instructed Moses to take Aaron and Aaron's son, Eleazar, and go up Mt. Hor. There, in the sight of the whole community, Moses removed Aaron's priestly garments and put them on Eleazar. With that, Eleazar became the high priest. He would now be the one to perform all the duties that had been assigned to Aaron and would cross over with the Israelites into the Promised Land. In Numbers 33:38–39, we are told Aaron died at age 123, on the first day of the fifth month of the fortieth year after the Israelites came out of Egypt.[5]

Our perfect high priest lives forever and intercedes for us.

No matter how hard Moses and Aaron may have tried, they, like all humans, were imperfect. While God had established various sacrifices under the Law to be offered as atonement for sin, they were imperfect sacrifices and could not take away sin.[6] Rather, the sacrifices the high priest offered when he entered the Holy of Holies served as an annual reminder of sins.[7] Not until Jesus came and offered Himself as the perfect sacrifice, once and for all time, could the requirements of the Law be fulfilled and the New Covenant brought into effect.[8]

How gratifying it is to know that the blood of Christ covered the sins of those who lived under the Law, just as it covers the sins of Christians today. The writer of Hebrews explained in Hebrews 9:15b (NIV): "he has died as a ransom to set them free from the sins committed under the first covenant." The prophet Jeremiah had foretold of this New Covenant God would establish, and with its coming, the Lord declared: "I will forgive their wickedness and will remember their sins no more" (Jeremiah

————— 7 —————

"The law is only a shadow of the good things that are coming—not the realities themselves. For this reason it can never, by the same sacrifices repeated endlessly year after year, make perfect those who draw near to worship. Otherwise, would they not have stopped being offered? For the worshipers would have been cleansed once for all, and would no longer have felt guilty for their sins. But those sacrifices are an annual reminder of sins. It is impossible for the blood of bulls and goats to take away sins" (Hebrews 10:1–4, NIV).

————— 8 —————

"Day after day every priest stands and performs his religious duties; again and again he offers the same sacrifices, which can never take away sins. But when this priest had offered for all time one sacrifice for sins, he sat down at the right hand of God, and since that time he waits for his enemies to be made his footstool. For by one sacrifice he has made perfect forever those who are being made holy" (Hebrews 10:11–14, NIV).

—————— 9 ——————

See Jeremiah 31:31–34 for the prophecy concerning the New Covenant, which God would make with the house of Israel. The writer of Hebrews cites part of this prophecy in Hebrews 10:11–18 and explains that Christ's one sacrifice made perfect forever those who are being made holy.

31:34b, NIV). What glorious news this must have been to God's people who lived under the Law! Finally, this New Covenant would bring true and eternal forgiveness and not merely atonement for their sins.[9]

What glorious news this remains for Christians today. Jesus's sacrifice completely covers our sins. We no longer need to offer sacrifices as the Israelites did under the Law because Christ was the perfect sacrifice. When we become Christians, we are truly forgiven of our sins, and as the Hebrew writer tells us, "where these have been forgiven, sacrifice for sin is no longer necessary" (Hebrews 10:18, NIV).

Thank you, God, for your indescribable gift of forgiveness made possible through your precious Son!

Blessed is the one whose transgressions are forgiven, whose sins are covered. Blessed is the one whose sin the LORD does not count against them and in whose spirit is no deceit.

—Psalm 32:1–2, NIV

If we claim to be without sin, we deceive ourselves and the truth is not in us. If we confess our sins, he is faithful and just and will forgive us our sins and purify us from all unrighteousness.

—1 John 1:8–9, NIV

Thoughts to Ponder

Even as the time to enter the Promised Land drew near, the people were almost taunting Moses and Aaron with the fact that where they were at the moment had no grain, figs, vines, or pomegranates. Who else had presented a similar argument to Moses? What happened to them?

_____

_____

_____

_____

_____

If the Law was imperfect, why did God put it in place at all if He planned to replace it later? What purpose did it serve? (See Galatians 3:19–29.)

_____

_____

_____

_____

In what ways does Christ fulfill for Christians today both the roles that Moses and Aaron had under the Law? How is He superior to them?

_____

_____

_____

_____

GOD'S PLAN IS GREATER THAN WE CAN IMAGINE

Chapter 40

Moses's Death Draws Near

Numbers 21:4–9; 27:12–23; Deuteronomy 3:23–29, HCSB

(Num. 21:4) Then they set out from Mount Hor by way of the Red Sea to bypass the land of Edom, but the people became impatient because of the journey. (5) The people spoke against God and Moses: "Why have you led us up from Egypt to die in the wilderness? There is no bread or water, and we detest this wretched food!" (6) Then the LORD sent poisonous snakes among the people, and they bit them so that many Israelites died.

(7) The people then came to Moses and said, "We have sinned by speaking against the LORD and against you. Intercede with the LORD so that He will take the snakes away from us." And Moses interceded for the people.

(8) Then the LORD said to Moses, "Make a snake image and mount it on a pole. When anyone who is bitten looks at it, he will recover." (9) So Moses made a bronze snake and mounted it on a pole. Whenever someone was bitten, and he looked at the bronze snake, he recovered.

◇◇◇

(Num. 27:12) Then the LORD said to Moses, "Go up this mountain of the Abarim range and see the land that I have given the Israelites. (13) After you have seen it, you will also be gathered to your people, as Aaron your brother was. (14) When the community quarreled in the Wilderness of Zin, both of you rebelled against My command to show My holiness in their sight at the waters." Those were the waters of Meribah of Kadesh in the Wilderness of Zin.

(15) So Moses appealed to the LORD, (16) "May the LORD, the God of the spirits of all flesh, appoint a man over the community

(17) who will go out before them and come back in before them, and who will bring them out and bring them in, so that the LORD's community won't be like sheep without a shepherd."

(18) The LORD replied to Moses, "Take Joshua son of Nun, a man who has the Spirit in him, and lay your hands on him. (19) Have him stand before Eleazar the priest and the whole community, and commission him in their sight. (20) Confer some of your authority on him so that the entire Israelite community will obey him. (21) He will stand before Eleazar who will consult the LORD for him with the decision of the Urim. He and all the Israelites with him, even the entire community, will go out and come back in at his command."

(22) Moses did as the LORD commanded him. He took Joshua, had him stand before Eleazar the priest and the entire community, (23) laid his hands on him, and commissioned him, as the LORD had spoken through Moses.

(Deut. 3:23) "At that time I begged the LORD: (24) Lord GOD, You have begun to show Your greatness and power to Your servant, for what god is there in heaven or on earth who can perform deeds and mighty acts like Yours? (25) Please let me cross over and see the beautiful land on the other side of the Jordan, that good hill country and Lebanon.

(26) "But the LORD was angry with me on account of you and would not listen to me. The LORD said to me, 'That's enough! Do not speak to Me again about this matter. (27) Go to the top of Pisgah and look to the west, north, south, and east, and see it with your own eyes, for you will not cross this Jordan. (28) But commission Joshua and encourage and strengthen him, for he will cross over ahead of the people and enable them to inherit this land that you will see.' (29) So we stayed in the valley facing Beth-peor.

Suggested Song

"Jesus, Keep Me Near the Cross"

(tinyurl.com/yf5dtub7)

Even with the Promised Land so close at hand, the Israelites were still unable to look beyond their present circumstances. Impatient with having to detour around Edom, they once again spoke against God and Moses, asking why they had been brought out of Egypt to die in the wilderness. Of course, they also complained about the water and the food. They had witnessed the abundant water so recently brought forth from the rock at Kadesh, yet they lacked the faith that God would continue to supply their needs. As for the manna,[1] they went so far as to declare their utter disdain for it, calling it "this wretched food."[2]

It's no wonder that God responded to their complaints with deadly venom. He had carried these people for so many years through inhospitable territory and sustained their lives with food that the psalmist would later describe as "the bread of angels."[3] With their stunning lack of gratitude, the Israelites were essentially throwing God's gift of manna back in His face.

Struck by the pain, suffering, and death caused by the snake bites, the people came to Moses. They confessed they had sinned when they spoke against God and against him, and they asked Moses to pray for them. God's response seems surprising. Instead of simply removing the snakes, He instructed Moses to create an image of a snake and mount it on a pole. Then, whoever got bitten had to look upon the bronze snake in order to live.

The Commissioning of Joshua

With the forty years of wandering quickly drawing to an end, God told Moses and Eleazar, Aaron's son and now the priest, to take a second census.[4] Included in the counting were all the Israelite men aged twenty and over who were able to serve in the army.[5] In addition to identifying the army members, this counting served several purposes. It helped determine the amount of land each tribe was set to inherit. The more people there were in a tribe, the more land that tribe would be allotted. Also, with this counting, Moses was able to ascertain that none of those whom God had condemned to die in the desert were still alive except for Caleb and Joshua. Finally, the time had come for the Israelites to take possession of their inheritance.

Moses desperately wanted to cross over the Jordan with the Israelites. He had devoted the last forty years of his life to

---

1

The Israelites ate manna for forty years until they entered the Promised Land (Exodus 16:35). They began to eat the produce of the land the day after they celebrated Passover while camped at Gilgal on the plains of Jericho shortly after they entered Canaan (Joshua 5:10–12).

2

Other versions state in Numbers 21:5: "Our soul loathes this worthless bread" (NKJV) and "we are disgusted with this miserable food" (NASB).

3

See Psalm 78:21–25. The entire Psalm gives an interesting historical account of the Israelites from the time of Jacob until David.

4

See Numbers 26 for the account of the second census Moses took shortly before the Israelites crossed into the Promised Land.

5

Note that the tribe of Levi was not counted with the rest of the Israelites because God had set them aside for His service, and they received no inheritance. They were counted separately, and their count included all males aged one month old and above. See Numbers 26:57–62 for how the Levites were counted.

An account of the Israelites defeating Sihon and Og is given in Numbers 21:21–35 and in Deuteronomy 2:26–3:11.

———— 7 ————

See Exodus 33:18–34:11 for the account of Moses asking to see God's glory and of God complying with his request.

———— 8 ————

See Numbers 31 for the account of Moses fulfilling God's command to take vengeance on the Midianites.

———— 9 ————

See Numbers 25 for the account of the Israelites being led astray into the worship of the Baal of Peor and the plague that God sent as a result. The number who died is given in verse 9. In verses 16–18, God instructed Moses to treat the Midianites as enemies and kill them.

bringing them to this point. He had endured untold trials and tribulations with them and had interceded on numerous occasions to keep God from totally destroying them. Now, with their recent battles against Sihon, king of the Amorites, and Og, king of Bashan,[6] they had begun to witness God's mighty power in conquering the nations in order to deliver their inheritance to them.

> Moses desperately wanted to cross over the Jordan with the Israelites.

Rarely did Moses write about himself personally, and rarely did he ask God for something for himself. Recall that he did so in Exodus 33:18 when he asked God to show him His glory. God granted him this wish to the extent that was possible for a human to witness.[7] Here in Deuteronomy 3:23–25, Moses made another request of God. Moses begged God to allow him to cross over and see the good land beyond the Jordan. He understood that God had only just begun to show His greatness with the defeat of these two kings, Sihon and Og, and he wanted to witness the mighty hand of God as He fought the battles for the Israelites and cleared the land before them. He wanted to see the years of his labor with the Israelites come to fruition as they claimed the inheritance God had promised Abraham so long ago.

This time, however, God denied Moses's request. Both he and Aaron had disobeyed God's command at the waters of Meribah in Kadesh. Moses had struck the rock rather than calling upon Him to act. With his words and his actions, Moses made it seem as if he and Aaron were responsible for the miracle rather than God. They had failed to honor God as holy before the eyes of the people.

Even faced with such disappointment, Moses continued to think of the welfare of the Israelite people. He asked God that they not be left like sheep without a shepherd. He knew all too well that, left to their own devices, the Israelites might never be able to claim their home in the Promised Land. They had shown themselves to be unfaithful on multiple occasions. They were too easily deterred by their circumstances and influenced by the ungodly people around them. They needed a strong leader who would be faithful to God.

In response, God had Moses commission Joshua to become their next leader. Like Moses, God had been preparing him for this leadership role since a young age. He would be the one to take the Israelites across the Jordan and lead them in the defeat of the nations that occupied the Promised Land.

God had one last mission for Moses before he died.[8] He was to take vengeance on the Midianites for the way they had treated the Israelites and for the role they had played in leading them astray in the worship of the Baal of Peor. This heartbreaking incident occurred right as the Israelites were poised to enter Canaan and is recorded in Numbers 22–25. Because of the Israelites' unfaithfulness to Him at Peor, God had sent a plague among them, which killed 24,000.[9]

God never leaves His people without a shepherd.

Because Moses had shouldered the load of leadership for so long, he may not have been able to think how things could continue without him. After accepting his role, he had devoted his life to leading, interceding, and preserving the lives of the Israelites in order to deliver them to the Promised Land. While Moses had been the one through whom God worked, the promise itself came from God. No doubt He could and would continue to fulfill His promise. Joshua, as Moses's aide, had been in training all along, and he would be the one to continue God's work.

God had a plan for saving the people as well. In due time, salvation would come, not only to the Israelites but to all people through His Son, Jesus Christ. Like the snake that Moses lifted on the pole, so Jesus would be lifted up on the cross. Rather than saving those who gazed upon Him from physical death, as the image of the snake had done, those who look to Jesus are saved

God's Protection of the Edomites, Moabites, and Ammonites

Why did the Israelites go around Edom even though they conquered other people who refused them passage? (See Numbers 21:1–3 for an account of the Israelites' defeat of the Canaanite king of Arad. See Numbers 21:21–35 and Deuteronomy 2:26–3:11 for an account of their defeat of Sihon, King of the Amorites, and Og, king of Bashan.)

There were certain lands God did not allow the Israelites to take because He had promised them to others long ago. The Edomites descended from Esau, the brother of Jacob (or Israel). God had given Esau the hill country of Seir as his own, and even though the Israelites did, at some point, pass through their land, God sternly warned them to be very careful. He would not give them any of their land, and the Israelites were to pay them in silver for the food and water they consumed. (See Deuteronomy

2:4–6 for God's warning concerning the land he had given to Esau.)

God also did not allow the Israelites to take any of the lands He had promised to the Moabites or to the Ammonites. These people were the descendants of Lot, the nephew of Abraham. (See Deuteronomy 2:9–12, 18–22 for God's warning concerning the land he had given to the Moabites and the Ammonites.)

Note: The *Ammonites* are not to be confused with the *Amorites*. While the Ammonites were descendants of Lot, the Amorites were descendants of Canaan, a son of Ham, who was one of Noah's three sons (Genesis 10:6, 15–18).

from spiritual death. Those who gazed upon the snake still died a physical death at a later date, but those who look upon our Lord Jesus need not fear a physical death. Because Jesus conquered death and rose again on the third day, His followers can know they will also rise again and live with Him for all eternity.

No one has ascended into heaven except he who descended from heaven, the Son of Man. And as Moses lifted up the serpent in the wilderness, so must the Son of Man be lifted up, that whoever believes in him may have eternal life.

—John 3:13–15, ESV

"Now is the judgment of this world; now will the ruler of this world be cast out. And I, when I am lifted up from the earth, will draw all people to myself." He said this to show by what kind of death he was going to die.

—John 12:31–33, ESV

Thoughts to Ponder

Why did the Israelites have to look upon the snake to live? What, if any, was the importance of the snake itself?

When Jesus came to earth centuries later, he found the people at that time were indeed "like sheep without a shepherd." How did He treat the people who flocked to Him? How were He and Moses similar in their roles on earth? How did they differ? See Matthew 9:35–38 and Mark 6:30–44.

How had God been preparing Joshua for his role as leader of the Israelites? What all did he do and witness during his apprenticeship?

Chapter 41

God Gives Moses a Song

Deuteronomy 31, HCSB

(1) Then Moses continued to speak these words to all Israel, (2) saying, "I am now 120 years old; I can no longer act as your leader. The LORD has told me, 'You will not cross this Jordan.' (3) The LORD your God is the One who will cross ahead of you. He will destroy these nations before you, and you will drive them out. Joshua is the one who will cross ahead of you, as the LORD has said. (4) The LORD will deal with them as He did Sihon and Og, the kings of the Amorites, and their land when He destroyed them. (5) The LORD will deliver them over to you, and you must do to them exactly as I have commanded you. (6) Be strong and courageous; don't be terrified or afraid of them. For it is the LORD your God who goes with you; He will not leave you or forsake you."

(7) Moses then summoned Joshua and said to him in the sight of all Israel, "Be strong and courageous, for you will go with this people into the land the LORD swore to give to their fathers. You will enable them to take possession of it. (8) The LORD is the One who will go before you. He will be with you; He will not leave you or forsake you. Do not be afraid or discouraged."

(9) Moses wrote down this law and gave it to the priests, the sons of Levi, who carried the ark of the LORD's covenant, and to all the elders of Israel. (10) Moses commanded them, "At the end of every seven years, at the appointed time in the year of debt cancellation, during the Festival of Booths, (11) when all Israel assembles in the presence of the LORD your God at the place He chooses, you are to read this law aloud before all Israel. (12) Gather the people—men, women, children, and foreigners living within your gates—so that they may listen and learn to fear the LORD your God and be careful to follow all the words of this law. (13) Then their children who do

not know the law will listen and learn to fear the LORD your God as long as you live in the land you are crossing the Jordan to possess."

(14) The LORD said to Moses, "The time of your death is now approaching. Call Joshua and present yourselves at the tent of meeting so that I may commission him." When Moses and Joshua went and presented themselves at the tent of meeting, (15) the LORD appeared at the tent in a pillar of cloud, and the cloud stood at the entrance to the tent.

(16) The LORD said to Moses, "You are about to rest with your fathers, and these people will soon commit adultery with the foreign gods of the land they are entering. They will abandon Me and break the covenant I have made with them. (17) My anger will burn against them on that day; I will abandon them and hide My face from them so that they will become easy prey. Many troubles and afflictions will come to them. On that day they will say, 'Haven't these troubles come to us because our God is no longer with us?' (18) I will certainly hide My face on that day because of all the evil they have done by turning to other gods. (19) Therefore write down this song for yourselves and teach it to the Israelites; have them recite it, so that this song may be a witness for Me against the Israelites. (20) When I bring them into the land I swore to give their fathers, a land flowing with milk and honey, they will eat their fill and prosper. They will turn to other gods and worship them, despising Me and breaking My covenant. (21) And when many troubles and afflictions come to them, this song will testify against them, because their descendants will not have forgotten it. For I know what they are prone to do, even before I bring them into the land I swore to give them." (22) So Moses wrote down this song on that day and taught it to the Israelites.

(23) The LORD commissioned Joshua son of Nun, "Be strong and courageous, for you will bring the Israelites into the land I swore to them, and I will be with you."

(24) When Moses had finished writing down on a scroll every single word of this law, (25) he commanded the Levites who carried the ark of the LORD's covenant, (26) "Take this book of the law and place it beside the ark of the covenant of the LORD your God so that it may remain there as a witness against you. (27) For I know how rebellious and stiff-necked you are. If you are rebelling against the LORD now, while I am still alive, how much more will you rebel after I am dead! (28) Assemble all your tribal elders and officers before me so that I may speak these words directly to them and call heaven and earth as witnesses against them. (29) For I know that after my death you will become completely corrupt and turn from the path I have commanded you. Disaster will come to you in the future, because you will do what is evil in the LORD's sight, infuriating Him with what your hands have made." (30) Then Moses recited aloud every single word of this song to the entire assembly of assembly of Israel:

[The Song of Moses follows in Deuteronomy 32:1–43.]

Shortly before his death, as the Israelites stood ready to cross over into the Promised Land, Moses wrote the book of Deuteronomy. In it, he recapped much of what had transpired during their forty-year journey. He also repeated or summarized many of the laws and instructions God had delivered to them earlier as a kind of refresher course.[1] Recall that most of those who comprised this present group of Israelites were either younger than twenty or had not yet been born when Moses originally received the Law at the mountain of God. He wanted to equip this generation as best he could before relinquishing control.

In his final words to the Israelites, Moses encouraged both the people and Joshua to be strong and courageous. He told them that God Himself would go before them in the conquest of the Promised Land and warned them not to become fearful or discouraged. God would be with them and would not leave them nor forsake them.

With that, Moses presented the book of the Law he had written to the priests and elders of the community. He charged them to read it aloud every seven years when it was the year for canceling debts during the Festival of Booths (also called the Feast of the Tabernacles). They were to summon everyone to hear the reading—men, women, children, and foreigners living among them—so that everyone would come to know the Lord, to fear Him, and to follow Him. Then, as now, God's Word was for all who would heed His commands.

Then, God summoned both Moses and Joshua and appeared before them in the pillar of cloud. He told them much of what would transpire in the future, how the Israelites would grow prosperous and turn away from Him. Disaster would befall them for doing evil in the sight of the Lord. To serve as a witness for Him against the Israelites when such difficulties arose, He instructed Moses to write down the words of a song. He was to

Suggested Song

"He Gave Me a Song"
(tinyurl.com/6bdfc7xs)

——— 1 ———

The word *deuteronomy* means "the repetition of the law." The two references below provide a brief summary of the book. According to these sources, the Pentateuch (the first five books of the Bible) formed one roll or volume and was not divided into separate books until much later. When Moses delivered to the priests "the book," he gave them all of the Pentateuch.
"Deuteronomy," *Smith's Bible Dictionary* (tinyurl.com/yrn276y2)
"Deuteronomy," *Easton's Bible Dictionary* (tinyurl.com/48cn25vh)

——— 2 ———

The articles below provide more insight into the complexities of how music is processed in the brain. It can involve different hemispheres in different people and seems to be a separate function from processing language. This could be why some people can remember words to songs when they have lost other of their memories.
"Music, Rhythm, and the Brain" (tinyurl.com/ywn7m5mn)
"Music and the Brain" (tinyurl.com/3spf78tn)

Ellicott's Commentary for English Readers (tinyurl.com/384tspwe) makes this observation concerning how in olden times, songs were an effective means of communicating knowledge in a way that people were likely to retain. Here is his comment on Deuteronomy 31:19:

(19) *Put it in their mouths, that this song may be a witness*. This method of perpetuating the truth was even better adapted to the times and to the condition of the people than the delivery of a written law. It was not possible to multiply copies of the law among them to any great extent; but the rhythmical form of the song would make it easy to be retained in their memories. There is reason to believe that Samuel, the first person who (so far as we know) effected anything of importance towards the establishment of a system of religious education in Israel, employed the same means for the purpose, viz., psalms and spiritual songs . . . And if they taught the psalms

teach it to the people so they could remember this song and pass it on to their children. The words would remind them of their heritage and of their God who delivered them.

A Song to Carry in Their Hearts

What a solemn occasion this must have been. As Moses handed over the scroll, he knew his life on earth was quickly drawing to an end. The community knew that as well, as did Joshua, who now bore the responsibility of leading the Israelite nation.

The air had to have been charged with great emotion as Moses stood before God and the people. Letting go is never easy, but beyond that, He feared for the Israelite people. He knew their rebellious nature and how easily they could turn away from serving God. He had been a strong and dedicated leader, yet even he had been unable to keep them from falling into the worship of other gods. Many had paid for their sins with their lives; in fact, almost an entire generation lay dead in the wilderness because they had failed to trust in the Lord.

The song God gave Moses shortly before his departure would serve as a lasting reminder of all He had done for the Israelites. Long after Moses was gone, the song he taught them that day would live on in their hearts. It was meant to serve as an admonition to the people, but it would also become a precious gift.

> Long after Moses was gone, the song he taught them that day would live on in their hearts.

At the time, there was only one copy of the book Moses had written containing the Word of God, and its access would be severely limited. Even if multiple copies had been available, it's likely that few people could read them. Songs served as an effective method anyone could utilize to both recall a message for their own edification as well as to convey a message to others. With this song, the people could actually carry the Word of God with them—a precious gift indeed!

What song is in your heart?

While we have ready access to the Bible today, songs remain a wonderful means of instruction and encouragement. We can use songs to remind us of our spiritual heritage, our many blessings, and of God's great love for us. Best of all, the songs we carry in our hearts are with us twenty-four hours a day!

Those who work with the elderly know that many retain their memory for songs and music, even when they have lost their short-term or long-term memories.[2] The gift of a song is truly a lasting gift, something that our Creator certainly understood.

What songs will you carry in your heart? Make it a point to listen to Christian music, read the poetry of the Psalms, and sing and hum your favorite worship songs as you go about your day. Fill your heart with songs of God, and then one day, if your eyes grow dim and your memory fades, it's quite possible that those beautiful songs will remain within your heart.

Let the message of Christ dwell among you richly as you teach and admonish one another with all wisdom through psalms, hymns, and songs from the Spirit, singing to God with gratitude in your hearts.

—Colossians 3:16, NIV

By day the LORD commands his steadfast love, and at night his song is with me, a prayer to the God of my life.

—Psalm 42:8, ESV[3]

to the people, as they learnt them under Samuel and David—especially historical psalms, like the 78th, 105th, and 106th—a very efficacious means of spreading the knowledge of God in Israel was in their hands.

Also, consider that the indwelling of the Holy Spirit, to the measure that Christians enjoy today, did not occur until after Jesus's resurrection. For God's people in Old Testament times, being able to memorize songs of praise and worship and carry them with them in their hearts was truly a precious gift. While this was no substitute for the Holy Spirit, certainly the songs in their hearts provided them with much-needed comfort and instruction. This article addresses some of the differences between Old and New Testament times: "How Did the Holy Spirit Operate in the Lives of OT Saints?" (tinyurl.com/bdzje5pm).

———— 3 ————
This verse is from the beautiful Psalm 42, which begins, "As the deer pants for streams of water" (NIV). It is one of several Psalms attributed to the sons of Korah.

Thoughts to Ponder

The book of Psalms, with 150 chapters, is one of the longest books in the Bible. It is a collection of prayers, poems, and hymns written by various people over a period of years. At least some of the psalms were meant to be set to music. Moses is credited with writing Psalm 90 and possibly others. Modern church songbooks often contain a variety of songs based on a psalm or a portion of one.

Do you have a favorite Psalm? How does it speak to you? Under what circumstances do you find yourself singing or reciting it?

_____

_____

_____

Although songs and singing are mentioned many times in the Old Testament, the New Testament contains relatively few references to either. Concerning Jesus and His disciples, Matthew 26:30 (NKJV) states: "And when they had sung a hymn, they went out to the Mount of Olives." (Mark 14:26 gives a parallel account of this occasion.)

What event had just transpired? What event would soon occur? Why do you think they chose to sing a hymn at this particular time?

_____

_____

_____

The account of Paul and Silas being thrown in prison is given in Acts 16:16–40. Verse 25 (NKJV) states: "But at midnight Paul and Silas were praying and singing hymns to God, and the prisoners were listening to them."

What impact do you think their singing had on Paul and Silas themselves and on their fellow prisoners? How do you know God heard their songs and prayers?

_____

_____

_____

Chapter 42

The Death of Moses

Deuteronomy 32:44–52; Deuteronomy 34, HCSB

(32:44) Moses came with Joshua son of Nun and recited all the words of this song in the presence of the people. (45) After Moses finished reciting all these words to all Israel, (46) he said to them, "Take to heart all these words I am giving as a warning to you today, so that you may command your children to carefully follow all the words of this law. (47) For they are not meaningless words to you but they are your life, and by them you will live long in the land you are crossing the Jordan to possess."

(48) On that same day the LORD spoke to Moses, (49) "Go up Mount Nebo in the Abarim range in the land of Moab, across from Jericho, and view the land of Canaan I am giving the Israelites as a possession. (50) Then you will die on the mountain that you go up, and you will be gathered to your people, just as your brother Aaron died on Mount Hor and was gathered to his people. (51) For both of you broke faith with Me among the Israelites at the waters of Meribath-kadesh in the Wilderness of Zin by failing to treat Me as holy in their presence. (52) Although from a distance you will view the land that I am giving the Israelites, you will not go there."

[In Deuteronomy 33, Moses pronounces his blessings on the Israelite tribes.]

(34:1) Then Moses went up from the plains of Moab to Mount Nebo, to the top of Pisgah, which faces Jericho, and the LORD showed him all the land: Gilead as far as Dan, (2) all of Naphtali, the land of Ephraim and Manasseh, all the land of Judah as far as the Mediterranean Sea, (3) the Negev, and the region from the Valley of Jericho, the City of Palms, as far as Zoar. (4) The LORD then said to him, "This is the land I promised Abraham, Isaac, and Jacob, 'I will give it to your descendants.' I have let you see it with your own eyes, but you will not cross into it."

(5) So Moses the servant of the LORD died there in the land of Moab, as the LORD had said. (6) He buried him in the valley in the land of Moab facing Beth-peor, and no one to this day knows where his grave is. (7) Moses was 120 years old when he died; his eyes were not weak, and his vitality had not left him. (8) The Israelites wept for Moses in the plains of Moab 30 days. Then the days of weeping and mourning for Moses came to an end.

(9) Joshua son of Nun was filled with the spirit of wisdom because Moses had laid his hands on him. So the Israelites obeyed him and did as the LORD had commanded Moses. (10) No prophet has arisen again in Israel like Moses, whom the LORD knew face to face. (11) He was unparalleled for all the signs and wonders the LORD sent him to do against the land of Egypt—to Pharaoh, to all his officials, and to all his land, (12) and for all the mighty acts of power and terrifying deeds that Moses performed in the sight of all Israel.

Suggested Song

"Hold to God's Unchanging Hand"

(tinyurl.com/52kfamk2)

The song Moses received from God and delivered to the Israelites would become an important part of their heritage. You can hear the passion in his voice when he admonished the people concerning the song: "They are not just idle words for you—they are your life. By them you will live long in the land you are crossing the Jordan to possess" (Deuteronomy 32:47, NIV). During his last few moments on earth, he wanted to impress upon them the importance of keeping these words in their hearts so they could live and prosper in the land they were to inherit.

That same day, God instructed Moses to climb one more mountain. From atop Mount Nebo, Moses was able to look across into the land that had been the goal of the Israelites' forty-year journey. Just as his brother, Aaron, had died on a mountain, so Moses died on Mount Nebo. Because the brothers had failed to honor God when bringing water from the rock at Meribah, God had declared that neither of them would be allowed to cross over into the Promised Land.

> That same day, God instructed Moses to climb one more mountain.

We can only speculate what Moses's thoughts were as he walked from the plains of Moab up the mountain to face the end of his life. He had accompanied his brother on his final walk and had witnessed his death, but Moses would make this walk alone. Whether the people were able to see him as he reached the top of the mountain is unknown.

The Lord Himself showed Moses the whole of the Promised Land. What a privilege to have the Great Creator as his tour guide, to point out the far boundaries of the land He had promised to Abraham, Isaac, and Jacob centuries earlier.[1] There, in the presence of God Almighty, Moses took his last breath and died atop the mountain. His work on earth was finished; he had completed what God had called him to do.

In His great wisdom, God buried Moses in an undisclosed location. His grave could neither be enshrined by potential worshipers nor desecrated by those who would count him an enemy. The Israelites mourned for him for thirty days, as they had for his brother Aaron.[2]

For the Israelites, Moses's death marked both the end of their long journey out of Egyptian slavery and the beginning of a new chapter in their history. With Joshua as their leader and the Lord going before them, they would soon cross the Jordan and begin their conquest of the Promised Land. God's daily gift of manna would cease. Finally, they would taste the produce of this wonderful land, a land "flowing with milk and honey."[3] It would all be as God had promised so long ago.

God Provided for Moses and the Israelites

Although God called upon Moses to do remarkable things during his lifetime, He always equipped him for the task at hand. The education Moses received in Egypt while being raised by Pharaoh's daughter enabled him to be the scribe of the Pentateuch. The years he spent in Midian tending the flocks of

—————— 1 ——————
You can find God's promise to Abram in Genesis 15:18–21. He renewed His promise to Isaac in Genesis 26:2–5 and to Jacob in Genesis 28:13–15.

—————— 2 ——————
See Numbers 20:29 concerning the thirty-day mourning period for Aaron. When Joseph carried the body of his father, Jacob, back out of Egypt to bury him, they mourned for him for seven days (Genesis 50:10).

—————— 3 ——————
See Joshua 5:10–12 for the account of the Israelites observing Passover in Canaan, eating the produce of the land, and then the manna ceasing to appear.

—————— 4 ——————
See Deuteronomy 29:5 for the passage concerning the Israelites' clothing and sandals not wearing out during their journey.

—————— 5 ——————
See Exodus 35:30–35, 36:1–2 for the account of God gifting the artisans.

Deuteronomy 34:1 states that Moses ascended Mount Nebo to the top of Pisgah. The Nebo and Pisgah peaks were part of the Abarim mountain range. They were evidently in close proximity to each other or were possibly parts of the same peak. From this vantage point, God showed Moses the land of Canaan, which the Israelites would soon possess.

Various commentaries and secular writings suggest Joshua and perhaps others accompanied Moses on his ascent up Mount Nebo. However, the scriptures do not say that anyone accompanied him. It seems that if someone had accompanied him, then his grave would not be in an unknown location, as the scriptures state.

As for his burial site, commentators disagree on whether God transported Moses's body to a valley below the mountain or whether He chose a depression or valley area atop

his father-in-law taught him much about living in the wilderness. While there, he became familiar with the territory, where one day, he would return with the Israelites in tow.

When God told Moses to go back to Egypt, He didn't send him alone. He called Aaron to accompany him, and He equipped him with a staff and a whole range of miracles to perform. He also provided Moses with the courage and boldness to stand before the most powerful ruler in the known world.

God also provided Moses with a strong and capable body in order for him to be able to physically accomplish and endure all that he was called to do. Even as a baby, his mother saw he was no ordinary child and went to great lengths to preserve his life. Now, here at the end of his life, the scriptures tell us Moses's body still retained its strength and vigor.

God provided in remarkable ways for the Israelites during their arduous journey as well. He guided them with the pillar of cloud. He sent them manna to eat and supplied them with water on numerous occasions. Miraculously, their clothes and sandals did not wear out as they wandered in the wilderness for forty years.[4] When He gave instructions for the Tabernacle to be built, He equipped Bezaleel and Aholiab with the knowledge and artistic ability to beautifully craft all that He had commanded.[5]

God continues to provide for us today.

Whatever it is that God has called you to do in this life, remember that He is always faithful. He will equip you with what you need to fulfill your calling. Whether it's physical ability, mental acuity, or monetary resources, God will find a way to provide you with what you need. He will not call you to a task without making available the tools you need to accomplish it.

Like Moses, we all have seasons in our lives, times that are appropriate for us to achieve certain things. As one season draws to a close, know that another is just beginning. While our seasons may not come in forty-year increments, recall that the most powerful and influential season of Moses's life occurred during the last forty of his incredible 120 years on earth.

Whatever your age or physical condition, relish where you are. Make each season of your life count in your service to God. Continually seek to fulfill what He has called you to do during this present season and know that He will provide for you just as He provided for Moses in every season of his life so long ago.

Teach us to number our days, that we may gain a heart of wisdom.

—Psalm 90:12, NIV[6]

Whatever you do, work at it with all your heart, as working for the Lord, not for human masters, since you know that you will receive an inheritance from the Lord as a reward. It is the Lord Christ you are serving.

—Colossians 3:23–24, NIV

And God is able to bless you abundantly, so that in all things at all times, having all that you need, you will abound in every good work.

—2 Corinthians 9:8, NIV

the mountain range. Secular writers suggest God placed Moses in a cave somewhere on the mountain. Still others suggest God had an angel bury Moses due to the scripture in Jude 1:9 concerning the archangel Michael disputing with the devil about the body of Moses. So it seems, just as the scriptures state in Deuteronomy 34:6, no one knows where Moses was buried, even to this day.

For more information on Mount Nebo, scroll down to "(prophet), Mount" under the listing for "Nebo" at *Smith's Bible Dictionary* (tinyurl.com/ymrfrfm5). You can also search online for images of Mount Nebo to get a better idea of the topography.

——— 6 ———

Psalm 90 is a prayer attributed to Moses. Some secular writers attribute eleven psalms to Moses, Psalm 90 through Psalm 100, although Moses's authorship cannot be verified.

Thoughts to Ponder

When Moses begged God to be allowed to cross over into the Promised Land, certainly part of his reason was his desire to see what the focus of his forty-year journey had been. But he also wanted to continue to accompany the Israelites because he was fearful that they would not do well without his leadership. How had God already planned for the continuance of their leadership? If Moses had been allowed to cross over, how might things have been different?

_____

_____

_____

_____

Do you think Moses was fearful as he climbed Mount Nebo, knowing he would die there? If you had an appointed time to die, how might you live your life differently?

_____

_____

_____

_____

God spoke to Moses face-to-face, as with a friend. When did Moses's relationship with God begin to develop? How did Moses foster that relationship? What can you do to further develop your relationship with God?

_____

_____

_____

_____

Chapter 43

Preparing the Way for the Messiah

Deuteronomy 18:15–22, HCSB

(15) "The LORD your God will raise up for you a prophet like me from among your own brothers. You must listen to him. (16) This is what you requested from the LORD your God at Horeb on the day of the assembly when you said, 'Let us not continue to hear the voice of the LORD our God or see this great fire any longer, so that we will not die!' (17) Then the LORD said to me, 'They have spoken well. (18) I will raise up for them a prophet like you from among their brothers. I will put My words in his mouth, and he will tell them everything I command him. (19) I will hold accountable whoever does not listen to My words that he speaks in My name. (20) But the prophet who dares to speak a message in My name that I have not commanded him to speak, or who speaks in the name of other gods—that prophet must die.' (21) You may say to yourself, 'How can we recognize a message the LORD has not spoken?' (22) When a prophet speaks in the LORD's name, and the message does not come true or is not fulfilled, that is a message the LORD has not spoken. The prophet has spoken it presumptuously. Do not be afraid of him."

◇◇◇

When God spoke to Moses from the burning bush, He only mentioned bringing the Israelites out of Egypt. If He had told Moses *all* that He needed him to do *and* that it would take him the rest of his life, Moses might have collapsed from the weight of His words!

Here's an overview of the many roles God called Moses to fulfill. You can probably think of more.

- He was a rescuer, saving the enslaved Hebrew people from their Egyptian oppressors.
- He was a judge and civic leader, maintaining order and keeping peace among the tribes of Israel.
- He served as a model for the people, showing them what it looked like to trust God and have a personal relationship with Him.
- He was a teacher, training the nation to live by the Law God gave him on Mount Sinai.
- He interceded for the people, begging for God's mercy when they sinned.
- He was a prophet, chosen by God to be His spokesperson so the people—and eventually the world—would know how holy, righteous, just, and merciful the Father is.

In each of these roles, Moses, in whom God's Spirit resided, foreshadowed the coming of the Savior, Jesus Christ. The reading for this lesson speaks specifically to Moses's role as a prophet.

Moses, the Forerunner of Christ

Recall that after the Israelites had arrived at Mount Horeb (or Mount Sinai), God spoke to them and delivered the Ten Commandments. Being in His presence and hearing His voice frightened them so much they asked if Moses could be their mediator. God agreed to this arrangement, so while the people stood far away, Moses drew near to God. Moses listened to God's words and conveyed His messages back to the people. In so doing, he acted as both an intercessor or go-between and as a prophet conveying God's Word.[1]

On this same occasion, God also spoke to the future when he told Moses, "I will raise up for them a prophet like you from among their brothers. I will put My words in his mouth, and he will tell them everything I command him" (Deuteronomy 18:18, HCSB).

That future prophet would be the Messiah. He was the One of whom God had spoken in the Garden of Eden, the offspring of Eve, who would ultimately crush Satan's head.[2] He was the One whom God had declared would come through the lineage of Abraham and bless all peoples on earth.[3]

While this particular generation of Israelites may or may not have understood what God meant by His reference to a prophet like Moses, future generations certainly would. Centuries later, when the Jews in Jerusalem were trying to figure out who John the Baptist was, they asked him if he was the "prophet." He assured them he was not.[4] Later, after people witnessed Jesus feeding the 5,000, they began to say, "Surely this is the Prophet who is to come into the world" (John 6:14, NIV).

When Jesus began His ministry, He called certain disciples to follow Him, the ones who would later be known as the apostles. After calling Philip, Philip then found Nathanael and told him, "We have found the one Moses wrote about in the Law, and about whom the prophets also wrote—Jesus of Nazareth, the son of Joseph" (John 1:45, NIV).

> "We have found the one Moses wrote about in the Law, and about whom the prophets also wrote—Jesus of Nazareth, the son of Joseph."

Jesus Himself affirmed that He was the one Moses had written about. He told the Jews who sought to persecute Him in John 5:46–47 (NIV), "If you believed Moses, you would believe me, for he wrote about me. But since you do not believe what he wrote, how are you going to believe what I say?"

——— 1 ———
See Exodus 20:18–21 for the account of the Israelites asking if Moses could speak with God and then tell them His messages.

——— 2 ———
See Genesis 3:15.

——— 3 ———
See Genesis 12:1–3 for God's call to Abram.

——— 4 ———
See John 1:19–34 for John's declaration to the Jews concerning Christ.

The Messiah is a prophet greater than Moses!

For all the ways Moses lived up to his calling, he wasn't perfect. When he struck the rock at Meribah and failed to give God credit for the miraculous flow of water, God refused to allow him to enter the Promised Land. Moses lived under the Law, and while his sin could be atoned for through sacrifices made on the altar, it could not be truly forgiven. As the writer of Hebrews later explained, it is not possible for the blood of bulls and goats to take away sins.[5]

Only Jesus, by living a life without sin and offering Himself as the perfect sacrifice, would be able to make true forgiveness possible. What Moses's life and calling foreshadowed, Jesus fulfilled completely:

- Only Jesus can rescue us from our bondage to sin (Romans 6:22–23).

- Jesus judges the nations (John 5:22–23) and His own people (2 Corinthians 5:10).

- Jesus served as a model for the relationship His followers can have with God (John 15:15, Hebrews 4:16, 1 Peter 5:7) and showed through His willingness to be our sacrifice what it means to live in obedience to the Father (Luke 22:42).

- Jesus teaches us God's will (Matthew 5–7, Matthew 28:16–20).

- Jesus continually intercedes for us before God (Romans 8:34, Hebrews 7:25).

- God chose Jesus, His own Son, to be His spokesperson so everyone would know how holy, righteous, just, and merciful the Father is (John 17:6–9, 26).

Jesus also fulfilled every requirement of the Law and, in so doing, ushered in the New Covenant. This covenant, under which we live today, is far superior to the Law that Moses

---

————— 5 —————
See Hebrews 10:1–4.

presented to the Israelites at Mount Sinai. And, as the writer of Hebrews points out, it is founded on better promises.[6] Because of Jesus and the New Covenant, we have the hope of eternal life.

After fulfilling His role on earth, Jesus ascended into heaven, where He now sits at God's right hand. As Moses did for the Israelites, He now intercedes for His people, and like Aaron, He serves as our great high priest. Thankfully, Jesus is the perfect version of each. "But because Jesus lives forever, his priesthood lasts forever. Therefore he is able, once and forever, to save those who come to God through him. He lives forever to intercede with God on their behalf" (Hebrews 7:24–25, NLT).

In addition to everything He did while on earth, Jesus sent us an incredible gift after His death! During Old Testament times, few people ever experienced the gift of the Holy Spirit's presence. Now, because of Jesus and the New Covenant He left us, this gift is available to all who love Him and obey Him. As He told His disciples in John 14:16 (NLT): "And I will ask the Father, and he will give you another Advocate, who will never leave you."

Indeed, God fulfilled His promise to raise up a prophet like Moses from the lineage of the Israelites. He raised up Jesus, His only begotten Son. He was everything that Moses was—and so much more! Through Him, we are saved completely, and by His covenant, we are assured of the hope of eternal salvation.

———— 6 ————
See Hebrews 8:6–13.

The next day John saw Jesus coming toward him and said, "Look! The Lamb of God who takes away the sin of the world! He is the one I was talking about when I said, 'A man is coming after me who is far greater than I am, for he existed long before me.'"

—John 1:29–30, NLT

I didn't know he was the one, but when God sent me to baptize with water, he told me, "The one on whom you see the Spirit descend and rest is the one who will baptize with the Holy Spirit." I saw this happen to Jesus, so I testify that he is the Chosen One of God.

—John 1:33–34, NLT

Epilogue

Moses, a Faithful Servant of God

When all was said and done, Moses led a remarkable life. Born a slave but raised as nobility, he returned from living as a fugitive to deliver the Israelite people from captivity and then lead them on to the Promised Land. Initially reluctant to accept the mission God set before him, once he did, Moses gave it his all. He would indeed prove himself to be a faithful servant of God.

God provided for Moses.

God equipped Moses physically such that at the end of his life, his eyes were not dim nor his strength abated. He lived to age 120, when, according to the psalm attributed to him, a normal life span averaged 70 to 80 years.[1] Moses, in fact, was just beginning his incredible forty-year journey at age eighty, an age when most people had passed on.

During the first eighty years of his life, God prepared Moses for what lay ahead. The education he received in Egypt served him well as he recorded all that God instructed him to write. His years among the Midianites tending the flocks of his father-in-law allowed him to explore the land where, one day, he would return with the Israelites. It also allowed him the opportunity to live in the wilderness, something which, no doubt, proved useful later.

Suggested Song

"The Lord Bless You and Keep You"

(tinyurl.com/mrxw74f4)

1

Psalm 90:10a (NKJV) states: "The days of our lives are seventy years; And if by reason of strength they are eighty years."

See Numbers 9:15–23 for an explanation of how the pillar of cloud functioned.

See Exodus 14:19–20 for the account of the cloud moving around behind the Israelites to protect them from the Egyptians.

See Deuteronomy 34 for the account of Moses's death. Another instance of God Himself handling matters for humans occurred in the Garden of Eden when God made garments of skin for Adam and Eve and clothed them before banishing them from the garden in Genesis 3:21–24. Such instances of God's personal involvement are rare, at least that are recorded in Scripture.

To find references to Moses, use a Bible concordance or search the Bible online. A Bible search on "Moses" at https://www.biblestudytools.com/ using the New King James Version yielded a total of 788 references (at the time). If you "filter" the results, you can see a total for each book of the Bible where he's mentioned. By subtracting those from Exodus, Leviticus, Numbers, and Deuteronomy (books written by Moses), you'll see he's mentioned approximately 113 times in the remaining books of the Old Testament. Additionally, he's mentioned

When God instructed Moses to confront Pharaoh, He didn't send him empty-handed. He supplied him with miracles to perform and allowed Aaron to accompany him. His brother often served as Moses's mouthpiece and provided him with moral support.

As the Israelites journeyed in the wilderness, God accompanied them every step of the way. His pillar of cloud went before them by day, guiding their path, and shone over them at night, providing protection.[2] During their escape from Egypt, the cloud moved around behind them, keeping the enemy army in darkness and away from the Israelites.[3]

God continued to bless Moses.

When Moses and Aaron sinned at the waters of Meribah, God denied them both the privilege of entering the Promised Land. It was the same sentence He had pronounced upon the Israelites who had broken faith with Him years earlier. Even though Moses was forced to accept this bitter disappointment, God still managed to bless him as He had no other.

From the vantage point of Mount Nebo, God granted Moses the privilege of looking over into the Promised Land. God Himself pointed out to Moses the boundaries where various tribes would soon locate. Then, after being allowed to see with his own eyes what he had been journeying toward for the last forty years, Moses died and was gathered to his people. He was buried by God in an undisclosed location. God took care of His friend.[4]

Thus ended one of the most remarkable and influential lives in all of the Old Testament. While some count it a sad thing that God did not allow Moses to cross over into the Promised Land, consider that Moses accomplished all that God had called him to do. Now, as in a relay race, he passed the baton of leadership on to Joshua. It would be his successor's turn to fulfill all that

> His rest would be well deserved.

God had called him to do. Finally, Moses could rest from the heavy responsibilities he had borne so admirably. His rest would be well deserved.

Moses's work continued after him.

The writings of Moses and the Law he presented to the Israelites laid the foundation for the rest of the Scriptures. From the days of Joshua through the time of the judges, the kings, and the prophets, the Old Testament repeatedly references Moses.[5] Three of the Psalms—78, 105, and 106—give summaries of the history of the Israelite people and include many details of their exodus out of Egypt and their subsequent journeys through the wilderness. Moses himself is credited with writing Psalm 90 and possibly several others.

The New Testament likewise contains numerous references to Moses and the Law, including several by Jesus.[6] These many references from both Testaments speak to the authority and validity of Moses's writings.

Christians today owe much to Moses. The scroll he handed over to the Levites before his death now comprises a great portion of our Bible.[7] He wrote more of our Bible by word count than any other author.[8] But more importantly, he brought the Law to God's people. This would set the scene for Christ to come into the world centuries later, and with Him would come eternal salvation.

After death, Moses appeared at Jesus's transfiguration.

In ending our study of Moses, let us consider the last time that the Scriptures record he appeared on earth. Centuries after Moses's death, our Lord Jesus climbed high atop a mountain with three of his disciples to pray.[9] He knew that the time of His crucifixion

approximately seventy-nine times in the New Testament. Note that the count may be different, depending on the version of the Bible you select.

───── 6 ─────

For examples of Jesus referencing Moses and the Law, see John 5:45–47 and John 7:19.

───── 7 ─────

See Deuteronomy 31:9–13 and 31:24–26 for the account of Moses handing the book he had written over to the Levites who carried the ark of the covenant. He instructed them to read it aloud to everyone every seven years, in the year for canceling debts, during the Feast of Tabernacles. For more information, see "Pentateuch" in *Smith's Bible Dictionary* (tinyurl.com/5xcv6zv7) and in *Easton's Bible Dictionary* (tinyurl.com/mr2xa2yz).

───── 8 ─────

According to word count in the original Hebrew language, Moses was the most prolific writer of our Bible, with his works accounting for over 20 percent. Considering that the Pentateuch (what is now Genesis, Exodus, Leviticus, Numbers, and Deuteronomy in our Bibles) was originally one book, he also wrote the longest book in the Bible. While the Apostle Paul wrote thirteen books of our New Testament, by word count, his writings account for a little over 5 percent of our Bible. See "Infographic: Who wrote

most (and least) in the Bible?"
(tinyurl.com/ym5aumw8)
for more information on this
topic. The site also contains
many interesting facts about
the Bible.
Note that Moses is also
credited with Psalm 90 and
maybe several others. It's also
possible he wrote the book
of Job.

——————— 9 ———————

An account of Jesus's
transfiguration is given in
three of the Gospels (Matthew
17:1–8, Mark 9:2–8, and Luke
9:28–36). Peter confirms being
an eyewitness to Christ's
majesty and hearing the voice
of God honor Jesus in 2 Peter
1:16–18.

Scriptures do not name
the site of the mountain of
transfiguration. According
to Roman Catholic tradition,
it was Mount Tabor. Others
name Mount Hermon as the
more likely site. These articles
provide more information
about these two mountains:
"What Is the Significance of
Mount Tabor in the Bible?"
(tinyurl.com/4p8jfs7j) and
"What Is the Significance of
Mount Hermon in the Bible?"
(tinyurl.com/3h29a2rs).

——————— 10 ———————

This article discusses the
transfiguration of Jesus
and its meaning: "25. The
Transfiguration (Matthew
17:1–13)" (tinyurl.com/
m6ky4dn7).

was near, and He needed to commune with His Father. As He did so, He took on His heavenly glory, such that His face and garments shone exceedingly bright. During that time, Moses and Elijah appeared there with Him and spoke to Him.

Jesus's transfiguration was a deeply meaningful event.[10] God declared to the disciples who were there that, indeed, Jesus was the Son of God. His appearance with Moses and Elijah also signaled that a transition of authority was about to occur. Moses had delivered the Law, which had acted as a guardian to bring God's people to Christ.[11] Elijah, along with a host of other prophets, had served as God's special spokespersons and messengers. Together, these two embodied the Law and the Prophets, for which the intent and focus of both had been to point the world toward the Messiah. With His death on the cross, Jesus would fulfill the commands of the Law as well as all that the prophets had foretold. His perfect sacrifice would usher in the New Covenant under which we live today.

While the presence of Moses and Elijah had to have been a welcome encouragement to Jesus, also consider what a great reward this was for these two men. They had faithfully served as forerunners to prepare the way. Now, they were privileged to stand on this mountaintop with the Messiah Himself. In sending them back to earth at this crucial time, God allowed them to witness their life's work being fulfilled and coming to fruition.

What a great honor God bestowed upon both Moses and Elijah by sending them back to minister to our Lord Jesus as He prepared for the greatest event in history. As for Moses, while God had not allowed him to cross over into the Promised Land while alive, He granted him the exceptional privilege of appearing after his death at Jesus's transfiguration. By accepting what God had called him to do, Moses became a friend of God in the process. In turn, God blessed His friend as only He could do.

> God blessed His friend as only He could do.

May God bless you as you walk with Him and continue your study of His glorious Word.

Now to him who is able to do immeasurably more than all we ask or imagine, according to his power that is at work within us, to him be glory in the church and in Christ Jesus throughout all generations, for ever and ever! Amen.

—Ephesians 3:20–21, NIV

——— 11 ———

In Galatians 3:19–29 (NKJV), Paul discusses the purpose of the Law. In verses 24–25, he states: "Therefore the law was our tutor to bring us to Christ, that we might be justified by faith. But after faith has come, we are no longer under a tutor."

Paul goes on to explain in verses 26–29 (NKJV) how Christians become heirs according to the promise: "For you are all sons of God through faith in Christ Jesus. For as many of you as were baptized into Christ have put on Christ. There is neither Jew nor Greek, there is neither slave nor free, there is neither male nor female; for you are all one in Christ Jesus. And if you are Christ's, then you are Abraham's seed, and heirs according to the promise."

Frequently Asked Questions

Why did God not allow Moses his wish to cross over into the Promised Land?

Moses and Aaron sinned openly before all the Israelite community when bringing water from the rock at Meribah.[1] God had told Moses to speak to the rock, but instead, he struck the rock twice. Even worse, he and Aaron gave themselves credit for the miracle when he said, "Must *we* bring you water out of this rock?" (Numbers 20:10b, NIV). Afterward, God told both of them in Numbers 20:12 (NIV): "Because you did not trust in me enough to honor me as holy in the sight of the Israelites, you will not bring this community into the land I give them." By failing to honor God with the miracle that was performed, they displayed a lack of trust in God. In short, they broke faith with God.

The Israelite community had committed the same type of sin against God when they refused to cross over into the Promise Land.[2] Even after all the miracles they had witnessed, they did not trust God to deliver on His promise to go before them. They feared the inhabitants of the land more than they believed in God's might. They broke faith with God, and because of it, God declared they would not be allowed to see the land He had promised to their fathers.

Moses begged God to forgive the people of their sins, which He did; however, God declared they would still bear the

---

1

The account of what happened at the waters of Meribah is recorded in Numbers 20:2–13.

2

See Numbers 14 for the account of the Israelites rebelling against God and refusing to enter the Promised Land.

consequences of their sins. He replied to Moses, "I have forgiven them, as you asked. Nevertheless, as surely as I live and as surely as the glory of the LORD fills the whole earth, not one of those who saw my glory and the signs I performed in Egypt and in the wilderness but who disobeyed me and tested me ten times—not one of them will ever see the land I promised on oath to their ancestors. No one who has treated me with contempt will ever see it" (Numbers 14:20–23, NIV).

When Moses and Aaron failed to honor God before the people, He declared there would be similar consequences for them. Neither of them would be allowed to enter the Promised Land. While Moses was granted the privilege of seeing it from afar, neither he nor Aaron ever set foot upon the land.

By God's own admission, Moses had developed a close relationship with Him.[3] No doubt Moses had confessed his error and begged God's forgiveness. In fact, it's likely he made a sacrificial offering for his sin. Why, then, did God refuse to grant him this wish? God could not do this because He had declared consequences, and He is a just God. He could not selectively allow Moses to forgo the consequences while binding them upon all the others.

If Moses wrote the first five books of the Bible, how did he write about his own death in Deuteronomy 34?

When Moses completed his writings and turned over the Book of the Law to the Levites, he handed them a single scroll.[4] It contained what would later be called the Pentateuch—Genesis, Exodus, Leviticus, Numbers, and Deuteronomy. To the Jews, this collective work would be known as the Torah. Presumably, Greek translators were the ones who later divided Moses's writings into the five separate works we have in our Bibles today and gave the books their individual titles.[5]

It's possible that God could have instructed Moses beforehand on what to write concerning his own death. However, it

---

[3] See Numbers 12:6–8 for God's admonishment of Miriam and Aaron, where He explained to them His relationship with Moses.

[4] See Deuteronomy 31:24–26 for the account of Moses handing his book over to the Levites.

[5] For more information, see "Pentateuch" in *Smith's Bible Dictionary* (tinyurl.com/5xcv6zv7) and in *Easton's Bible Dictionary* (tinyurl.com/mr2xa2yz).

seems more likely that Joshua wrote the last bit of Deuteronomy. As God's appointed successor to Moses, it would have been fairly easy for him to access the scroll and add this portion to the end. Moreover, Moses's obituary is not written from a personal viewpoint and doesn't sound like something Moses would write about himself. The tone of the writing is one of great respect toward Moses. The wording is much more in keeping with how Joshua would later refer to Moses in his own book, particularly in calling him "the servant of the Lord."

What is the meaning of the scripture in Jude concerning the body of Moses?

Here is the scripture:

> Yet Michael the archangel, in contending with the devil, when he disputed about the body of Moses, dared not bring against him a reviling accusation, but said, "The Lord rebuke you!"
>
> —Jude 1:9, NKJV

Bible commentators do not have a satisfying explanation for this scripture. Some feel the reference to the devil desiring to possess Moses's body is one passed down verbally in Jewish tradition. Regardless, in the book of Daniel, Michael was the great prince or chief angel who stood watch over the Israelite people.[6] It makes sense that he would be the one to stand guard over the body of Moses.

We know from the transfiguration of Christ that the soul of Moses was safe from the devil's grasp because God allowed him to appear on the mountain with Jesus. Why, then, would the devil want Moses's body? Quite possibly, if he could make its whereabouts known to humans, they would turn his tomb into a sacred site.[7] Much like the golden calf, this would help turn the focus of the people's worship away from God and cause them to violate God's commands to not honor other gods or bow down to any images. Certainly, Moses, who fought so hard against

---

6

See Daniel 10:13, 21; 12:1 for references concerning the angel Michael.

7

The body of the prophet Daniel provides an excellent example of why Moses's burial site was better left unknown. Bitter quarrels arose over Daniel's remains, and at one point, his bier was transferred each year across the Choaspes River, residing one year on one side and the next year on the opposite side. His body was thought to bring prosperity to those living nearby. A Persian shah finally stopped the practice, declaring it disrespectful to the prophet. He had the bier fastened with chains to a bridge and erected a chapel. Many other incidents have been reported concerning Daniel's remains, and it's unknown whether any of the sites named as his tomb actually contain his bones. For more information, see the article: "Daniel, Tomb of" in *The 1901 Jewish Encyclopedia* (tinyurl.com/5f6t5b9k).

Leviticus 4 describes sin offerings. When God's directives were followed, the offerings the priests made on behalf of others provided atonement for their sins, and they were forgiven. (See verses 19–20, 26, 31 and 35.) Leviticus 5 describes other circumstances which required offerings, and again, atonement would be made and forgiveness granted. (See verses 10, 13, 16, and 18.)

9

See Hebrews 10:1–4 (NIV): "The law is only a shadow of the good things that are coming—not the realities themselves. For this reason it can never, by the same sacrifices repeated endlessly year after year, make perfect those who draw near to worship. Otherwise, would they not have stopped being offered? For the worshipers would have been cleansed once for all, and would no longer have felt guilty for their sins. But those sacrifices are an annual reminder of sins. It is impossible for the blood of bulls and goats to take away sins."

10

The yearly Day of Atonement is described in Leviticus 16. In verse 34 (NKJV), God commanded that it was to be done year after year: "This shall be an everlasting statute for you, to make atonement for the children of Israel, for all their sins, once a year."

idolatry, would never want his tomb to be revered in such a way either.

The greater lesson in this scripture is how Michael responded to the devil. The archangel fully understood the tremendous power Satan wields over this world. He also understood that Satan is no match for our God. Yahweh reigns supreme; He has the power to fully withstand Satan. Wisely, Michael put the dispute into God's hands. What a great lesson for us today—allow God to handle evil as only He can do.

How were people saved who lived under the Law?

The writer of Hebrews (presumably Paul) contrasts the Law, which Moses presented to God's people, with the New Covenant, which came into effect after the death of Christ. Under the Law, the people were commanded to offer certain sacrifices for their sins. These sacrifices atoned for their sins, and God granted the people forgiveness.[8] These sacrifices, however, could not permanently take away their sins.[9] Once a year, every year, the high priest was required to enter the Most Holy Place in the Tabernacle and make a special atonement for all the sins of the Israelites.[10]

To better understand how the atonement process worked, you can think of the sacrifices made under the Law as being similar to the payments made on an interest-only loan. When you take out an interest-only loan, your payments are only for the interest due during that time period. All of the principal on your debt remains outstanding. Usually, the interest-only period lasts for only a few years before you're required to start paying on the principal or refinance. Theoretically, you could pay on such a loan forever and never repay any of your debt, provided you could find a lender willing to hold such a loan. The interest payments made during the interest-only period simply keep you in good standing and prevent foreclosure on your loan.

That's how it was for God's people who lived under the Law. The debt that sin incurred was too great for any of them to ever repay. Their sacrifices only covered the interest due at the time but could never eliminate their debt. God was willing to grant them such a loan because He already had a plan in place. He knew that one day Someone would be willing and able to repay their debt in full for them—His Son, Jesus Christ. When Jesus died on the cross, His sacrifice covered not only the sins of all who would believe on His name in the future living under the New Covenant but also the sins of the faithful who had died under the Law.[11]

How are people saved under the New Covenant?

Christians today no longer offer animal sacrifices. Jesus offered Himself as the perfect sacrifice for the sins of the world. He did this once and for all time. With the shedding of His blood and His death upon the cross came forgiveness—true forgiveness. No further sacrifice for sin will ever be needed. The price has been paid.[12]

Jesus lived a perfect life and fulfilled all the requirements of the Law. The Apostle Paul explains in Colossians 2:14 (HCSB) that Jesus "erased the certificate of debt, with its obligations, that was against us and opposed to us, and has taken it out of the way by nailing it to the cross." When Jesus poured out His blood (He did this with His death on the cross), He established a New Covenant.[13]

We avail ourselves of this great gift of salvation by doing what God told Jesus's disciples to do long ago on the Mount of Transfiguration. After He proclaimed to them, "This is my Son, whom I love; with him I am well pleased," He then instructed the disciples: "Listen to him!" (Matthew 17:5b, NIV). We listen to Jesus today by studying the inspired Word of God, the Bible. As we come to understand all that Jesus has done for us, our listening leads us to love Him. Our love for Him then leads us

———— 11 ————
See Hebrews 9:15 (ESV): "Therefore he is the mediator of a new covenant, so that those who are called may receive the promised eternal inheritance, since a death has occurred that redeems them from the transgressions committed under the first covenant."

———— 12 ————
Hebrews 10:1–18 explains how Jesus's sacrifice was made once and for all time.

———— 13 ————
During His Last Supper, Jesus explained that the cup He shared with His disciples represented His blood. With His death and the shedding of His blood would come the New Covenant. See Luke 22:20 and 1 Corinthians 11:25.

———— 14 ————

See Acts 8:26–39 for the account of the conversion of the Ethiopian eunuch.

———— 15 ————

Followers of the Way was an early designation for the followers of Jesus, who were later called Christians. Jesus taught that the way to the Father was through Him. In this beautiful passage in John 14:1–7, as He was preparing His disciples for His death, He told them, "I am the way, the truth, and the life. No one comes to the Father except through Me" (John 14:6, NKJV).

Acts 8:1–4 tells of the great persecution of the early church and Saul's role in it. Verse 3 (NKJV) tells us: "As for Saul, he made havoc of the church, entering every house, and dragging off men and women, committing them to prison." As a result, believers fled to other areas, and as they scattered about, they preached the Word everywhere they went.

———— 16 ————

For the account of Stephen, see Acts 6:8–7:60. Acts 7:58 states that those who stoned Stephen laid their clothes at the feet of a young man named Saul. Later, after his conversion, Paul stated in Acts 22:20 (NKJV), "And when the blood of Your martyr Stephen was shed, I also was standing by consenting to his death, and guarding the clothes of those who were killing him."

to obey what He has commanded. As Jesus told His disciples in John 14:23 (NIV), "Anyone who loves me will obey my teaching. My Father will love them, and we will come to them and make our home with them."

The Ethiopian Eunuch

The New Testament contains numerous examples of people accepting Jesus as their Savior. The Ethiopian eunuch was someone who searched the Scriptures, seeking understanding.[14] This man was an important official in charge of the treasury of Candace, the Queen of the Ethiopians. He had been to Jerusalem to worship and was on his way home. As he was sitting in his chariot reading from the prophet Isaiah, an angel of the Lord sent Philip to him. The eunuch asked Philip to explain to him the scripture he was reading. Philip began with that very passage and went on to tell him the rest of the story, the good news of Jesus.

As they came to a place that had water, the eunuch said, "See, here is water. What hinders me from being baptized?"(Acts 8:36b, NKJV). He ordered his chariot to stop. Then both he and Philip went down into the water, and Philip baptized him. After they came up out of the water, the Spirit of the Lord suddenly took Philip away, possibly to go teach someone else, while the eunuch continued on his way rejoicing.

The Apostle Paul

The Apostle Paul provides another example of someone who accepted Jesus as his Savior, only he started from a very different place than the eunuch. Originally called by his Hebrew name of Saul, he was so convinced that the followers of the Way were wrong and in violation of the Law that he set about to persecute them.[15] He sought their death and watched as Stephen, a follower of Jesus, was being stoned to death, guarding the clothes of those who were killing him.[16]

Saul would ultimately prove useful in our Lord's service, but first, he had to be converted to Christianity. The Lord got his attention by speaking to him while he journeyed to Damascus and temporarily blinding him with a bright light. Then He sent a disciple named Ananias to go minister to Saul and to lay his hands upon him in order to restore his sight.[17] Acts 9:18 (NKJV) tells us that when this occurred, "something like scales" fell from his eyes "and he received his sight at once; and he arose and was baptized."

From that point forward, Saul became as zealous for the name of Jesus as he had been against Christianity before his conversion. He later began using his Roman name of Paul as he traveled to the Gentiles and preached the good news of Jesus.[18] Like Moses, Paul was an educated person. This served him well as he reasoned with people, spoke to his audiences, and trained other evangelists. The letters he wrote comprise a great portion of our New Testament.[19]

The Apostle Peter

Finally, the Apostle Peter provides us with an excellent summary concerning how to be saved. Shortly after Jesus had ascended back into heaven, Peter spoke to a large group who had gathered on the day of Pentecost. He explained to them that Jesus was the fulfillment of the prophecies concerning the Messiah, and then he told them, "Therefore let all the house of Israel know assuredly that God has made this Jesus, whom you crucified, both Lord and Christ" (Acts 2:36, NKJV).

When the people heard this, they were cut to the heart and asked what they should do. Peter told them, "Repent, and let every one of you be baptized in the name of Jesus Christ for the remission of sins; and you shall receive the gift of the Holy Spirit" (Acts 2:38, NKJV). The Scriptures tell us from that point on, these new believers steadfastly followed the apostles' teachings. They prayed and fellowshipped with one another. In short,

--- 17 ---

Ananias was hesitant to go minister to Saul because he knew of the harm he had done to Jesus's followers. The Lord reassured Ananias and told him, "Go, for he is a chosen vessel of Mine to bear My name before the Gentiles, kings, and the children of Israel" (Acts 9:15, NKJV).

--- 18 ---

This article discusses Saul later going by the name of Paul: "When and Why Was Saul's Name Changed to Paul?" (tinyurl.com/3d9b2vz3).

For a summary of his life, see the article "The Life of Paul" (tinyurl.com/2p83jz85). At this same site, https://www.biblestudy.org/, you can search for other interesting articles about Paul.

--- 19 ---

The Apostle Paul authored at least thirteen books of our New Testament: Romans, 1 and 2 Corinthians, Galatians, Ephesians, Philippians, Colossians, 1 and 2 Thessalonians, 1 and 2 Timothy, Titus, and Philemon. The book of Hebrews does not name its author, but many attribute it to Paul as well. This article gives a brief summary of each of these books: "14 Letters in Bible Attributed to St. Paul or His Followers" (tinyurl.com/4pfa5tat).

By word count, the writings of Paul account for over 5 percent of our total Bible and over 23 percent of the

New Testament. Of the New Testament writers, only Luke wrote more. This article discusses the authors of the Bible and gives a brief biography of each: "The 35 Authors Who Wrote the Bible" (tinyurl.com/ybmtrxxj).

This article considers the Bible as a whole: "Infographic: Who wrote most (and least) in the Bible?" (tinyurl.com/ym5aumw8).

——— 20 ———
See Acts 2:40–47 for the account of how the early church grew.

they did not revert to their old ways but went on to live a life devoted to serving Christ.[20]

If we are saved by our faith in Jesus, what is the purpose of baptism?

By studying the Old Testament scriptures and the Law, we learn that no matter how penitent someone was for their sins, that wasn't enough. None of the sacrifices were able to completely take away sin until Jesus came and offered Himself. By the same token, devoting oneself to God, doing good deeds, and following His directives are not enough either. No one, then or now, is able to live a perfect life, and at some point, we all sin. Our study of Moses bears that out. He did so much that was right, yet his sin kept him out of the Promised Land. It's not possible for us to do enough on our own to earn salvation.

Thankfully, God had mercy on us. He extended His grace to us by sending His Son into the world. Jesus's sacrifice would be enough for everyone, but it's up to us to avail ourselves of this indescribable gift. We are free to either accept or reject Jesus. If we reject Him, there's no other way to eternal salvation. Jesus declared in John 14:6 (NLT), "I am the way, the truth, and the life. No one can come to the Father except through me." The Apostle Peter later reaffirmed this when he said of Jesus, "There is salvation in no one else! God has given no other name under heaven by which we must be saved" (Acts 4:12, NLT).

Because of God's grace, we are saved through our faith in Jesus. The Apostle Paul stated this beautifully in Ephesians 2:8–10 (NLT): "God saved you by his grace when you believed. And you can't take credit for this; it is a gift from God. Salvation is not a reward for the good things we have done, so none of us can boast about it. For we are God's masterpiece. He has created us anew in Christ Jesus, so we can do the good things he planned for us long ago."

Baptism is a way for us to symbolically begin our new life in Christ Jesus. Paul explains in Romans 6:3 that those who are baptized into Christ Jesus are baptized into His death. When we do that, we die to sin, put off our old, sinful ways, and rise up out of the water to walk a new life.[21] That's not to say we'll never sin again—because we will. However, sin can no longer condemn us to a spiritual death because now we live under grace. As John explained in 1 John 1:5–7, as long as we continue to walk in the light, Jesus's blood cleanses us from all sin. He also tells us in verse 9 (NIV) of that chapter: "If we confess our sins, he is faithful and just and will forgive us our sins and purify us from all unrighteousness."[22]

When we are baptized into Christ, we put on Christ. Paul explained it this way in Galatians 3:27 (NLT): "And all who have been united with Christ in baptism have put on Christ, like putting on new clothes." We symbolically put off our old clothing that's been tattered and stained by sin and put on the beautiful new clothing of Christ. Baptism shows we belong to Him—every one of us, regardless of our gender or earthly heritage. Moreover, we shall be heirs with Him to eternal life, and God's promise to Abraham will belong to us as well![23]

May you continue to read and study your Bible to learn more about God's Word and His will for your life. Remember to always search the Scriptures to determine what is true.

———— 21 ————
Read the rest of Paul's explanation in Romans 6:3–14.

———— 22 ————
See 1 John 1:5–10 for John's admonition to walk in the light.

———— 23 ————
See Galatians 3:26–29 for more of what Paul said on the subject.

> "If we confess our sins, he is faithful and just and will forgive us our sins and purify us from all unrighteousness."

Heaven and earth will pass away, but my words
will never pass away.

—Mark 13:31, NIV

Also by Marilynn E. Hood

Daniel: Esteemed by God

Finding Peace in a Changing World

Does God care when things go wrong in our lives? Daniel and his friends must have asked themselves that question as they faced captivity, unfair politics, and even death sentences. Time after time, Daniel asked God for help—for hope—and God answered! Although the accounts in Daniel may seem far removed from the reality of life today, the truth is that the God who guided and protected His people back then is the same God who cares for you today.

The powerful stories and prophecies in the book of Daniel are exciting and, at times, confusing. In truth, not even Daniel himself understood everything he wrote about. But here's the good news: He didn't have to understand everything to have a close relationship with God; he simply needed to believe God and trust Him.

Daniel: Esteemed by God reveals the beautiful message of God's faithful love and continual presence in our lives. What Daniel and his friends discovered remains true in today's constantly changing world: God is in control. By relying on Him, you can find peace, even in the direst of circumstances.

Designed to be accessible for Bible students and novices alike, this book—with its short chapters, complete scripture references, and thought-provoking questions—makes this Old Testament book personally relevant. Most importantly, *Daniel: Esteemed by God* will help you better understand how to have a close relationship with God and experience His love in a deeper way.

"*Daniel: Esteemed by God* is a welcome and refreshing guide to understanding more of the tiny divine insights we are privileged to experience, if we have our spiritual eyes, ears, and minds attuned for the reception."
—**Dan Miller**, author of *Wisdom Meets Passion*

"Marilynn Hood masterfully shows the hand of God at work in Daniel and how that same hand is at work for us…. *Daniel: Esteemed by God* is a book for our times."
—**Debbie W. Wilson**, author of *Little Women, Big God*

MarilynnHood.com/daniel

info@courageousheartpress.com

Resources

Throughout this book, tiny URLs have been used to keep the text clean. The full links are provided here along with the resources cited.

Setting the Scene

[Sidebar] *Quick Reference Dictionary*, *Bible Study Tools*, https://www.biblestudytools.com/dictionary.

[Sidebar] "Bible Timeline: Complete Biblical Timeline," *Bible Hub,* https://biblehub.com/timeline/.

Chapter 1: The Baby Drawn Out of the Water

2.   "Animals Living In and Around the River Nile," *River Nile*, http://rivernile.info/animals.php.

[Sidebar] Barrier, Julie, "Queen Hatshepsut, Moses' Egyptian Mother," *Preach It, Teach It*, https://preachitteachit.org/articles/detail/queen-hatshepsut-moses-egyptian -mother/.

Chapter 2: Moses Escapes From Egypt

Thoughts to Ponder, Question 2: "Bible Timeline: Complete Biblical Timeline," *Bible Hub,* https://biblehub.com/timeline/.

Thoughts to Ponder, Question 2: "Pharaoh Timeline," *World History Encyclopedia,* https://www.worldhistory.org/timeline/pharaoh.

[Sidebar] "Midian: Atlas," *Bible Hub*, http://bibleatlas.org/full/midian.htm.

[Sidebar] Rudd, Steve, "Exodus Route Map," *The Interactive Bible*, March 11, 2007, https://www.bible.ca/archeology/maps-bible-archeology-exodus-route.jpg.

Chapter 3: Moses Finds a Family Among the Midianites

6.   "Jethro," *Smith's Bible Dictionary*, *Bible Study Tools,* https://www.biblestudytools.com/dictionaries/smiths-bible-dictionary/jethro.html.

6.   Campbell, Mike, "Reuel," *Behind the Name,* 2023, https://www.behindthename.com/name/reuel.

Thoughts to Ponder, Question 3: "Commentaries: Genesis 25:1," *Bible Hub*,
     http://biblehub.com/commentaries/genesis/25-1.htm.

[Sidebar] Bratcher, Dennis, "Travelers and Strangers: Hospitality in the Biblical World," *Christian Resource Institute*, 2021, www.crivoice.org/travelers.html.

Chapter 4: Moses's Call to Leadership

[Sidebar] "Dispensation," *Quick Reference Dictionary*, *Bible Study Tools*,
     https://www.biblestudytools.com/dictionary/dispensation/.

Chapter 5: God Reveals His Plan to Moses

2.   Aling, Charles, PhD, "Joseph in Egypt: Part IV," *Associates for Biblical Research*, 2010,
     https://biblearchaeology.org/research/chronological-categories/patriarchal-era/3751
     -joseph-in-egypt-part-iv.

Thoughts to Ponder, Question 1: "Is Jehovah the true name of God?" *Got Questions Ministries*,
     accessed January 9, 2023, https://www.gotquestions.org/Jehovah.html.

Thoughts to Ponder, Question 1: Sproul, R.C., ed., "Exodus: Ex 3:15," *ESV Reformation Study Bible*, *Bible Gateway*, https://www.biblegateway.com/resources/reformation-study-bible/
     Exod.3.15.

[Sidebar] "The Traditional Mt. Sinai," *Wyatt Archaeological Research*,
     https://wyattmuseum.com/the-traditional-mt-sinai/2011-212.

[Sidebar] Jacobs, Joseph, M. Seligsohn, and Wilhelm Bacher, "Sinai, Mount," *1906 Jewish Encyclopedia*, https://jewishencyclopedia.com/articles/13766-sinai-mount.

Chapter 6: God Equips Moses for His Role

1   "The Speech Problem of Moses," *Innvista Library*, https://innvista.com/culture/religion/
     bible/compare/the-speech-problem-of-moses/.

[Sidebar] "Egypt: Atlas," *Bible Hub*, https://bibleatlas.org/egypt.htm.

[Sidebar] "List of ancient great powers," *Wikipedia*, https://en.wikipedia.org/wiki/List_of_ancient
     _great_powers.

[Sidebar] Jarus, Owen, "Ancient Egypt: History, dynasties, religion and writing," *Live Science*,
     August 26, 2022, https://www.livescience.com/55578-egyptian-civilization.html.

[Sidebar] "Bible Timeline: Complete Biblical Timeline," *Bible Hub*, https://biblehub.com/timeline/.

Chapter 7: Moses Leaves for Egypt

[Sidebar] "What is the Abrahamic Covenant?," *Got Questions Ministries*, accessed January 9, 2023,
     https://www.gotquestions.org/Abrahamic-covenant.html.

Chapter 9: Moses Questions God

Thoughts to Ponder, Question 3: Bernock, Danielle, "What Are the Names of God Found in the
     Bible?" *Christianity.com*, September 9, 2022, https://www.christianity.com/wiki/god/what
     -are-all-the-names-of-god.html.

Thoughts to Ponder, Question 3: "What Are the Different Names of God, and What Do They Mean?" *Got Questions Ministries*, accessed January 9, 2023, https://www.gotquestions.org/names-of-God.html.

Chapter 10: The Plagues Begin

[Sidebar] Mark, Joshua J., "Magic in Ancient Egypt," *World History Encyclopedia*, February 24, 2017, https://www.worldhistory.org/article/1019/magic-in-ancient-egypt/.

[Sidebar] "How Were Pharaoh's Magicians Able to Perform Miracles?" *Got Questions Ministries*, accessed January 9, 2023, https://www.gotquestions.org/Pharaohs-magicians-miracles.html.

Chapter 11: Gnats and Flies

1. "Commentaries: Exodus 8:16," *Bible Hub,* https://biblehub.com/commentaries/exodus/8-16.htm.

2. "Commentaries: Exodus 8:24," *Bible Hub,* https://biblehub.com/commentaries/exodus/8-24.htm.

[Sidebar] Mark, Joshua J., "Egyptian Gods—The Complete List," *World History Encyclopedia*, April 14, 2016, https://www.worldhistory.org/article/885/egyptian-gods—-the-complete-list/.

Chapter 13: Locusts

1. "Bible: Exodus 10:10," *Bible Hub*, https://biblehub.com/exodus/10-10.htm.

2. Reimann, Matt, "In one year, 12 trillion locusts devastated the Great Plains—and then they went extinct," *Timeline*, February 15, 2017, https://timeline.com/in-the-1870s-12-trillion-locusts-devastated-the-great-plains-and-then-they-went-extinct-6f7c51a15d90.

Chapter 14: Darkness and a Final Warning

[Sidebar] "Commentaries: Exodus 10:21," *Bible Hub,* https://biblehub.com/commentaries/exodus/10-21.htm.

[Sidebar] "Khamsin," *Britannica*, https://www.britannica.com/science/khamsin.

Chapter 15: God Establishes the Passover

2. "Commentaries: Exodus 12:3," *Bible Hub,* https://biblehub.com/commentaries/exodus/12-3.htm.

3. "Hyssop," *Quick Reference Dictionary*, *Bible Study Tools*, https://www.biblestudytools.com/dictionary/hyssop/.

4. Riggs, David, "Redemption from Beginning to End," *Oak Ridge Church*, oakridgechurch.com/riggs/redempti.htm.

[Sidebar] "Gird one's loins," *Dictionary.com*, 2023, https://www.dictionary.com/browse/gird-one-s-loins.

[Sidebar] "Chapter 17: Answering Questions About Garments," *Nazarene Israel*, 2023, https://nazareneisrael.org/book/nazarene-scripture-studies-vol-5/answering-questions-about-garments/.

Chapter 18: Crossing the Red Sea

[Sidebar] "What Is the Shekinah Glory," *Got Questions Ministries*, accessed January 9, 2023, https://www.gotquestions.org/shekinah-glory.html.

Chapter 19: A Song of Praise to the Lord

[Sidebar] Kranz, Jeffrey, "All the Songs in the Bible," *OverviewBible*, July 2, 2014, https://overviewbible.com/bible-songs/.

Chapter 20: The Israelites Grumble

1. "Distance from Cairo to Jericho," *Distance Calculator*, accessed January 9, 2023, https://www.distancecalculator.net/from-cairo-to-jericho.

4. "Wilderness of Sin," *Encyclopedia of the Bible*, *Bible Gateway*, https://www.biblegateway.com/resources/encyclopedia-of-the-bible/Wilderness-Sin.

Chapter 21: Manna and Quail

1. "What Are the Modern Equivalents of Biblical Weights and Measures," *Got Questions Ministries*, accessed January 9, 2023, https://www.gotquestions.org/biblical-weights-and-measures.html.

Chapter 22: Water from a Rock and the Battle at Rephidim

2. "Rephidim," *Smith's Bible Dictionary*, *Bible Study Tools*, https://www.biblestudytools.com/dictionaries/smiths-bible-dictionary/rephidim.html.

2. "Rephidim," *International Standard Bible Encyclopedia*, *Bible Study Tools*, https://www.biblestudytools.com/encyclopedias/isbe/rephidim.html.

3. "Meribah," *Smith's Bible Dictionary*, *Bible Study Tools*, https://www.biblestudytools.com/dictionaries/smiths-bible-dictionary/meribah.html.

4. "Who was Hur in the Bible," *Got Questions Ministries*, accessed January 9, 2023, https://www.gotquestions.org/Hur-in-the-Bible.html.

4. "Is Ben-Hur in the Bible," *Got Questions Ministries*, accessed January 9, 2023, https://www.gotquestions.org/Ben-Hur-in-the-Bible.html.

5. "Exodus 17," *Ellicott's Commentary for English Readers*, *Bible Hub*, https://biblehub.com/commentaries/ellicott/exodus/17.htm.

Chapter 23: The Beginnings of a Judicial System

2. "Salem," *Encyclopedia of the Bible*, *Bible Gateway*, https://www.biblegateway.com/resources/encyclopedia-of-the-bible/Salem.

Chapter 26: Moses Intercedes for the Israelites

1. "What Is the Significance of Mount Horeb in the Bible," *Got Questions Ministries*, accessed January 9, 2023, https://www.gotquestions.org/mount-Horeb.html.

2. "What Is the Dispensation of Law," *Got Questions Ministries*, accessed January 9, 2023, https://www.gotquestions.org/dispensation-of-Law.html.

[Sidebar] "What Is the Covenant Code or the Book of the Covenant (Exodus 20:22–23:33)," *Got Questions Ministries*, accessed January 9, 2023, https://www.compellingtruth.org/Covenant-Code.html.

[Sidebar] "Book of the Covenant," *Jewish Virtual Library,* https://www.jewishvirtuallibrary.org/book-of-the-covenant.

[Sidebar] "Covenant, Book of The," *International Standard Bible Encyclopedia*, *Bible Study Tools*, https://www.biblestudytools.com/encyclopedias/isbe/covenant-book-of-the.html.

Chapter 28: The Golden Calf

4. "Commentaries: Exodus 32:6," *Bible Hub*, https://biblehub.com/commentaries/exodus/32-6.htm.

7. Hirsch, Emil G., M. Seligsohn, Joseph Jacobs, and Louis Ginzberg, "Hur," *1906 Jewish Encyclopedia*, https://www.jewishencyclopedia.com/articles/7942-hur.

Chapter 29: Moses Smashes the Tablets

7. "What Is the Purpose of Jesus Interceding for Us in Heaven," *Got Questions Ministries*, accessed January 9, 2023, https://www.gotquestions.org/Jesus-interceding.html.

Chapter 31: The New Tablets

3. "The Purpose of the Old Law," *La Vista Church of Christ,* December 30, 2014, http://www.lavistachurchofchrist.org/cms/the-purpose-of-the-old-law/.

Chapter 32: Becoming a Nation

9. "What is the importance of the Lord's supper/Christian Communion?," *Got Questions Ministries*, accessed January 9, 2023, https://www.gotquestions.org/communion-Christian.html.

[Sidebar] "Encampment of the Tribes of Israel in the Wilderness," *Conforming To Jesus Ministry*, https://www.conformingtojesus.com/charts-maps/en/wilderness_camp_of_the_tribes_of_israel.htm.

Chapter 33: Leaving the Mountain of God

4. "Taberah," *Encyclopedia of the Bible, Bible Gateway,* https://www.biblegateway.com/resources/encyclopedia-of-the-bible/Taberah.

4. "Kibroth Hataavah," *Encyclopedia of the Bible, Bible Gateway,* https://www.biblegateway.com/resources/encyclopedia-of-the-bible/Kibroth-Hataavah.

[Sidebar] "Journey," *Easton's Bible Dictionary, Bible Gateway,* https://www.biblegateway
.com/resources/eastons-bible-dictionary/Journey.

Chapter 34: Miriam and Aaron Criticize Moses

[Sidebar] David, Charles Patrick, MD, PhD, "Leprosy (Hansen's Disease)," *Medicine Net,* April 29,
2022, https://www.medicinenet.com/leprosy/article.htm.

[Sidebar] "Leprosy in the Bible," *The Leprosy Mission International,*
https://www.leprosymission.org/what-is-leprosy/leprosy-in-the-bible.

Chapter 37: Korah's Rebellion

9. "Encampment of the Tribes of Israel in the Wilderness," *Conforming To Jesus Ministry,*
https://www.conformingtojesus.com/charts-maps/en/wilderness_camp_of_the_tribes_of
_israel.htm.

Thoughts to Ponder, Question 2: "Who were the sons of Korah in the Old Testament?," *Got
Questions Ministries,* accessed January 9, 2023, https://www.gotquestions.org/sons-of
-Korah.html.

Thoughts to Ponder, Question 3: "What Does It Mean That God Is Not Mocked," *Got Questions
Ministries,* accessed January 9, 2023, https://www.gotquestions.org/
God-is-not-mocked.html.

Chapter 38: God Reaffirms His Leaders

Thoughts to Ponder, Question 2: "Signs & Symbols of the Bible (Incense)," *Jesus Way 4 You,*
https://jesusway4you.com/2017/09/28/signs-symbols-of-the-bible-incense/.

[Sidebar] Lipnick, Jonathan, "What Is The Holy Of Holies?," *Israel Institute of Biblical
Studies,* January 10, 2017, https://blog.israelbiblicalstudies.com/holy-land-studies/
what-was-the-holy-of-holies/.

Chapter 41: God Gives Moses a Song

1. "Deuteronomy," *Smith's Bible Dictionary, Bible Study Tools,*
https://www.biblestudytools.com/dictionaries/smiths-bible-dictionary/deuteronomy.html.

1. "Deuteronomy," *Easton's Bible Dictionary, Bible Study Tools,* https://www.biblestudytools
.com/dictionaries/eastons-bible-dictionary/deuteronomy.html.

2. Jun, Passion, MD, "Music, Rhythm, and the Brain," *Brain World Magazine,* January 22, 2022,
https://brainworldmagazine.com/music-rhythm-brain.

2. Ruder, Debra Bradley, "Music and the Brain," *Harvard Medical School*, https://neuro.hms.harvard.edu/centers-and-initiatives/harvard-mahoney-neuroscience -institute/about-hmni/archive-brain-1.

[Sidebar] "Deuteronomy 31," *Ellicott's Commentary for English Readers, Bible Hub*, https://biblehub.com/commentaries/ellicott/deuteronomy/31.htm.

[Sidebar] "How did the Holy Spirit operate in the lives of OT saints?," *Bible.org*, January 1, 2001, https://bible.org/question/how-did-holy-spirit-operate-lives-ot-saints.

Chapter 42: The Death of Moses

[Sidebar] "Nebo," *Smith's Bible Dictionary, Bible Gateway*, https://www.biblegateway.com/ resources/smiths-bible-names-dictionary/Nebo.

Epilogue: Moses, A Faithful Servant of God

7. "Pentateuch," *Smith's Bible Dictionary, Bible Study Tools*, https://www.biblestudytools.com/ dictionaries/smiths-bible-dictionary/pentateuch-the.html.

7. "Pentateuch," *Easton's Bible Dictionary, Bible Study Tools*, https://www.biblestudytools.com/ dictionaries/eastons-bible-dictionary/pentateuch.html.

8. Kranz, Jeffrey, "Infographic: Who wrote most (and least) in the Bible?," *OverviewBible*, November 5, 2014, https://overviewbible.com/author-wrote-most-bible/.

9. "What Is the Significance of Mount Tabor in the Bible," *Got Questions Ministries*, accessed January 9, 2023, https://www.gotquestions.org/Mount-Tabor.html.

9. "What Is the Significance of Mount Hermon in the Bible," *Got Questions Ministries*, accessed January 9, 2023, https://www.gotquestions.org/mount-Hermon.html.

10. Ross, Allen, "25. The Transfiguration (Matthew 17:1–13)," *Bible.org*, March 31, 2006, https://bible.org/seriespage/25-transfiguration-matthew-171-13.

Frequently Asked Questions

5. "Pentateuch," *Smith's Bible Dictionary, Bible Study Tools*, https://www.biblestudytools.com/ dictionaries/smiths-bible-dictionary/pentateuch-the.html.

5. "Pentateuch," *Easton's Bible Dictionary, Bible Study Tools,* https://www.biblestudytools.com/ dictionaries/eastons-bible-dictionary/pentateuch.html.

7. Singer, Isidore, PhD, Projector and Managing Editor, "Daniel, Tomb of," *The 1901 Jewish Encyclopedia, Study Light*, https://www.studylight.org/encyclopedias/eng/tje/d/daniel -tomb-of.html.

18. "When and why was Saul's name changed to Paul?," *Got Questions Ministries*, accessed January 9, 2023, https://www.gotquestions.org/Saul-Paul.html.

18. "The Life of Paul," *Bible Study*, https://www.biblestudy.org/beginner/learn-basic-bible -timeline/life-of-apostle-paul.html.

19. Hartnagel, Nancy, CNS, "14 letters in Bible attributed to St. Paul or his followers," *Catholic Courier*, December 21, 2009, https://catholiccourier.com/ articles/14-letters-in-bible-attributed-to-st-paul-or-his-followers/.

19. Kranz Jeffrey, "The 35 Authors Who Wrote the Bible," *OverviewBible,* August 9, 2018, https://overviewbible.com/authors-who-wrote-bible/.

19. Kranz, Jeffrey, "Infographic: Who wrote most (and least) in the Bible?," *OverviewBible,* November 5, 2014, https://overviewbible.com/author-wrote-most-bible/.

About The Author

Marilynn E. Hood is a Christian who has studied the Bible for most of her life. She draws upon her own personal learning journey and years of teaching experience in presenting these lessons on the life of Moses.

Marilynn holds an MBA from Texas A&M University, where she later joined the faculty in the Department of Finance and taught the principles of personal finance to thousands of students. She also taught the principles of insurance in the CERTIFIED FINANCIAL PLANNER™ Program offered by Texas A&M University's Department of Agricultural Economics.

Marilynn is the author of *Money for Life* and *Daniel: Esteemed by God*. Having retired from university teaching, she and her husband of fifty-two years, David Hood, currently reside on their farm near Bryan, Texas. They are the parents of three children and, more importantly, the grandparents to six wonderful grandchildren and one adorable great-granddaughter.

MarilynnHood.com
Facebook.com/MarilynnHoodAuthor